CORNERSTONE

BUILDING ON YOUR BEST

THIRD EDITION

ROBERT M. SHERFIELD
The Community College of Southern Nevada

RHONDA J. MONTGOMERY
The University of Nevada, Las Vegas

PATRICIA G. MOODY
The University of South Carolina

Prentice Hall

Upper Saddle River, New Jersey
Columbus, Ohio

Library of Congress Cataloging-in-Publication Data

Sherfield, Robert M.
    Cornerstone : building on your best / Robert M. Sherfield, Rhonda J. Montgomery, Patricia G. Moody.—3rd ed.
        p.   cm.
    Includes bibliographical references and index.
    ISBN 0-13-091369-3
    1. Success—Psychological aspects.   2. Self-actualization (Psychology)   3. Academic achievement.   I. Montgomery, Rhonda J.   II. Moody, Patricia G.   III. Title.

BF637.S8 M597 2002
378.1'98—dc21

00-068682

Dedication

Cornerstone is dedicated to our families and close friends who have helped us, nurtured us, believed in us, and encouraged us to become the best we can be.

For Robb: My friend, confidant, and rock, Brian R. Epps

For Rhonda: My soulmate, Mick Montgomery, and my inspiration, Jackie Montgomery

For Pat: My personal hero, my mother, Annie Laura Bryan Ginn

Vice President and Publisher: Jeffery W. Johnston
Acquisitions Editor: Sande Johnson
Editorial Assistant: Cecilia Johnson
Production Editor: Holcomb Hathaway
Design Coordinator: Diane C. Lorenzo
Cover Designer: Thomas Borah
Cover Art: © Sibley Peteet Design
Production Manager: Pamela D. Bennett
Director of Marketing: Kevin Flanagan
Marketing Manager: Christina Quadhamer
Marketing Assistant: Barbara Rosenberg

This book was set in Scala by Aerocraft Charter Art Service. It was printed and bound by Banta Book Group. The cover was printed by Banta Book Group.

Photo Credits, by page: 2 Corbis Images; 5 Len Rubinstein/Index Stock Imagery; 7 PhotoDisc; 8 L. Kolvoord/The Image Works; 10 Sepp Seitz/Woodfin Camp & Associates; 14 Loren Santow/Tony Stone Images; 18 Jacques Chenet/Woodfin Camp & Associates; 28 Corbis Images; 31 Spencer Grant, The Picture Cube; 34 Sepp Seitz/Woodfin Camp & Associates; 37 P. Beringer/The Image Works; 58 Corbis Images; 61 Matthew McYay/Stock Boston; 65 Paul Mozell/Stock Boston; 69 Michael Newman/PhotoEdit; 88 Corbis Images; 91 EyeWire Images; 93 Bob Daemmrich/Stock Boston; 98 J. Nourok/PhotoEdit; 102 (top) Ira Wyman/Sygma; 102 (mid) Mandella D. Brauchli/Sygma; 102(bot) Bargas/Sygma; 105 Gary Conner/ PhotoEdit; 118 Corbis Images; 121 Paula Lerner/Woodfin Camp & Associates; 126 Deborah Davis/Tony Stone Images; 135 PhotoDisc; 144 Corbis Images; 147 EyeWire Images; 149 Gary A. Conner/PhotoEdit; 150 David H. Wells/The Image Works; 153 Stewart Cohen/Tony Stone Images; 160 J. Marshall/The Image Works; 166 Corbis Images; 169 EyeWire Images; 171 EyeWire Images ; 176 Gary A. Conner/PhotoEdit; 178 EyeWire Images; 188 Corbis Images; 191 PhotoDisc; 193 Deborah Davis/PhotoEdit; 195 PhotoDisc; 206 EyeWire Images; 209 Mark Richards/PhotoEdit; 211 Phyllis Picardi/StockBoston; 216 Corbis Images; 219 Bob Daemmrich/The Image Works; 222 Esbin-Anderson/The Image Works; 233 Nick Gunderson/Tony Stone Images; 240 Corbis Images; 243 Bob Daemmrich/Stock Boston; 252 Barbara Stitzer/PhotoEdit; 253 Gregg Mancuso/Stock Boston; 255 Bob Daemmrich/The Image Works; 276 Corbis Images; 279 Francie Manning/The Picture Cube; 283 Sepp Seitz/ Woodfin Camp & Associates; 285 Michael Newman/PhotoEdit; 291 Paula Lerner/Woodfin Camp & Associates; 302 Corbis Images; 305 C. J. Allen/Stock Boston; 308 Ellis Herwig/Stock Boston; 309 Bob Daemmrich/Stock Boston; 311 Loren Santow/Tony Stone Images; 332 Corbis Images; 335 PhotoDisc; 338 PhotoDisc; 342 John Boykin/PhotoEdit; 343 R. Hutchins/PhotoEdit; 345 Charles Gupton/ Tony Stone Images; 347 Day Williams/Photo Researchers, Inc.; 354 Corbis Images; 357 PhotoDisc; 361 Bob Daemmrich/StockBoston; 365 David Young-Wolff/PhotoEdit; 372 EyeWire Images

10 9 8 7 6 5 4 3

ISBN 0-13-091369-3

Contents

4   THINK   88

Critical and Creative Thinking Skills

5   PRIORITIZE   118

Time, Money, and Resources

6   LISTEN   144

The Art of Listening

7   RECORD   166

The Essentials of Note Taking

To Our Students

Cornerstone was born out of our desire to help new college students develop the skills that would enable them to be successful in college. Seldom will you read a textbook as honest and straightforward as we have tried to make this one. The words that you read and the activities provided in this worktext have not come easily to us. They are the result of our collective experiences over our many years of teaching and administration in higher education. We hope our words will touch you deeply and provide you insight that will enable you to make it to graduation and beyond.

Education is not preparation for life, education is life itself.

—*JOHN DEWEY*

We hope that our words will give you peace as well as cause you some discomfort; teach you and challenge you; hold you and let you go. It is also our hope that you will approach these activities with new eyes; yours is a different world now. To experience that world, you'll need to be open and willing to participate. Without your participation, the power of this book is lost. With your participation, it holds unlimited possibilities for bringing change, improving skills, and setting you off on a lifetime of success.

Within the pages of this worktext you will find many activities such as *Where Are You at This Moment?* that will help you explore where you are and where you are going. Each chapter includes a feature called *Insider's View,* stories from students across the United States discussing issues found within the chapter. You will also find a feature, *From the World of Work,* that includes essays from professionals in a variety of careers.

Journal pages are included with this text. When used properly, they can be a valuable communication tool between you, your peers, and your instructor. Take your time to reflect honestly and openly on the questions asked. Only through your own soul-searching and self-revelation will the features of this book help you improve your skills as a college student and assist you in becoming a productive citizen.

We wish you luck in building your future on the cornerstones that will carry you for the rest of your life.

Robb, Rhonda, and Pat

About the Authors

ROBERT M. SHERFIELD

Robert Sherfield has been teaching public speaking, theater, and study skills and working with first-year orientation programs for over 17 years. Currently, he is Co-Director of the Faculty Center of Learning and Teaching, and a professor at the Community College of Southern Nevada, teaching study skills, orientation courses, and drama.

An award-winning educator, Robb was recently named Educator of the Year at the Community College of Southern Nevada. He twice received the Distinguished Teacher of the Year Award from the University of South Carolina and has received numerous other awards and nominations for outstanding classroom instruction and advisement. In 1998, 1999, and 2000, he was nominated by students for, and named to, *Who's Who Among American Educators.*

Robb's extensive work with student success programs includes experience with the design and implementation of these programs—including one program that was presented at the International Conference on the Freshman Year Experience in Newcastle upon Tyne, England.

In addition to his coauthorship of *Cornerstone: Building on Your Best,* he has also coauthored *Roadways to Success* (Prentice Hall, 2001), the trade book *365 Things I Learned in College* (Allyn & Bacon, 1996), and *Capstone: Succeeding Beyond College* (Prentice Hall, 2001).

Robb's interest in student success began with his own first year in college. Low SAT scores and a mediocre high school ranking denied him entrance into college. With the help of a success program, Robb was granted entrance into college, and went on to earn a doctorate and become a college faculty member. He has always been interested in the social, academic, and cultural development of students, and sees this book as his way to contribute to the positive development of first-year students across the nation.

RHONDA J. MONTGOMERY

Rhonda Montgomery is an Associate Professor in the William F. Harrah College of Hotel Administration at the University of Nevada, Las Vegas, and has been teaching in higher education for 15 years. Rhonda has been responsible for developing and incorporating first-year orientation/study skills curricula into existing introductory courses and programs.

Currently, Rhonda is teaching a first-year orientation/study skills course as well as hospitality education. Because she believes in the holistic development of first-year students, she volunteers to teach first-year students each semester and uses a variety of experiences such as field trips, exercises, and case studies to aid in their retention and success.

Rhonda has received several awards for her teaching and advising. She is also an active member of Phi Eta Sigma, a National Freshman Honorary Association. Rhonda is the coauthor of seven texts including *Cornerstone: Building on Your Best, Roadways to Success* (Prentice Hall, 2001), *365 Things I Learned in College* (Allyn & Bacon, 1996) and *Capstone: Succeeding Beyond College* (Prentice Hall, 2001). She has also presented at The National Conference on the Freshman Year Experience and spoken extensively to first-year students and educators about building success into their curriculum.

PATRICIA G. MOODY

Patricia G. Moody is Dean of the College of Hospitality, Retail and Sport Management at the University of South Carolina, where she has been a faculty member for over 20 years. An award-winning educator, Pat has been honored as Distinguished Educator of the Year at her college and as Collegiate Teacher of the Year by the National Business Education Association, and has been a top-five finalist for the Amoco Teaching Award at the University of South Carolina. In 1994, she was awarded the prestigious John Robert Gregg Award, the highest honor in her field of over 100,000 educators.

Pat frequently speaks to multiple sections of first-year students, incorporating personal development content from her trademark speech, "Fly Like an Eagle," as well as numerous strategies for building self-esteem and for achieving success in college. She also works with first-year classes on subjects such as goal setting, priority management, and diversity.

A nationally known motivation speaker, Pat has spoken in 42 states, has been invited to speak in several foreign countries, and frequently keynotes national and regional conventions. She has presented "Fly Like an Eagle" to thousands of people from Olympic athletes to corporate executives to high school students. Her topics include Thriving in the Changing Corporate Environment, Perception Is Everything: Powerful Communications Strategies, Gold Star Customer Service, and The Great Balancing Act: Managing Time at Home and at Work.

An avid sports fan, she follows Gamecock athletics and chairs the University of South Carolina Athletics Advisory Committee.

Preface

Why Cornerstone?

WHAT CAN THIS BOOK AND THIS COURSE DO FOR YOU?

This book and this course are intended to shake you up—to *cause* change! Yes, to cause change. We hope that this book will help you see more clearly the possibilities the future holds; that the activities included here will help you anticipate and cope with the many new situations you will face; that in the days and weeks to come you will use this book as a guide to help you contend with change, discover more about yourself, develop study and prioritizing skills, develop critical and creative thinking skills, learn more about careers, cope with stress, and develop an appreciation for diversity. We hope that our words together—yours and ours—will help you make your goals and dreams come true. This book is primarily about decisions and changes: decisions and changes that you will face in the days and months ahead, decisions and changes that may affect the rest of your life, decisions and changes that *you* will make. This book is about learning how to bring the best you have to each situation. *Cornerstone* is about building on your best!

We chose the title *Cornerstone* because a cornerstone is, according to the *American Heritage Dictionary,* "the indispensable and fundamental basis of something." We consider this course the cornerstone for your success in college. In a building, a cornerstone is laid to establish a firm foundation. Often, a ceremony attends the laying of a cornerstone, and treasured documents and valuables may be placed within the cornerstone. Today is a celebration; a celebration of your future, of your potential, and of the joys and triumphs yet to come. Today, you are laying the cornerstone for the rest of your life. Take your time, use only the best materials available to you, plan your structure carefully, let others help you along the way, and you will have built a lasting monument celebrating your achievements.

As you read about—and possibly struggle with—the concepts and challenges presented here, you will find many opportunities to write and personalize this worktext. Some of the activities may seem personal and may make you uncomfortable, but if you undertake them seriously, you will gain valuable tools that will help you be successful. The chapters contain many common elements: quotations; *Where Are You at This Moment?;* interactive writing opportunities; activities; journal exercises; student testimonials; stories of students and graduates; statements from professionals in *From the World of Work;* an online study guide; and *Cornerstones* for success.

Each chapter is included to assist you in making the most of your college experience. Below, you will find a few tips and suggestions to help make your journey easier and more beneficial.

QUICK TIPS ON HOW TO READ A TEXT

An entire section of Chapter 8 is devoted to the art of reading a text and remembering its content. Here, we provide some simple, quick suggestions on getting the most from the pages of this book.

- **Survey the entire chapter before you read it.**
    - As you survey, read the major titles and subtitles.
    - Notice the content and headings of text boxes, graphs, and charts.
    - Read the introduction to the chapter.
    - Read the Results (objectives of the chapter).
    - Note the typographical clues as you read (**bold words**, *italicized words,* words in color, Capitalized Words, and so forth).
    - Read the last paragraph or summary of the chapter.
    - Read the Cornerstones at the end of the chapter.
- **Begin reading the chapter in detail.**
    - Always read with a pencil or highlighter.
    - Highlight only the most important points.
    - Make margin notes.
    - Use a notebook and take extensive notes as you read the material.
    - Determine the main idea of each paragraph or section.
    - Paraphrase each paragraph in your notebook.
    - Study every graph, chart, table, and text box.
- **As you read, turn each heading into a question to be answered when you complete the chapter.**
- **When you have completed the chapter, read it again.**
- **Always read and study in the most conducive atmosphere for you.** If you need quiet, find quiet. If you like soft music, play music. However, if you are doing what you have always done, you may want to consider changing environments. Example: If you have always studied with music and you continually perform poorly and don't remember what you have read or studied, perhaps you need to read and study in a quieter place.
- **Look up words that you do not know or understand as you read along.** Write the definitions in the margin of your text.
- **Take a 5-minute break every 20 to 25 minutes.**
- **Move ahead and read Chapter 8 before you begin the first chapter assigned.**

TIPS ON JOURNALING

Journaling has been around as long as humans have been around. Early cave dwellings are filled with drawings and designs that tell stories and share information about people and their past. Your journaling efforts in this text will do no less. Properly done, this text will allow you to create a history of your first year in college. You will, in essence, be creating a written history of who you were and what you believed and how you felt during your first-year experience.

Journaling is an important aspect of the *Cornerstone* program. Each chapter asks that you complete three journal entries at the end of the chapter. Your professor may not use all three entries, but some professors may use additional entries such as E-mail journals. We consider the chapter activities that ask in-depth questions a form of journaling also.

Understand that the more time you spend journaling and completing the chapter exercises and the more honest you are with yourself, the more beneficial your journaling and experience will become.

Why Journal?

- To recover from the past
- To explain the present
- To interact with our feelings
- To dream about the future
- To assess where we are at the present moment
- To nurture our spiritual lives

How Long Does Journaling Take?

- As long as it takes. There is no time limit, and journaling will be different for every person.
- If you have never kept a journal before, set aside at least 20 minutes for each journaling project.
- Know that the more you journal, the more time it usually takes.

When Should I Journal?

- Regularly
- At least three times per week
- During a time when you are least likely to be interrupted

Where Should I Journal?

- Journaling requires silence and careful thought, so choose a place where you can concentrate.
- Choose a place where you will not be interrupted.

Thoughts

What Should I Journal?

- The truth, and only the truth
- Your feelings
- Your desires and dreams and wishes
- Your fears and challenges

Journaling Beyond *Cornerstone*

Cornerstone asks you to reflect on the material in the text or on the website. You may wish to consider creating your own first-year journal in a separate binder. If you choose to do so, you may want to consider the following topics or headings for your writings:

- Daily thoughts and actions
- Your history
- Pilgrimage (your personal growth)
- Dreams
- Musings
- Family
- School
- Finances

Thoughts

Acknowledgments

Professional Acknowledgments: Dr. Stuart Mann, Dean, The William F. Harrah College of Hotel Administration, University of Nevada, Las Vegas; Dr. Carol Harter, President, University of Nevada, Las Vegas; Patti Shock, Department Chair, Tourism and Convention Administration, University of Nevada, Las Vegas; Dr. John Palms, President, The University of South Carolina; Dr. Jerome Odom, Provost, The University of South Carolina; Dr. Robert Silverman, Interim President, The Community College of Southern Nevada; Theo Byrns, Vice President, The Community College of Southern Nevada; Dr. Don Smith, Dean of Arts and Letters, The Community College of Southern Nevada; Steve Konowalow, Professor, The Community College of Southern Nevada; Dr. Charles Mosley, Department Chair, English, The Community College of Southern Nevada.

We also offer our sincere gratitude to the following professionals who helped us, encouraged us, and provided significant support to us: Cheryl E. Schwartz, Javier Ortiz, Steve Spearman, Curtis Roe, Bob Binkowski, Arnoldo Gonzalez, Lois Pasapane, Molly Widdicombe, Linda Chenault, Garcia Tate, Steve Brannon, Joe Perdue, Tim Rice, Roosevelt Richardson, Lucinda Moyano, Nancy Markee, Janice Gardner, Missy Parker, Chris Fiorentino, Bryan Delph, Martiza Correa, Joe Anna Hibler, and Jim Farmer.

The following educators offered significant contributions to the development of this book with their insightful and constructive reviews: Elaine H. Byrd, Utah Valley State College; Penny Schempp, Western Iowa Community College; Charlene Latimer; Sandra M. Bovain-Lowe, Cumberland community College; Jeffrey A. Miller; Leslie L. Duckworth, Florida Community College at Jacksonville; Katherine A. Wenen-Nesbit, Chippewa Valley Technical College; Ronald W. Johnsrud, Lake City Community College; Joseph R. Krzyzanowski, Albuquerque TVI; Janet Cutshall, Sussex County Community College; Marnell Hayes, Lake City Community College; Elzora Holland, University of Michigan, Ann Arbor; John Lowry-King, Eastern New Mexico University; and Betty Smith, Univer-sity of Nebraska at Kearney.

Finally, a very special thanks to the following faculty, who took the time to share their expertise with us in the feature *Voices from the Field,* in our Instructor's Manual: Dee. F. Bostick, Midlands Technical College; Carol Cooper, Miami Dade Community College; JoAnn Credle, Northern Virginia Community College; Hugh Horan, New Mexico Highlands University; Steve Konowalow, Community College of Southern Nevada; William Larson, University of Tennessee-Knoxville; Nancy T. McGlasson, University of Tennessee-Knoxville; Joan O'Connor, New York Institute of Technology; Bennie Perdue, Miami Dade Community College; Hattie Pinckney, Florence Darlington Technical College; Kay Young, Jamestown Community College; Andria Shoates, Northern Virginia Community College; Wister M. Withers, Northern Virginia Community College; and Marie Zander, New York Institute of Technology.

CORNERSTONE

BUILDING ON YOUR BEST

Life is about change, and about movement, and about becoming

Change.

something other than what you are at this very moment.

CHAPTER 1

Change

Mark was the son of textile workers. Both of his parents had worked in the mills for almost 30 years. They lived in the rural south about 35 miles from the nearest metropolitan area. His high school graduated a small number of students yearly. Mark had decided to attend a community college some 30 miles from home for his first two years and then transfer to a larger, four-year college. Money, time, grades, goals, and family commitments led to his decision.

Mark was not a good student in high school. He finished with a D– average and his SAT scores and rank in his class *were in the lowest 25th percentile.* In fact, initially he had been *denied entrance to the community college.* The college granted him provisional acceptance only if he enrolled in, and successfully completed, a summer preparatory program. During the summer, Mark enrolled in the prep program, *never realizing what lay ahead.*

Mark's first class that semester was English. The professor walked in, handed out the syllabus, called the roll, and began to lecture. Lord Byron was the topic for the day. The professor sat on a stool by the window, leaned his elbow on the ledge, and sipped a cup of coffee as he told the story of how Byron's foot had been damaged at birth. He continued to weave the details of Byron's life poetically, through quotes and parables, until the 50-minute period had quietly slipped away. After an hour's break, Mark headed across campus for history. The professor entered with a dust storm behind her. She went over the syllabus, and before the class had a chance to blink, she was involved in the first lecture. "The cradle of civilization," she began, "was Mesopotamia." The class scurried to find notebooks and pens to begin taking notes. *Already they were behind, Mark included.* Exactly 47 minutes after she had begun to speak, the professor took her first breath. "You are in history now. You elected to take this class and you will follow my rules," she told the first-year students sitting in front of her. "You are not to be late, you are to come to this class prepared, and you are to read your homework. If you do what I ask you to do, you will learn more about Western civilization than you ever thought possible. *If you do not keep up with me,*

> **Mark was not a good student in high school. He finished with a D– average . . .**

you will not know if you are in Egypt, Mesopotamia, or pure hell! Class dismissed!"

Without a moment to spare, Mark ran to the other end of campus for his next class. He walked into the room in a panic, fearing he was late. To his surprise, the instructor was not yet in class. *The class waited for more than 10 minutes before the professor entered.* "You need to sign this roster and read chapter one for Wednesday," he said. "You can pick up a syllabus on your way out." *Mark was shocked. Was the class over?* What about the bell? The students in the class looked at each other with dismay and quietly left the room, wondering what Wednesday would hold. On the 30-mile trip home, Mark's mind was filled with new thoughts . . . *Lord Byron, Mesopotamia, professors who talked too fast, professors who did not talk at all, the cost of tuition, the size of the library.* He knew that something was different, *something had changed.* He couldn't put his finger on it. It would be years later before he would realize that the change was not his classes, not his schedule, not the people, not the professors—but himself; *Mark had changed.* In one day, he had tasted something intoxicating, something that was addictive. *He had tasted a new world.*

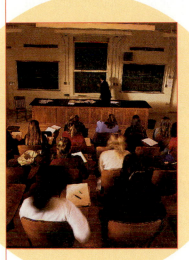

Mark had to go to work that afternoon, and even his job had changed. He had always known that he did not want to spend the rest of his life in the factory, but this day the feeling was stronger. His job was not enough, his family was not enough, the farm on which he had been raised was not enough anymore. *There was a new light for Mark, and he knew that because of one day in college, he would never be the same.* It was like tasting Godiva chocolate for the first time—Hershey's kisses were no longer enough. It was like seeing the ocean for the first time and knowing that the millpond would never be the same. *He couldn't go back. What he knew before was simply not enough.*

My name is Robert Mark Sherfield, and 24 years later, as I coauthor your text, I am still addicted to that new world. Spartanburg Methodist College changed my life, and I am still changing—with every day, every new book I read, every new class I teach, every new person I meet, and every new place to which I travel, I am changing.

at this moment?

STATEMENT	SCORE	Strongly Disagree	Disagree	Don't Know	Agree	Strongly Agree
1. I know why I'm in college.		1	2	3	4	5
2. I am confident about my ability to succeed in college.		1	2	3	4	5
3. I know what it takes to succeed in college.		1	2	3	4	5
4. I know how to make the necessary changes to succeed in college.		1	2	3	4	5
5. I focus on the positive aspects of change.		1	2	3	4	5
TOTAL		0–5	6–10	11–15	16–20	21–25

FEEDBACK

0 – 5	Extensive changes need to occur to ensure success.
6 – 10	Substantial changes need to occur to ensure success.
11 – 15	Considerable changes need to occur to ensure success.
16 – 20	Moderate changes need to occur to ensure success.
21 – 25	Minor changes need to occur to ensure success.

GOALS FOR CHANGE

Based on this feedback, my goals and objectives for change are . . .

Goal Statement _____

Action Steps 1. _____

2. _____

Goal Statement _____

Action Steps 1. _____

2. _____

Goal Statement _____

Action Steps 1. _____

2. _____

Results ● ● ●

Reading this chapter, completing the exercises, and reflecting on change will result in your:

- Identifying why college is important to you.

- Identifying reasons for attending college.

- Discussing how college changes people.

- Analyzing recent changes in your personal life.

- Preparing for changes in the coming days.

- Preparing for life changes.

- Recognizing and dealing with the physical and emotional effects of change.

- Incorporating into your life the cornerstones for dealing with change.

Why College?

Well, here you are, in college. Time to party? Time to get away from the children? Time to find a significant other? Time to study? Time to ponder the meaning of life? All these may be reasons to attend college. There are more than three and a half million first-year students in the nation's colleges right now; each one may have a different reason for being there. Some students are pursuing a high-paying job, developing a specific skill, retraining for the job market, following an old dream. Others are recently divorced and trying to acquire skills that were not taught 15 years ago. Some are in college because of pressure from their parents. And yes, there are those who say that they are in college to party and have a good time. Perhaps you've met a few of them already. And let us not forget the tens of thousands who say they are enrolled to experience developmental, interactive pedagogy and scientific relativity . . . NOT!

The college experience is different for every person. Some people love every minute of it, some people see it as a necessary evil to getting that wonderful job. Some see the college experience as a way of expanding horizons, and others see it as a two- or four- (or five-) year prison sentence!

The college experience is different for every person.

List the major reasons why you are in college today. Be honest with yourself!

1. _____

2. _____

3. _____

4. _____

Were all four blanks easy to fill? Did you do it quickly? As you discuss these reasons in class, you will find that many of your classmates are attending college for many of the same reasons you listed. If your class holds true to form, most of your classmates responded, "to get a

T
he real object of education is to give one resources that will endure as long as life endures; habits that time will not destroy; occupations that will render sickness tolerable, solitude pleasant, age venerable, life more dignified and useful, and death less terrible. —*S. SMITH*

better job and make more money." In 1999, the American Council on Education and the Cooperative Institutional Research Program reported that 73.2 percent of first-year students polled responded to this question with the answer, "to be able to get a better job." Seventy-five percent answered, "to make more money."

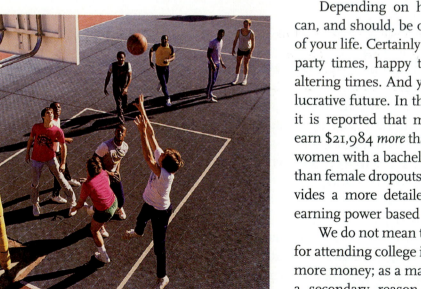

Involvement in extracurricular activities can enhance your college experience and help you adjust to change.

Depending on how you approach it, college can, and should, be one of the most exciting times of your life. Certainly college brings stressful times, party times, happy times, tearful times, and life-altering times. And yes, college can lead to a more lucrative future. In the book *Understanding* (1999), it is reported that men with a bachelor's degree earn $21,984 *more* than male high school dropouts; women with a bachelor's degree earn $17,527 more than female dropouts. The accompanying table provides a more detailed overview of differences in earning power based on sex and education level.

We do not mean to suggest that the only reason for attending college is to get a better job or to make more money; as a matter of fact, we feel that this is a secondary reason. Many other considerations may be at least as important as money to a person's decision to attend college, among them knowledge, spiritual development, sports, socialization, peer or parental pressure, and job training. Some of these reasons are practical, and some have a more altruistic appeal. Were any of these items listed as one of *your* reasons for attending college?

One response you probably won't find on your list of reasons for attending college—or on the lists of your classmates—is "I want to change." Although most people do not come to college for the express

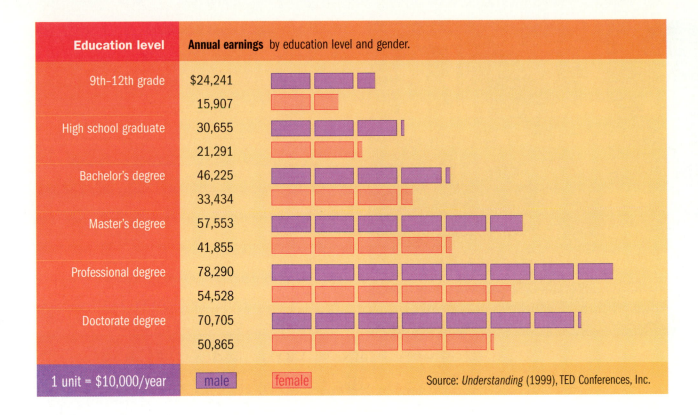

Education level	Annual earnings by education level and gender.								
9th–12th grade	$24,241								
	15,907								
High school graduate	30,655								
	21,291								
Bachelor's degree	46,225								
	33,434								
Master's degree	57,553								
	41,855								
Professional degree	78,290								
	54,528								
Doctorate degree	70,705								
	50,865								
1 unit = $10,000/year	male female								Source: *Understanding* (1999), TED Conferences, Inc.

purpose of changing, change is certain to happen during your college years. The key to dealing with change is to realize that change is the only thing in this world that is assured, short of death and taxes.

Whatever your reasons for attending college, if you embrace the notion that change is going to occur and respond to change by guiding it along, nurturing your new relationships with peers and professors, learning to study effectively, becoming involved in campus activities, and opening your mind to different views and ideologies, college will be a "moment in time" that you can carry with you for the rest of your life. You will be building on your best.

The Significance of Your College Experience

In your lifetime many events, people, places, and things will alter your views, personality, goals, and livelihood. Few decisions, people, or travels will have a greater influence on the rest of your life than your decision to attend college and the years you spend in structured higher learning. College can mean hopes realized, dreams fulfilled, and the breaking down of social and economic walls that may be holding you captive.

Before reading any further, jot down some thoughts about college life, what you value about being in college, what you expect from your institution, and what your college expects from you.

Regardless of your background or reasons for attending college, the experience of change is something you'll share with everyone. Will you be able to open yourself up to new people and new situations?

While in college, I want to achieve . . .

1. Better study habits
2. New friends
3. Improve my self-esteem
4.

I feel college is significant to my life because . . .

1. I will improve my way of thinking
2. I will gain a better and richer future
3. Earn a little more respect from peers & family
4.

From my college I expect . . .

1. To have a better understanding of me & my surroundings
2. To have a better paying job
3. To be content in my job
4.

Education is the knowledge of how to use the whole of oneself. Many use one or two faculties out of a score with which they are endowed. One is educated who knows how to make a tool of every faculty; how to open it, how to keep it sharp, and how to apply it to all practical purposes. —*H. W. BEECHER*

My college expects me to . . .

1. Study more & better
2. Perform better
3. Improve my training and thinking
4.

Noted authors and experts on the first-year student experience John Gardner and Jerome Jewler (2000) suggest that students undergo several life-altering changes and developments during their college years. Some of the changes they cite are:

- Your self-esteem grows
- Your political sophistication increases
- Your intellectual interests expand
- Your views become more flexible
- You are more concerned with wellness and health care

Our observations of college students reveal these changes also. If your professor were to make a video of you as first-year students and allow you to view it as seniors, you would be astounded at the changes in you. Beyond changes in appearance you would see development in attitudes, values, judgment, and character. Generally, college tends to teach students to be

Insider's view

Two years ago, I moved from my homeland of Niigata, Japan, to the United States. For the first time in my life, I was not living with my parents and I moved away from my close circle of friends and my support group. That was a major life change for me, the most major change I had ever faced or probably will ever face.

When I began college at CCSN, I was also faced with more changes. For the first time ever, I was in classes with people who were very, very different from me. I was shocked to see people who were older than me. In my school in Japan, this just did not happen. Another change from Japanese schools was the amount of discussion that took place in class. Again, I was shocked that I would actually have to participate and make statements in class.

Because I had just begun to speak English, I was shy and somewhat withdrawn. I was scared and separated from my family and friends. At first, people did not speak to me because they saw me as different. However, little by little, things began to get better. As classes progressed, I was placed into discussion or study groups and I began to get to know people. Ironically, it was the older students, the ones that I had been so shocked by, who struck up the first con-

versations with me. Because of their caring and concern, I began to speak more and meet more people. This has made a great deal of difference to me.

I have to say that the most frightening thing about coming to college was all of the decisions that I have had to make on my own. What classes will I take? What will my major be? When will I schedule my classes? For the first time, neither the school nor my parents were making decisions for me. I was afraid that I might make a big mistake if I did not take their advice. I quickly learned that I could depend on my advisors, the faculty members, and other students to help me. I would give you the same advice. Use the resources that you have at your college. Those resources can stop you from making many mistakes that first-year students like me make.

Coming to another country, making new friends, learning a new language, adapting to new customs, and sitting in classes with people from all over the world are huge changes. It has not been easy, but I know that this is where I need to be and that hotel management is what I want to do. The changes were worth it because I know that I can survive on my own, live on my own, and prosper with the love and support of my family and friends.

Eri Tsuchida, age 21
Major: Hotel Management
The Community College of Southern Nevada, Las Vegas, Nevada

Change is a learning process. If you are not changing, you are not learning or growing. In my position, I have to read and keep up on new issues and marketing concepts daily. Technology changes so quickly that I can't afford to get behind; that would be fatal in my profession.

One of the things that I like to do, and find useful in dealing with change, is to use the resources I have and draw from my colleagues in the office. Both help keep me focused and help me set goals. I also have to pay attention to what is going on and changing in my company, while at the same time, complete the tasks at hand. So, I had to learn how to do my daily job and plan for change at the same time. The best way that I have found to do this is to stay well informed about current trends and issues and have as much information as possible.

As you enter college, you will find that change is a daily activity. When you are in the college setting, you are faced with challenges and opportunities that will help you for the rest of your life. In the college environment, you are not necessarily protected. If you don't show up for classes, you're out of college. That is a change. College students are faced with the fact that one's actions have consequences. College helps you deal with that. It helps you understand how the world works. It polishes character.

Javier F. Ortiz, *Marketing Specialist*   Verizon Communications, Irving, Texas

more gentle, more accepting, more open, and more willing to get involved in their community and to share their resources; often, college creates in students the desire to continue to learn. Many college professors utilize a class portfolio to grade a student's progress. Keeping your class portfolios will enable you to have a visual record of your educational progress.

No one, not all the researchers in the world, not your authors, not your professors, not even your friends, can put a real value on the experience that college provides or the degree of change you will undergo. The value differs for each student, and it is private. You may share with others the benefits of your higher education, but fundamentally, the results of these years are quietly consumed by your character, your actions, and your values. Some people will change a little, some people will change a lot. For all, however, change is coming.

What Do You Want?
Thinking about Your Choices

Today, you face many decisions. Some of them will affect the rest of your life. Some changes and decisions will be of your own making; others will be beyond your control. Some will be easily altered; others will hold for the long run.

Before you read further, think about where you are at this very moment and where you want to be in the coming years. Remember the quotation, ("If you don't know where you are going, that's probably where you'll end up.") The following activity is one of the first cornerstones of this book. It requires you to look at your current status, your peers, your past, and your aspirations and is intended to guide you in evaluating your life, attitudes, and thoughts. Take your time, be honest with yourself, and think in terms of realistic goals.

1. *Define success.*

   Success is the element obtained thru hard work and says to society that you are a survivor.

2. *Name one person whom you deem successful. Why is that person successful?*

   Paula Anaya - H.S. Counselor - She is a sweet + smart person. Good all around human being

3. *List one accomplishment that would signify your success.*

   College graduation with a job right after.

4. *What will you have to change to achieve this accomplishment?*

   My lifestyle + attitude

5. *How will you approach these changes?*

   With Patient understanding

6. *What part will your college experience and education play in helping you reach this accomplishment?*

   Learning, experiencing, focusing, adjusting, concentrating

Changes in the Days to Come

One of the first changes you will notice about college is the degree of freedom you are given. There are no tardy notes to be sent to the principal's office, no hall passes, no mandates from the state regarding attendance, and, usually, no parent telling you to get up and get ready for school. You may have only one or two classes in a day. "Great!" you say, and maybe you're right. This freedom can be wonderful, but it can also be dangerous. Many people do their best when they are busy and have a limited amount

Thoughts ● ● ●

of time to accomplish a task. College can give you more freedom than you are used to. You need to learn how to handle it quickly, before the freedom that is intended to liberate you destroys you. Learning how to set priorities for your time, money, and resources is a critical step to successfully handling this freedom. Chapter 5 will help you with priority management.

Another change coming your way involves the workload for your courses. The workload is likely to be greater than what you are used to. You may be assigned a significant amount of reading as homework. Although

You gain strength, experience, and confidence by every experience where you really stop to look fear in the face . . . . You must do the thing you think you cannot. *—ELEANOR ROOSEVELT*

you may have only two classes in one day, the rule of thumb is that for every hour spent in class, a minimum of 2 hours should be spent in review and preparation for the next class. Quick math: if you are taking five classes and are in class for 15 hours per week, you need to spend 30 hours studying; this makes a 45-hour week—5 hours more than a normal work week for most people! Not I, you may say, and you may be right. It all depends on how wisely you use your time and how difficult the work is. However tempting, don't make the mistake of putting off assignments for very long. Waiting until the last minute may cause serious problems for you sooner or later; probably sooner. And, think about your schedule before you register to make sure that you have enough time to deal with the demands of the courses you have selected. Many professors now have their syllabi on the web, thus enabling you to review their course requirements before you schedule their class. Talk to friends, residence hall assistants, and returning students about your schedule; see what they think about it. Make informed decisions about your class schedules.

Understanding and using technology can help you research, write, and communicate.

Another change of paramount importance is the increased focus and attention paid to technology by your college professors. Your high school will probably have introduced you to many different computing concepts and applications. However, for those of you who are returning to college after a few years in the workforce or for those whose high schools did not have a strong computer emphasis, take every opportunity to learn as much about computers and technology as possible. You may be asked to submit assignments electronically, conduct research on the Internet, use a CD-ROM with one of your textbooks, or design your own statistical program for a research project. If you do not type, this is the first order of business. Enroll in a keyboarding class or a continuing education class in typing. You'll thank yourself for this essential skill.

You have probably already noticed a difference between your college professors and your high school teachers in terms of teaching style and relationships with students. You may have encountered a teaching assistant, usually a graduate student who serves as an instructor in first-year and sophomore-level classes. Unlike teaching assistants, college professors take on many different roles. They are involved in research, community and college service, teaching, and committee work.

A significant change you may face in the days and weeks to come is the amount of diversity in the people around you. You may have come from a high school with a fairly homogeneous student body. If you went to school in a metropolitan area such as New York, Atlanta, Los Angeles, Boston, Chicago, Dallas, or Washington, D.C., you may be used to a diverse student body. Regardless of your background, you will meet students, peers, and classmates whose views, values, customs, language, sexual orientation, race, ethnicity, and origin are 100 percent different from yours. You will encounter people who are atheistic and people who are ultra-religious; people who are pro-life and people who are pro-choice; people who are against the death penalty and people who support capital punishment; people who abhor interracial relationships and people to whom race does not matter. If you come from a region or from a family in which these positions are not openly expressed, you must prepare yourself for change and realize how much you can learn from diversity. Chapter 12 is dedicated to understanding diversity.

Remember, the healthiest way to deal with change is to realize that it happens daily and to prepare for it.

abhor
interracial
status quo

Common Characteristics of Any Change

Several characteristics are common to any change, regardless of its cause.

CHANGE IS NEVER EASY

Even the best changes in our lives, such as starting college, earning a promotion, having a baby, getting married, moving away from home, or buying a home, come with a degree of stress and anxiety. To deal effectively with change, we need to realize that even good change is often hard.

CHANGE IS ALMOST ALWAYS MET WITH RESISTANCE

Human beings are creatures of habit. We tend to resist change, especially if the change affects a security that has been enjoyed for a long period of time.

THE PERSON WHO INITIATES CHANGE IS ALMOST ALWAYS UNPOPULAR

The person who initiates change, the change agent, frequently is an outsider or is relatively new to a situation. By suggesting that change could improve a situation, this person threatens the status quo. Olesen (1993) suggests that when change occurs, everyone begins at zero, everyone begins anew. Thus, people who have been secure for years fear losing that security, and the person proposing change often becomes the subject of rumor and <u>innuendo</u>.

CHANGE CREATES UNFAMILIAR GROUND

We are more comfortable with what is familiar to us; the unfamiliar can be scary and sometimes dangerous. We may be inclined to shy away from change because it creates unfamiliar ground. It may be helpful to recognize that every new step is basically unfamiliar—for you and everyone around you. Not to take the step only limits your possibilities and weakens your opportunities. It is important to learn how to move out of the comfort zone, where you feel secure and warm. A ship may be safe in the harbor, but that is not what ships are made for.

CHANGE TAKES COURAGE

Often, because of the resistance and negative reactions of others, a change agent will remain quiet. It takes courage to initiate change. Even if a change will eventually benefit others, you sometimes have to risk unpopularity and <u>ridicule</u> to initiate change. Professors or fellow classmates who force you to evaluate a long-held belief are often viewed negatively. Don't ignore or reject these people because of your differences. Some of our most valued lessons come from people we may disagree with.

Physical and Emotional Reactions to Change

By the time you've read this far, you've probably gone through a few changes. Were they exciting? Were they stressful? When you experience change, your body typically goes through a process of physical and emotional change as well. Learning to recognize these symptoms in order to control them can help you control the stress that can accompany change. You may already have experienced some of these emotional and physical changes since arriving at your college. Take a moment now to reflect on your first few days in your new surroundings.

1. *How did you feel on entering your first class in college?*

   Neutral

2. *If you are married or have children, how did you feel when you had to leave your family today?*

I felt like I didn't want to leave them at all. I felt sad and that I was abandoning them

3. *How did you feel when you received your first syllabus outlining the content of a course?*

Like here I go again and I hope I do good.

4. *If you are living on campus, what physical changes occurred just before you met your new roommate? If you are living at home, how did you feel leaving today?*

Neutral and I didn't want to.

For most of you, these events caused a degree of stress and anxiety because you were experiencing change. Chapter 13 will help you learn to deal with the stress associated with college and everyday events.

Don't be shocked if your body and spirit begin to feel:

- Nervousness
- Stress
- A sense of being on the edge
- Fear
- Fatigue
- Guilt
- Homesickness
- Denial
- Anger
- Depression

These feelings are normal when you go through a powerful change, but they are temporary. If any of these feelings become overwhelming or life-threatening, seek counseling, talk to your friends, go to your advisor, or speak with your professors. These people are your support group; use them. Don't wait until it is too late to ask for help. Don't hide your feelings and pretend that nothing is wrong. Change is not easy. One of the most crucial steps in successfully dealing with change is realizing that it can cause problems.

It is also important to understand that many experts on change equate the feelings and emotions one encounters during major life changes with the feelings and emotions one faces when dealing with death. Some change experts suggest that a major life change is like a "little death."

Thoughts ● ● ●

In her pioneering research and study entitled *On Death and Dying* (1969), Elisabeth Kübler-Ross found that a person facing his or her own death or the death of a close loved one goes through a series of emotions. Those emotions and feelings come in stages:

1. Immobilization
2. Denial
3. Anger
4. Bargaining
5. Depression
6. Testing
7. Acceptance

Change experts suggest that these are the emotions that one might encounter when faced with a major life change, such as the loss of a job or career, a move away from home, the start of college, a divorce, or a cross-country transfer.

Understanding that these emotions and feelings are natural may aid you in coping with major life changes.

However, not all reactions to change will be negative. You may also begin to experience some of the following emotions:

Change can introduce you to new people, ideas, cultures, and experiences.

- A renewed sense of excitement
- Heightened awareness
- A more dynamic energy level
- Increased sensitivity to others
- Greater optimism
- A feeling of belonging
- Happiness

More than likely, you will find that you are going through a wide range of emotions and feelings. This is normal; don't get overwhelmed.

I n human life there is a constant change of fortune; and it is unreasonable to expect an exemption from this common fate. —*PLUTARCH*

Preparing for and Dealing with Change

Take a moment to reflect on what changes you might expect to experience this semester. Then list each change in one of the wedges on the change wheel below: record the change that you consider most stressful or the biggest change in the largest wedge; put the smallest change or the change that causes the least stress in the smallest wedge.

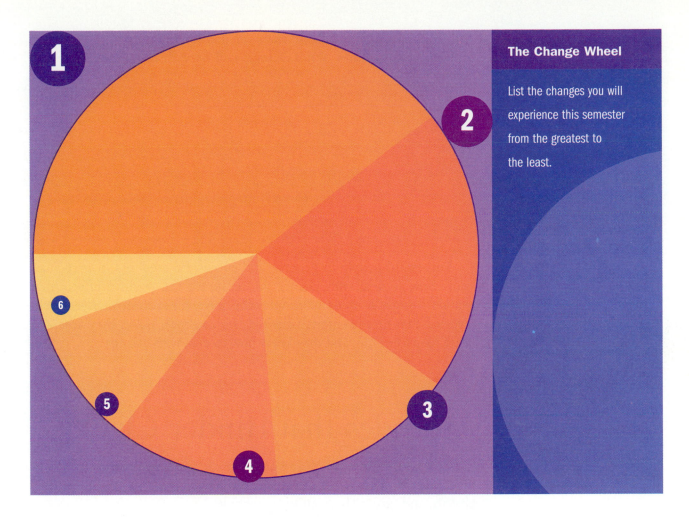

The Change Wheel

List the changes you will experience this semester from the greatest to the least.

Your world is different now that you are in college. People are different, attitudes are different, and classes are different. List some of the most obvious differences between your high school and your present institution.

1. I study and talk with more adults
2. My study habits are more detailed
3. I have more awareness and focus more on life.
4. I have become more careful & responsible
5. _____

Beyond the changes just listed, what changes have taken place in your personal life?

1. I have more friends
2. Partied more (just a little)
3. Had a Baby & got married.
4. _____
5. _____

Take a moment to think about where you want to be in one year, two years, or when you graduate. What changes will have to take place for this to happen?

_____

_____

_____

_____

_____

Successful people in general, and successful students in particular, know how to deal with change and embrace the positive effects that change brings. A study of people who were more than 100 years old revealed that these centenarians had two common traits: they accepted death as part of life, and they knew how to deal with change.

Attitudes that Hinder Change

You can develop attitudes that hinder change and stop growth. Such attitudes are dangerous because they rob you of opportunity, happiness, growth, and goals. These attitudes include:

- The "I can't" syndrome
- Apathy, or the "I don't care" syndrome
- Closed-mindedness
- Unfounded anxiety
- Fear of taking chances
- Loss of motivation
- The "let someone else deal with it" syndrome

If you can learn to control and watch out for these negative attitudes, you will begin to view change as a wonderful and positive lifelong event.

Changing Behaviors

There has to be some reason why you are sitting in a college classroom right now. There is something that you want to change or you would not be here. Maybe you are here to upgrade your technological skills, change your study habits, or learn how to maintain relationships. Whatever your reasons, consider the following suggestions as you continue changing and building on your best.

GET INVOLVED IN THE CHANGE

Most people let change happen to their lives; they don't try to direct the focus or the outcome of the change. Successful students get involved in the change that is happening in their lives and try to direct it toward a desirable outcome.

LET GO

The successful student knows how to let go of past events, places, and people who are not assisting in creating the desired future outcome.

HOLD ON

Holding on to people, memories, trinkets, and dreams that make you feel good and help you see today and tomorrow more clearly is healthy. The successful student knows when to hold on and when to let go. Both actions may be difficult, but both are necessary for dealing with change.

ASK FOR HELP

One of the most effective ways to deal with change is to ask for help, so don't be afraid or ashamed to do so. Many people will be having experiences similar to yours. Asking for help is the first step in finding a person to whom you can relate and with whom you feel comfortable.

DEVELOP A SENSE OF HUMOR

Laughter is one of the most powerful medicines available. Remember to laugh, smile, lounge around outside, admire the oak trees in the fall or flowers in the spring, eat a pizza, go to the movies. Too often, we forget to nourish our souls; we forget to feed our spirit a daily diet of beauty, and it grows tired and weary. Laughing and refusing to take life too seriously can provide the shot in the arm you need to make it through the week.

FOCUS ON THE OUTCOME

To deal effectively with change you need to look beyond the moment of fright or anxiety, to develop the ability to see the outcome. There has to be rain before there can be a rainbow. Moving beyond immediate gratification and realizing the potential long-term gain is a positive way to approach change.

SEARCH FOR TRUTH

Successful students know that they do not possess all the answers to every question; no one does. If you can look at change as a way of searching for the truth and deeper meaning, change will become less frightening, even though the truth can sometimes be unsettling.

TAKE RISKS

Although it does not come easily, learning to take calculated risks can be a tool for positive and steady growth.

HAVE AN OPEN MIND

Some of the most successful students deal with change by being open-minded, unbiased, and ready to listen to all sides.

VIEW CHANGE AS GROWTH

If your life is peaceful all the time, you are probably not growing or changing. Of course, everyone experiences times when things go according to plan and there is little change or anxiety; this is normal. But, if nothing has changed in your life in the past five years, you are most likely stagnating. Change means growth and as such, it is healthy; without change, there can be no progress.

COMMUNICATE WITH PEOPLE

One of the most effective and healthy ways to deal with change is to talk with others about it. Tell your friends and family what you're going through. Seek out people who may be going through, or may have recently gone through, the same changes.

MAINTAIN PERSPECTIVE

"This, too, shall pass." You may have to rely on this motto for a while to help you realize that change will not always be this stressful or this painful. Think clearly. Think about all the changes you've experienced in the past and how small they seem now compared with what they felt like when you were going through them. Keep things in perspective and deal with them accordingly. Enjoy the ride—"You shall pass this way but once."

A Moment in Time

The transition from one place to another is never easy, even when it is what you want. Entering college has forced you to assume new roles, develop new friendships, meet new people, work under different circumstances, and perhaps adjust your lifestyle. These changes form the very essence of the college experience; they create wonderful new experiences. Now is the time for you to seek new truths, associate with new and different people, read books that you will never have time to hold in your hands again, develop a solid philosophy of life, explore new religions, go to plays, buy season football tickets, join a club, read a book of poetry, go on a picnic with friends, sing, laugh, cry, write home, and love much. The winds of change are coming—*fly!*

Thoughts ● ● ●

BLUEPRINTS FOR CHANGE

NAME

DATE

C01P22

As a first-year student, identify one major area of change with which you have had difficulty.

_____

_____

_____

What emotions have you experienced because of this change?

_____

_____

_____

Have these emotions had a positive or negative impact on your response to this change? Why or why not?

_____

_____

_____

Identify two people in your life, such as a friend, parent, professor, sibling, or partner, who have experienced major life changes. Make an appointment to speak with these people. What questions will you ask them to assist you in your life changes?

Person 1 _____

Person 2 _____

Questions:

_____

_____

_____

_____

What words of wisdom did these people offer that shed some light on your issues? How can you apply this information in your own life?

_____

_____

_____

_____

_____

Having reviewed and reflected on the ways to change behavior, turn back to the change wheel you completed earlier in the chapter. Choose the biggest or the most stressful change that you identified on the wheel. Using the information provided above and throughout this chapter, identify several ways that you can effectively deal with this major change in your life.

1. _____

2. _____

3. _____

One Minute *Journal*

In one minute or less, jot down the major ideas that you learned from this chapter.

_____

_____

_____

_____

_____

_____

_____

_____

_____

_____

COMPANION Website *Journal*

Log on to **www.prenhall.com/montgomery**, choose the version of this book you are using, and then choose Chapter 1 on the menu. Next, choose "Links" on the left side of the screen. Explore one of the websites offered and summarize your findings.

_____

_____

_____

_____

_____

_____

_____

_____

_____

_____

_____

Refer to page 6 of Chapter 1.
Review your **GOALS FOR CHANGE**.
Respond in writing as to the progress
you have made toward reaching one
of your three stated goals.

GOAL STATEMENT

PROGRESS

How is your life changing because of this goal?

CORNERSTONES

for dealing with change

Remember, *challenges* can be *opportunities.*

Get involved and direct the change.

Changes are *worth the effort.*

Keep your sense of *humor.*

Talk to friends and family.

Change increases *energy.*

Change means growth.

Focus on the *positive.*

Be *courageous.*

Be *objective.*

Our world is a college, events are teachers, happiness is

Grow.

graduation, and character is the diploma.   N. D. Hillis

CHAPTER 2

Grow

This story began about ten years ago, when I met Leeah, a shy, sullen, withdrawn young woman, the daughter of an acquaintance. I had met Leeah's mother, a hotel housekeeper, while conducting training for the hotel staff, and knew that Leeah's mother had high hopes for her daughter. I thus took an interest in Leeah.

Leeah's family lived under *difficult circumstances.* Her father had abandoned the family when Leeah was a small child; her mother had supported the seven of them by working as a housecleaner. Leeah's mother was concerned for her daughter's future. Leeah had had few opportunities, little direction, and little encouragement— *almost everything was working against her.*

I asked Leeah about her plans after graduation from high school. Leeah responded that she would like to go to college but could not afford it. I asked to see Leeah's transcript and learned that she was ranked very high in her graduating class. *Leeah had more opportunities to go to college than she could imagine.*

I helped Leeah apply for grants and scholarships and gave her a job as a student assistant. It soon became obvious that Leeah was a *serious student.* She studied at every opportunity; she read voraciously, from classics to current events; she asked questions; and she observed everything. *She was like a sponge, literally soaking up knowledge.* Gradually, she began to change. She became more friendly and outgoing, her confidence seemed to increase, and she smiled more

> **I asked Leeah about her plans . . . Leeah responded that she would like to go to college but could not afford it.**

often. *Leeah was becoming a classic example of the powerful difference that education plus motivation, goal setting, and improved self-esteem can make in a person's life.*

Leeah matured rapidly and began to take on more responsibility. Although she had been awarded an endowed scholarship, which provided full tuition and room and board, she worked two jobs. She upgraded her wardrobe, bought a car, and became totally independent. She still conferred with me occasionally, but Leeah made most of her own decisions. She was *growing quickly and positively,* and she was beginning to know who she was and what she wanted. *More important, she began to realize what she could become.* All her professors quietly marveled at the dramatic changes in her.

When Leeah took my class as a junior, she was introduced to goal setting, motivation strategies, and using adversity as a strength. She listened quietly, asked questions, and quickly designed her own blueprint for success. Her self-esteem was at a high level. *Leeah was on her way because she had a clearly defined plan and she was willing to pay the price to reach her goals.*

Prior to graduation, Leeah applied to several prestigious graduate schools and was accepted at *every one.* She graduated *with honors* and was awarded several scholarships for graduate school. She continued to work two jobs during the sum-

mer; she wanted to save money for her expenses so that she would not have to work during the semester and could concentrate on her studies. Leeah was *highly motivated, goal directed, and focused* on her plans.

Several years later, Leeah stopped by my office. She had earned her CPA credentials and was a full-fledged accountant working for a Big Eight accounting firm. Dressed in a classic suit and carrying a briefcase, Leeah stood up straight, smiled with confidence, and spoke assertively. I was struck by the awesome difference between this

Leeah and the one I had met those many years ago. *Today, Leeah owns her own accounting firm, and several CPAs work for her.* She is a great example of the power of motivation and goal setting.

at this moment?

STATEMENT	SCORE	Strongly Disagree	Disagree	Don't Know	Agree	Strongly Agree
1. I am a highly motivated person at this time.		I	2	3	4	5
2. I prepare for my success every day.		I	2	3	4	5
3. I avoid letting my fears stand in my way.		I	2	3	4	5
4. I take the time to write my goals down and post them.		I	2	3	4	5
5. I like who I am and where I am going.		I	2	3	4	5
TOTAL		0–5	6–10	11–15	16–20	21–25

FEEDBACK

0 – 5   Extensive changes need to occur to ensure success.

6 – 10   Substantial changes need to occur to ensure success.

11 – 15   Considerable changes need to occur to ensure success.

16 – 20   Moderate changes need to occur to ensure success.

21 – 25   Minor changes need to occur to ensure success.

GOALS FOR CHANGE

Based on this feedback, my goals and objectives for change are . . .

Goal Statement _____

Action Steps 1. _____

          2. _____

Goal Statement _____

Action Steps 1. _____

          2. _____

Goal Statement _____

Action Steps 1. _____

          2. _____

Results

Reading this chapter, completing the exercises, and reflecting on your motivation, self-esteem, and goals will result in:

- Identifying your personal core values.
- Discussing the impact of your values on your personal goals.
- Discussing the importance of motivation in your life.
- Discussing the potential role of adversity in your success.
- Discussing the role of fear and desire in motivation.
- Using visualization of your goals to help you achieve them.
- Differentiating between short-term and long-term goals.
- Writing goals, objectives, and action steps for accomplishing your own personal strategic plan.
- Discussing the importance of self-esteem.
- Evaluating your own self-esteem.
- Listing and using strategies for improving self-esteem.

The Impact of Values on Motivation and Goal Setting

If you have been highly motivated to accomplish a goal in the past, this achievement was probably tied to something you valued a great deal. Most of what we do in life centers around what is truly important to us. You cannot get excited about achieving a goal or be disciplined enough to stick to it unless you definitely want to make it happen. If you really want to make the swim team, for example, you have to pay the price of long hours of practice, getting up early in the morning, and swimming when others are sleeping or playing. If you hate swimming, but you set a goal to make the swim team because your father was a champion swimmer and expects the same of you, you are not likely to achieve this goal. Your goals must relate to your personal value system.

Values, self-esteem, motivation, and goal setting are all mixed up together, making it difficult to separate one from the other. What you try to accomplish is directly connected to those things, ideas, and concepts that you value most.

Values are central beliefs and attitudes that make you a unique person, while greatly impacting your choices and your personal lifestyle.

If you cherish an attitude or belief, many of your actions will be centered around this ideal.

You were not born with your basic values. Your values were shaped to a great extent by your parents, the school you attended, the community where you grew up, and the culture that nourished you. Because of your personal background, you have developed a unique set of values. To make good decisions, set appropriate goals, and manage your priorities, you must identify those values that are central to who you are today. Until you clarify what you really value, you may try to accomplish what is important to someone else, and you will tend to wander around and become frustrated. Values, goals, and motivation bring direction to your life and help you get where you want to go.

Some people value education and knowledge more than anything. Others place a high priority on religion and spirituality, while others may place the highest priority on material possessions such as a big house, expensive car, and elegant clothes. Still others may place the greatest value on winning the race, scoring the most points, and setting records.

You will find that your values continue to change as you grow and mature. The core questions you should answer as you make value decisions are: What is right for me? Am I making this choice for the right reason and not because someone else wants me to do it?

You are likely to achieve goals that relate to your own personal value system and that are truly important to you. Have you thought much about your own goals? Are they your goals, or has someone else set them for you?

Do You Value College?

It may shock some people, but there are those who enroll in college and spend their money and time but do not value college or its benefits. Crazy? Most people would say yes, but consider the following: "Forty percent of students who start in four-year programs never finish their degrees. In two-year colleges, half or more of the entering class will drop out by the end of the first year" (Gardner, 2000).

W hen a man's willing and eager, the gods join in. —*AESCHYLUS*

This is not a new trend. In 1989, the Higher Education Research Institute reported that 32 percent of students attending 2,432 participating institutions did not return for their sophomore year.

Indeed, many factors may play a part in students' stopping or dropping out of college. A lack of motivation and active goal setting are among those factors.

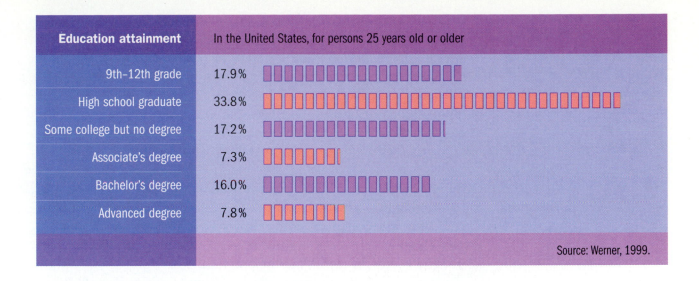

Education attainment	In the United States, for persons 25 years old or older	
9th–12th grade	17.9%	
High school graduate	33.8%	
Some college but no degree	17.2%	
Associate's degree	7.3%	
Bachelor's degree	16.0%	
Advanced degree	7.8%	

Source: Werner, 1999.

Examine the chart above. You will find that the majority of people in the United States have no college degree.

Obtaining a college degree requires a high level of motivation and a keen awareness of goal setting and achievement.

Attitude—The First Step in Getting What You Want

How many people have you met who turned you off immediately with their negative attitudes? They whine about the weather or their parents; they verbally attack people who differ from them; they degrade themselves with negative remarks. Listen for the negative comments people make, and the messages they send out about themselves. When people continually feed their brains negative messages, their bodies respond accordingly.

You may feel that you have had enough of attitude. Your parents talked to you about it, your teachers hounded you about it. But it is important! The impact of a bad attitude on your self-esteem is overpowering, and the importance of a good attitude should not be underestimated. Focusing on the positive can bring dramatic changes in your life.

We all know that life sometimes deals bad blows, but your goal should be to be positive much more often than you are negative. Positive attitudes go hand in hand with energy, motivation, and friendliness. People with positive attitudes are more appealing; negative people drive others away.

Listen to yourself for a few days. Are you whining, complaining, griping, and finding fault with everything and everybody around you? Do you blame your roommate for your problems? Is your bad grade the professor's fault? Are your parents responsible for everything bad that ever happened to you? If these kinds of thoughts are coming out of your mouth or are in your head, your first step toward improved self-esteem is to clean up your act.

To be successful at anything, you have to develop a winning attitude. You have to eliminate negative thinking. Begin today: tell yourself only positive things about yourself; build on those positives; focus on the good things; work constantly to improve.

Winners get up early with an attitude of "I can't wait for this day to start so I can have another good day." OK, OK—so you may not get up

Thought for every morning: *this is going to be a great day for me!*

early, but you can get up with a positive attitude. Tell yourself things that will put you in the right frame of mind to succeed. When you are talking to yourself—and everybody does—feed your brain positive thoughts. Think of your brain as a powerful computer; you program it with your words, and your body carries out the program.

Pay attention to the messages you send out to others as well. What kinds of remarks do you make about yourself and about others when you are with your friends? Do you sound positive or negative? Do you hear yourself saying positive things?

Preparing for Success

1. Prepare for success the evening before—organize your clothes and books and make a list of things you need to do the next day. (You'll read more about this in Chapter 5.)

2. Eat properly, get enough rest, and exercise. Winners know that a fit mind requires a fit body.

3. Get up early (at least occasionally), sing in the shower, and think about positive outcomes.

4. Talk to yourself using positive "I" statements: "I will have a good day today"; "I will perform well today because I have prepared to do well"; "I will be happy and positive and outgoing."

5. Read motivational books as well as biographies of famous people who overcame adversity to reach their goals. Reading will help keep you motivated while expanding your knowledge!

6. Practice your religion and seek spiritual wellness.

CHOOSE YOUR FRIENDS CAREFULLY

Although your motivation and attitude belong to you and are uniquely yours, they can be greatly influenced by the people with whom you associate. People do tend to become like the people with whom they spend time.

As a new college student, you have a clean slate where friends are concerned. You need to choose your very best friends carefully. Of course you want to spend time with people who have interests in common with yours. That's a given. But you also want your friends to have ambition, good work habits, positive attitudes, and high ethical standards. Seek out people who read good books, watch educational television programs, are goal oriented, and don't mind taking a stand when they believe strongly about something. Find friends who will work out with you, go to the library with you, attend plays and concerts with you. One of the best ways to make the most of your college education is to befriend people who have interests and hobbies that are new to you. Staying focused is much easier if you surround yourself with positive, motivated, goal-oriented people.

How are the friends you are making in college influencing your decisions?

Overcoming Doubts and Fears

Fear is a great motivator; it probably motivates more people than anything else. Unfortunately, it motivates most people to hold back, to doubt themselves, to accomplish much less than they could, and to hide the person they really are.

One of the biggest obstacles to reaching your potential may be your own personal fears. If you are afraid, you are not alone; everyone has fears. It is interesting to note that our fears are learned. As a baby, you had two fears: a fear of falling and a fear of loud noises. As you got older, you added to your list of fears. And, if you are like most people, you let your fears dominate parts of your life, saying things to yourself like: "What if I try and fail?" "What if people laugh at me for thinking I can do this?" "What if someone finds out that this is my dream?"

You have two choices where fear is concerned. You can let fear dominate your life, or you can focus on those things you really want to accomplish, put your fears behind you, and go for it. The people most successful in their fields will tell you that they are afraid, but that they overcome their fear because their desire to achieve is greater. Barbra Streisand, recording artist and stage performer, becomes physically nauseated with stage fright when she performs, yet she faces these fears and retains her position as one of the most popular entertainers of our time.

They who have conquered doubt and fear have conquered failure.

—*JAMES ALLEN*

Name one of the smallest fears you have now. What can you do to overcome it?

_____

_____

_____

_____

_____

What is your greatest fear? Why do you think you have this fear?

_____

_____

_____

_____

_____

What steps do you think you can take to overcome this fear?

_____

_____

_____

_____

_____

MOVING OUT OF YOUR COMFORT ZONE

Successful people face their fears because their motivation and ambition force them out of their comfort zones. Your comfort zone is where you know you are good, you feel confident, and you don't have to stretch your talents far to be successful. If you stay in your comfort zone, you will never reach your potential and you will deny yourself the opportunity of knowing how it feels to overcome your fears.

Deciding to go to college probably caused you some level of discomfort and raised many fears: "What if I can't make good grades?" "What if I flunk out?" "What if I can't make the team?" "What if I can't keep up with the kids just out of high school?" "What if I can't do my job, go to school, and manage a family at the same time?" The mere fact that you are here is a step outside your comfort zone—a very important step that can change your life dramatically.

Everyone has a comfort zone. When you are doing something that you do well, and you feel comfortable and confident, you are in your comfort zone. When you are nervous and afraid, you are stepping outside your comfort zone. When you realize you are outside your comfort zone, you should feel good about yourself because you are learning and growing and improving. You cannot progress unless you step outside your comfort zone.

DEALING WITH ADVERSITY AND FAILURE

To be motivated, you have to learn to deal with failure. Have you ever given up on something too quickly, or gotten discouraged and quit? Can you think of a time when you were unfair to yourself because you didn't stay with something long enough? Did you ever stop doing something you wanted to do because somebody laughed at you or teased you? Overcoming failure makes victory much more rewarding. Motivated people know that losing is a part of winning: the difference between being a winner and being a loser is the ability to try again.

If you reflect on your life, you may well discover that you gained your greatest strengths through adversity. Difficult situations make you tougher and more capable of developing your potential. Overcoming adversity is an essential part of success in college and in life.

Think of a time in your life when you faced difficulties but persisted and became stronger as a result. Perhaps you failed a course, didn't make an athletic team, lost a school election, had a serious illness, broke up with a long-term boyfriend or girlfriend, or experienced your parents' divorce. If you are a nontraditional student you may have been fired from a job or passed over for a promotion, suffered through a divorce, or experienced a death in the family.

Describe your experience of adversity.

_____

_____

_____

What did you learn from this experience?

_____

_____

_____

_____

How can you use this experience as a reminder that you can overcome adversity, learn to grow from it, and become a better person as a result of it?

_____

_____

_____

_____

_____

Thoughts ● ● ●

The Goal-Setting Process

Goal setting itself is relatively easy. Many people make goals, but fail to make the commitment to accomplish those goals. Instead of defining their goals in concrete, measurable terms, they think of them occasionally and have vague, unclear ideas about how to attain them. The first step toward reaching a goal is the commitment to pay the price to achieve it. Opportunities abound everywhere; commitment is a scarce commodity.

When you are ready to make a commitment to achieve your goals, write them down, along with steps for accomplishing deadlines that must be honored. These goals are your targets. Now you are ready to act, to begin accomplishing your goals, and you need to do so without delay. Be prepared to fail, because you surely will fail some of the time, but you must be equally committed to getting up and trying again. Your commitment to success must be so strong that quitting would never even occur to you.

Insider's View

As children, we might have imagined many things. Were we fair maidens or handsome princes? Were we going to be hairstylists or firefighters, nurses or doctors, lawyers or movie stars? As you think back, you may ask yourself, when did I first start dreaming about "becoming" something? Even more importantly, as you look back, you may begin to ask yourself, when did I set my first goal and start working toward that goal?

Goals can help you realize your dreams. A goal is really nothing more than a dream with a plan. Goals can help bring purpose to your life and help you discover a great deal about yourself. The thing that I found out about goals is that you have to set them for yourself. No one can set a goal for you. They have to be attainable. I found that if you start with small goals and work toward larger ones, they are easier to accomplish.

A goal must also be something that you want. If setting a goal makes you unhappy, then you won't be committed to that goal. If someone else sets that goal for you, then you will not have the commitment to that goal either. A goal is a personal commitment to yourself. It is a contract with your soul.

I think that the hardest part about goal setting for me was learning that we have to give up some things in order to reach our goals. Few things come without a price. I also had to learn that when we set goals, we may be afraid or apprehensive, but that is normal. It is always normal to have some fear when we begin a new journey or a new path. So, relax, have confidence, believe in yourself and your goals, and you'll be amazed at what your "plan" can help you accomplish.

However, one of the most important lessons that I learned is that a goal without the inner motivation is worthless. You can write as many goals as you like, put them on 1,000 sheets of paper and post them around the world, but unless you find the driving force that makes you go after these goals, they will remain just words on a sheet of paper. Just remember, a dream can become a reality when you decide to make it a goal and go for it with all of your heart.

Bethany Noble, *age 32*

Major: Dental Hygiene
Palm Beach Community College,
Boca Raton, Florida

Do, Be, or Have Exercise

What do I want to do?

_____

_____

What do I want to be?

_____

_____

What do I want to have?

_____

_____

CHARACTERISTICS OF ATTAINABLE GOALS

It is usually easier to set goals than to achieve them. To be able to set attainable goals, you need to know their characteristics. Attainable goals must be

- **Reasonable.** Your goals need to be based on your abilities, desires, and talents. If you made terrible grades in English composition and hate to sit at a computer, you shouldn't set a goal to become a writer. On the other hand, if you are a star athlete and love to work with young people, your goal might be to become a coach.

- **Believable.** To achieve a goal, you must really believe it is within your capacity to reach it. You may want a sailboat very badly, but the cost may be prohibitive. If you want it, but don't believe you can get it, you are probably fooling yourself—at least at this stage of the game.

A goal is anything you can do, be, or have.

- **Measurable.** A goal needs to be concrete and measurable in some way. If you set a vague goal, such as "I want to be happy," you cannot know if you've attained your goal, because you have no way of measuring it.

- **Adaptable.** Your goals may need to be adapted to changing circumstances in your life. You may begin with a goal and find that you have to change direction for one reason or another. Maybe you don't like this goal once you learn more about it or perhaps some insurmountable obstacle arises. You might have to adjust your expectations and the goal itself in order to achieve it.

- **Controllable.** Your goals should be within your own control; they should not depend on the whims and opinions of anyone else. For example, if your goal is to learn to play golf well enough to score 90, you need to control your practice and the times you play; you do not want to practice based on the needs of your roommate, who may have strengths and weaknesses different from yours.

- **Desirable.** To attain a difficult goal, you must want it very badly. You cannot make yourself work for something just because someone else wants it. If you have always dreamed about becoming a teacher of young children, set this as your goal; it will be extremely difficult for you to stay on course to become a medical researcher because your parents want you to follow in their footsteps.

Look at your responses in the Do, Be, or Have Exercise. Measure them against the characteristics of attainable goals. Do you think the goals you discussed are within your reach? Can you control events that could prevent you from attaining them? Do you really believe you can do what you want to do? Can you measure your success? Can these goals be adjusted if necessary? Do you really want to do, be, or have the things you listed?

HOW TO WRITE GOALS

Webster's New Collegiate Dictionary defines a goal as "the end toward which effort is directed." The process of goal setting involves deciding what you want and working to get it. Goals can be short term or long term. Short-term goals can usually be accomplished within six months or a year, although they could be accomplished in a much shorter time. "Within six months I will save enough money to spend a week skiing in Vail" is a short-term goal; "Within six years, I will become a certified public accountant (CPA)" is a long-term goal.

When you write goals you need to include a goal statement, action steps, and target dates. The goal statement should be specific and measurable, that is, it should entail some tangible evidence of its achievement. An example of a goal statement is "I will lose 10 pounds in six weeks." You can make goal statements from intangibles if you can devise a way to measure the desired outcome. For example, "I will develop a more positive attitude by the end of six weeks as evidenced by at least three people commenting on my improved attitude and by my dealing positively with at least three negative situations weekly."

After you write the goal statement, you'll need to create specific action steps that explain exactly what you are going to do to reach your goal. Then decide on a target date for reaching your goal.

The next step in writing goals is to write a narrative about what your goal accomplishments will mean to you. If your goals don't offer you significant rewards, you are not likely to stick to your plan. Lastly, write two reasons *why* you deserve the goal.

When you have accomplished your goals, you need to begin the process again. Successful people never get to a target and sit down; they are always becoming. They reach one goal and begin dreaming, planning, preparing for the next accomplishment.

● ● ● **Thoughts**

Although the documentation may be hard to find, I would be willing to bet that even cave dwellers were at times unmotivated. Just think about it. By day they hunted and gathered their family's meals, and by night they protected them from becoming meals. Their benefits were lousy—no holidays and not a stock option or 401-K plan in sight. And they probably had never heard of a 40-hour work week. Archaeologists have actually found cave-wall drawings that seem to say, "Is this all there is?"

As college students, you may be asking yourself the same question, "Is this all there is?" or "Is education really worth it?" After nights of study accompanied by the inevitable oral reports, you may occasionally want to just turn off the alarm, curl up in bed, grab a box of chocolate Snackwells, and watch "I Love Lucy" reruns. If you do, you are not alone, and the feeling does not decrease when you get into your chosen profession. Throughout our lives, we must learn to re-charge, re-engage, and re-motivate. The rewards for completing tasks at hand are the only things that change.

Throughout my several different, yet related careers, I have re-charged by studying areas that are new and exciting to me. Going back to school and taking additional courses were energizers. The courses usually did not even relate to what I was doing professionally at the moment. However, what I was learning eventually allowed me to parlay my skills into several exciting and lucrative positions, including Convention Manager for a national association and a Consultant and Personal Development Trainer.

Wanda Daniel, Ed.D., *Consultant and Personal Development Trainer,* Impression Management International, Atlanta, Georgia

Now you are ready to begin the exciting adventure known only to goal setters, using the worksheets on pages 45–46. To help you get started, we'll discuss below some common areas for which you might want to set goals. Think about goals in these terms: you can have a boat, you can be a member of the student government, you can play a musical instrument—a goal can apply to any area of your life. Use the questions in the box on page 47 to help you decide what goals to set. After reading these sections, however, you might want to venture off in a different direction. That's perfectly all right, since these are your goals.

Categories for Goals

Personal or Self-Improvement. Set a goal that relates to your personal life. For example, you might want to work on punctuality.

Goal: I will be on time and prepared for all my classes this semester.

Academic. You might set a goal of reaching a certain grade point average. A word of caution: don't set an average of 4.0 as your goal if you have always been a B student; strive first for a B+. Remember the "a little better every day" philosophy.

Goal: I will earn at least a B+ on my first English exam.

Family. You might want to do something nice for your parents or for a younger sibling.

Goal: I will go home for my brother's birthday and will spend the weekend doing whatever he wants to do.

Career. You could decide on a major or choose some electives that will allow you to explore new areas of interest.

Goal: I will take an elective in sports management next semester to determine if this major appeals to me.

Financial. Now is a good time to focus on managing your money, even if you don't have a great deal of it. Set a goal that will help you to establish good financial management practices.

Goal: I will save $400 by December so I can buy my family gifts.

Community Service. Set a goal to become involved in community service. Serving other people can be as rewarding for you as it is for those you help.

Goal: I will volunteer 10 hours of my time each week to the Madison Hospital in the area of children's physical therapy.

Social. You might want to work on certain social skills, such as restaurant etiquette or dancing, or you might want to limit your social life to certain activities.

Goal: I will take a course in dancing to improve my social skills.

Health. Set goals that will help you to relieve stress and stay in top condition. You might set goals that involve exercise, proper diet, or enough rest.

Goal: I will limit my fat intake to 36 grams per day.

Spiritual. Set goals to keep you spiritually fit. Anything that makes you feel alive and well can be part of your spiritual goal, such as walking on the beach or watching a touching movie.

Goal: I will participate in at least three activities each week that are spiritually rewarding and renewing for me.

setting goals

GOAL STATEMENT

Name _____

_____

_____

ACTION STEPS

1. _____

2. _____

3. _____

4. _____

TARGET DATE ◎

_____

NARRATIVE STATEMENT

_____

_____

_____

_____

_____

_____

_____

_____

_____

_____

_____

I deserve this goal because:

1. _____

_____

2. _____

_____

I hereby make this promise to myself.

date _____ signature _____

GOAL STATEMENT

Name _____

_____

_____

ACTION STEPS

1. _____

2. _____

3. _____

4. _____

TARGET DATE

NARRATIVE STATEMENT

_____

_____

_____

_____

_____

_____

_____

_____

_____

_____

I deserve this goal because:

1. _____

_____

2. _____

_____

I hereby make this promise to myself.

date _____ signature _____

Evaluation Plan for Your Goals

- Do I really want to achieve this goal enough to pay the price and to stick with it?

- What is the personal payoff to me if I achieve this goal?

- Who will notice if I achieve this goal? Does that matter to me?

- How realistic is this goal? Am I way over my head for this stage of my development?

- Do I need to reduce my expectations so I won't be disillusioned in the beginning, and then increase the difficulty of my goal only after I have reached the first steps?

- Can I control all the factors necessary to achieve this goal?

- Is this goal specific and measurable?

- Does this goal contribute to my overall development? Is this goal allowing me to spend my time in the way that is best for me right now?

- How will I feel when I reach this goal?

- Will my parents and friends be proud that I accomplished this goal?

- Will the achievement of this goal increase my self-esteem?

The Impact of Self-Esteem on Your Motivation

Some people are not as motivated as they might be because they suffer from poor self-esteem. Self-esteem is how you feel about yourself—the value you place on who you are as a person—and it impacts everything you do. Your grades, relationships, extracurricular activities, and motivation can all be impacted by your self-esteem.

You might think of self-esteem as a photograph of yourself that you keep locked in your mind. It is a cumulative product developed through many experiences and through relationships with many people.

People who demonstrate a high degree of self-esteem and confidence usually have five characteristics.

Characteristics of Self-Esteem

1. A sense of security	3. A sense of belonging	5. A sense of personal competence
2. A sense of identity	4. A sense of purpose	

These characteristics are considered key to a person's ability to approach life with confidence, maintain self-direction, and achieve outstanding accomplishments. As a high school senior or on the job, you might have felt pretty good about yourself, but since you have entered a new environment, you may find that your self-esteem is lower. It is natural to be nervous or to feel threatened as you move into a new environment. If your self-esteem is healthy, you will soon feel comfortable again.

All of us have had experiences that have negatively affected our self-esteem and kept us from being as successful and happy as we could be. Can you think of experiences in your past that have had a negative impact on your self-esteem?

Before reading any further, familiarize yourself with these important things to remember about self.

Self
WHAT MAKES ME WHO I AM

- Your self is made up of all experiences, beliefs, opinions, and attitudes that relate to you.

- Taking care of, protecting, and improving the self is the foundation of everyone's behavior.

- The protection of self causes people to position themselves in the best light.

- Your self needs your acceptance as much as it needs the acceptance of others.

- Most of your behaviors are consistent with how you feel about your self.

- Your self is constantly changing as you accept new ideas and discard old ones. (This idea is encouraging, because it means that you can change your self-esteem and make it better. It also suggests the necessity of constantly working on your self-esteem because as you change, your self-esteem will change too.)

- If you change your feelings about your self, your behavior will change. Learning to love your self will most likely result in better grades, improved relationships, and more direction and focus in your life.

- Your self needs routine, consistency, and patterns; therefore, introducing change to your self may bring some resistance. (Change is the hardest thing for human beings to face, even when they want it and when they know that, in the long run, it will be for the best.)

Influences on Self-Esteem

The concept of the child within has been a part of our culture for more than 2000 years. Psychotherapists have used different names for this concept: Donald Winnicott called it the "true self," Carl Jung used the "divine child," and Emmett Fox used the "wonder child"; many others refer to it as simply the inner child.

The child within is the very best part of us. It is our joy, enthusiasm, energy, and spontaneity; it determines whether we are fun-filled and happy, as well as fulfilled and productive. Troubled, dysfunctional families damage the inner child, resulting in anxiety, fear, emptiness, confusion, and low self-esteem. No matter what your past, however, you can learn to improve your self-esteem and, along with it, your happiness and success.

Many young girls believe that girls can't do math as well as boys; young men who show emotion may be ridiculed for not "being a man"; some boys believe that girls are more academically oriented than boys. These and similar notions, perpetuated by society, can contribute to the development of poor self-esteem and a damaged inner child.

Many people, especially women, are unhappy with their appearance, and these feelings often engender low self-esteem. Bulimia and anorexia may arise when thinness is inextricably linked to a person's feeling good about herself—these disorders are found primarily in women. College students carry the extra baggage of a societal value that links self-esteem and appearance, again, particularly for women. Sandra Haber, a New York City psychiatrist, specializes in eating disorders. Haber believes that what we see in the mirror is what we take into all our roles. In other words, how we see ourselves equates to our self-esteem.

Many people are obsessed with their outer shell and believe that if they can be thin enough or wear the right clothes or have big muscles, they will somehow miraculously be loved by others. Recently there has been an increase in the number of young boys taking steroids to pump themselves up, even though they know it can be dangerous to their health. Paying attention to physical appearance is important and can improve your feelings about yourself, but emphasis on appearance without attention to mental and emotional well-being will rarely bring about lasting change.

Alcoholism, drug dependency, abusive relationships, and promiscuous sexual behavior are other symptoms of low self-esteem. No one is born with low self-esteem. Many of the root causes of low self-esteem begin in childhood and are often in the form of "messages" given to us by parents, teachers, peers, and others. Since many of these thoughts related to poor self-esteem originated many years ago, you need to realize that correcting these problems may take time. The result is worth the effort, however, if you learn to love and value yourself.

Behaviors Associated with Poor Self-Esteem

Some of the most frequently observed behaviors associated with poor self-esteem are listed here. Place a check by the characteristics you recognize in yourself.

_____✔_____ *Am critical of myself and others*

_____✔_____ *Have guilty feelings*

_____ *Set unrealistic goals*

_____✔_____ *Have many physical complaints*

_____✔_____ *Hold extreme views of life*

_____ *Have little belief in my capabilities*

_____✔_____ *Am destructive*

_____ *Abuse substances*

_____✔_____ *Put myself down*

_____✔_____ *Am self-destructive*

_____ *Have difficulty facing reality*

_____✔_____ *Worry unreasonably*

_____✔_____ *Feel that I must always* ~~be dressed~~ perfectly   [handwritten: physically look]

_____ *Place too much importance on wearing brand-name clothing*

_____✔_____ *Always arrive late*

_____ *Always arrive early*

_____ *Have difficulty establishing intimacy*

_____✔_____ *Am preoccupied with what others may think of me*

_____ *Cannot adequately face the demands of life*

Now look over your responses and list the three items that you think have the most negative impact on your self-esteem.

1. _____

2. _____

3. _____

Using the goal-setting process discussed earlier, devise a goal plan to work on these areas.

Improving Your Self-Esteem

WHY SHOULD YOU DO IT?

You may be wondering what the point of all this is—why should you worry about self-esteem when you already have concerns about grades, work, laundry, relationships, and a million other things? Who has time for all this extra stuff? Maybe you think you can wait to worry about your self-esteem when you finish college. The reason you need to be concerned now is that your grades, work, social life—everything—are tied up with your self-esteem.

Several outstanding psychiatrists and professors stress the importance of addressing self-esteem in the educational process, believing that self-esteem goes hand in hand with academics. Carl Rogers (1972), a noted psychiatrist who has developed many psychological theories and ideas about self-esteem, wrote, "Sometimes I feel our education has as one of its major goals the bringing up of individuals to live in isolation cages." Leo Buscaglia (1982), a well-known professor who has taught for years on the subjects of love and relationships, asks, "How many classes did you ever have in your entire educational career that taught you about you?"

Your relationships with others—friends, parents, children, professors, bosses, spouses—depend on how well you have developed your own self-esteem. You are not an isolated human being. Every day you must relate to others, and your self-esteem will influence the kinds of relationships you build. You will continue to meet new people and face new challenges with the people you know as you grow and mature, and these challenges are likely to increase in complexity. Unless you are planning to live a life alone in the woods, you will rely on your ability to relate positively to all kinds of people. The basis for those relationships lies within you, in your self-esteem.

WAYS TO INCREASE YOUR SELF-ESTEEM

Take Control of Your Own Life

If you let other people rule your life, you will always have poor self-esteem. You will feel helpless and out of control as long as someone else has power over your life. Part of growing up is taking control of your life and making your own decisions. Get involved in the decisions that shape your life. Seize control—don't let life happen to you!

Adopt the Idea that You Are Responsible for You

The day you take responsibility for yourself and what happens to you is the day you start to develop your self-esteem. When you can admit your mistakes and celebrate your successes knowing you did it your way, you will learn to love yourself much better.

Refuse to Allow Friends and Family to Tear You Down

You may have family or friends who belittle you, criticize your decisions, and refuse to let you make your own decisions. Combat their negativity by admitting your mistakes and shortcomings to yourself and by making up your mind that you are going to overcome them. By doing this, you are taking their negative power away from them.

Control What You Say to Yourself

"Self-talk" is important to your self-esteem and to your ability to motivate yourself positively. Your brain is like a powerful computer and it continually plays messages to you. If these self-talk messages are negative, they will have a detrimental impact on your self-esteem and on your ability to live up to your potential. Make a habit of saying positive things to yourself: "I will do well on this test because I am prepared." "I am a good and decent person, and I deserve to do well." "I will kick the ball straight."

Take Carefully Assessed Risks Often

Many people find risk taking very hard to do, but it is one of the very best ways to raise your self-esteem level. If you are going to grow to your fullest potential, you will have to learn to take some calculated risks. While you should never take foolhardy risks that might endanger your life, you must constantly be willing to push yourself out of your comfort zone.

Don't Compare Yourself to Other People

You may never be able to "beat" some people at certain things. But it really does not matter. You only have to beat yourself to get better. If you constantly tell yourself that you "are not as handsome as Bill," or "as smart as Mary," or "as athletic as Jack," your inner voice will begin to believe these statements, and your body will act accordingly. One of the best ways to improve self-esteem and to accomplish goals is simply to get a little better every day without thinking about what other people are doing. If you are always practicing at improving yourself, sooner or later you will become a person you can admire—and others will admire you, too!

Develop a Victory Wall or Victory File

Many times, you tend to take your accomplishments and hide them in a drawer or closet. Put your certificates, letters of praise, trophies, and awards out where you can see them on a daily basis. Keep a file of great cartoons, letters of support, or friendly cards so that you can refer to them from time to time.

Keep Your Promises and Be Loyal to Friends, Family, and Yourself

If you have ever had someone break a promise to you, you know how it feels to have your loyalty betrayed. The most outstanding feature of one's character is one's ability to be loyal, keep one's promises, and do what one has agreed to do. Few things can make you feel better about yourself than being loyal and keeping your word.

Win with Grace—Lose with Class

Everyone loves a winner, but everyone also loves a person who can lose with class and dignity. On the other hand, no one loves a bragging winner or a moaning loser. If you are engaged in sports, debate, acting, art shows, or math competitions, you will encounter winning and losing. Remember, whether you win or lose, if you're involved and active, you're already in the top 10 percent of the population.

If you read news articles or magazines, you will find some reference to low self-esteem. According to numerous experts, many violent acts, unwanted pregnancies, and spousal and child abuse cases are attributed to low self-esteem.

Locate and read the following article: "You're OK, I'm Terrific: Self-Esteem Back-fires," *Newsweek,* July 13, 1998, p. 69. Summarize the main points from the article.

_____

_____

_____

_____

_____

What emotions related to self-esteem did this article elicit? How do you feel when people attribute their actions to low self-esteem?

Thinking

_____

_____

How do you agree or disagree with the premises stated in this article relative to how young people are impacted by receiving excessive amounts of praise?

_____

_____

_____

Think about your own education and life and how self-esteem has impacted both thus far. In Column A below, list two positive remarks that someone has made to you. In Column B, tell how these remarks affected you.

Column A
Positive Remarks

_____

_____

Column B
Impact of Remarks

_____

_____

Now, in Column A, describe two negative remarks that someone has made to you or about you. In Column B, tell how the negative remarks affected you.

Column A
Negative Remarks

_____

_____

Column B
Impact of Remarks

_____

_____

Change

On a separate sheet of paper, list five to seven ways that you can take negative remarks and use them to improve your self-esteem.

LIFE

One Minute *Journal*

In one minute or less, jot down the major ideas that you learned from this chapter.

_____

_____

_____

_____

_____

_____

_____

_____

_____

COMPANION Website *Journal*

Log on to **www.prenhall.com/montgomery**, choose the version of this book you are using, and then choose Chapter 2 on the menu. Next, choose "Links" on the left side of the screen. Explore one of the websites offered and summarize your findings.

_____

_____

_____

_____

_____

_____

_____

_____

_____

Refer to page 32 of Chapter 2.
Review your **GOALS FOR CHANGE**.
Respond in writing as to the progress
you have made toward reaching one
of your three stated goals.

GOAL STATEMENT

PROGRESS

How is your life changing because of this goal?

CORNERSTONES

for motivation, goal setting, & self-esteem

Develop a *high standard* of academic, personal, and social *integrity*.

Use the power of *positive thinking*.

Step *outside* your comfort zone.

Base your goals on your *values*.

Broaden your circle of friends.

Turn negative thoughts *loose*.

Don't give in to defeat.

Picture yourself *happy*.

Know what you want.

We are led to truth by our weaknesses as well as our strengths.

Learn.

Parker Palmer

Paul was nervous about his first day in the history class *because he had never done very well in "lecture" classes.* As he entered the room of strangers, he chose a seat close to the window about halfway back from the professor's lectern. The professor arrived, issued and explained the syllabus, and true to form, *indicated that the class would be conducted in the lecture format* with very little chance for participation or activities. *Paul's anxiety grew even more.*

As the professor began to lecture on the causes of the Second World War, *it was all that Paul could do to keep up with the information,* and it was even harder for him to remain focused. He struggled through the first few classes *only to realize that this semester's history class was simply not going to get any better.* He wondered to himself, "Why can't my history class and professor be more like my poetry class and professor?"

Paul had never taken poetry before. But in that class, the professor seldom lectured, *but often used music, posters, works of art, magic markers, copper wire, and even statues to teach* and impart the significance of the material. Paul had not wanted to take the poetry class, but it was the only literature alternative that would work in his schedule. It *turned out to be the class that he enjoyed the most* and the class in which he received the highest grade.

Paul was talking to some of his friends one evening about his classes and he mentioned *how*

> **Paul had not wanted to take the poetry class . . . it turned out to be the class he enjoyed the most.**

dynamic the poetry class had become. "I never thought that someone could take a handful of clay, some wire, and classical music and use it to make me understand poetry. One day," Paul said, "she read this poem called *Holocaust Museum.* There are lines in the poem that go like this:

> Wandering through the bleak, dusk interior
>
> lighting,
>
> I was paralyzed coming upon the shoes . . .
>
> The shoes of millions dead,
>
> lying mateless, alone, brown and
>
> crumbling.
>
> Heaped in piles, mirroring the millions
>
> of bodies, burned and stacked like
>
> cords of wood.

"When she finished the poem, she put on a CD of Rachmaninov's Symphony No. 2, threw some clay on our desks, gave us some wire and a square of cloth, *and told us to sculpt those lines of the poem.*" Paul's friends were laughing now, not believing him. "I'm not blowin' smoke, that's what she did." His friends *were in disbelief that this would happen in a poetry class.*

Paul got very serious for a moment and said, "It was the first time in my life that I ever understood anything like that. *It was the first time that I ever held poetry in my hands.*" "If only I could hold history in my hands," Paul thought, "this semester would be the best ever."

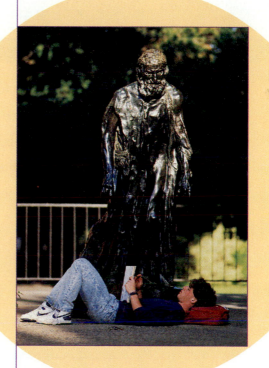

The ultimate mystery is one's own self.
—*SAMMY DAVIS, JR.*

STATEMENT	SCORE	Strongly Disagree	Disagree	Don't Know	Agree	Strongly Agree
1. When I study, I use a variety of ways to learn new material.		1	2	3	4	5
2. I work on improving my weaker learning styles.		1	2	3	4	5
3. I work on improving my study habits.		1	2	3	4	5
4. I know how to improve my grades by using a variety of learning styles.		1	2	3	4	5
5. I know how my personality affects my learning.		1	2	3	4	5
TOTAL		0–5	6–10	11–15	16–20	21–25

FEEDBACK

0 – 5   Extensive changes need to occur to ensure success.

6 – 10   Substantial changes need to occur to ensure success.

11 – 15   Considerable changes need to occur to ensure success.

16 – 20   Moderate changes need to occur to ensure success.

21 – 25   Minor changes need to occur to ensure success.

GOALS FOR CHANGE

Based on this feedback, my goals and objectives for change are . . .

Goal Statement _____

Action Steps 1. _____

2. _____

Goal Statement _____

Action Steps 1. _____

2. _____

Goal Statement _____

Action Steps 1. _____

2. _____

Results

Reading this chapter, completing the exercises, and reflecting on your learning styles and personality typology will result in your:

- Defining multiple intelligences.

- Understanding the basic concepts of multiple intelligences.

- Defining learning styles.

- Identifying your dominant learning style.

- Defining personality typing.

- Identifying your personality type.

- Identifying ways to use your learning style and personality type to best advantage when studying.

- Identifying ways to strengthen your less dominant learning styles and personality types when studying.

- Applying multiple intelligence theory to your study strategies.

Understanding Our Strengths

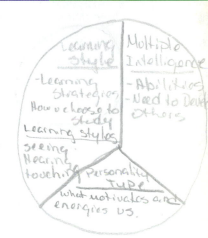

Paul's situation is not uncommon. While many students do not like the lecture format, others relish it. Some students learn best by touching and doing, while others learn best by listening and reflecting. Some students learn best with a group of people sitting outside under the trees, while others must be alone in the library. There are many factors that may influence the way we learn and process information.) Paul learned poetry best by "touching" it and getting involved with it. He began to use his tactile, or hands-on, skills to understand the poem's meaning. He may not have understood the depth of that poem if his only exposure to it had been a lecture.

To be what we are, and to become what we are capable of becoming, is the only end in life. —*ROBERT L. STEVENSON*

You may be asking yourself, "Is there one 'best' way of learning?" The answer is no. The way one learns depends on so many variables. Learning styles, your personal intelligences, and personality typing all play a part in the way you process new information. This chapter will explore the benefits of knowing your learning style and your personality type and the benefits of exploring your intelligences.

Identifying your learning style can be an important step in succeeding at any level in college. If you don't know how you learn and the best way to learn, your ability to succeed in college is greatly reduced.

Throughout my years in education, I have never been great at studying and have never made good grades. To be truthful, a lot of that time, I never really cared. My major was procrastination! I quickly learned that if I did not change, I had a guaranteed future flipping burgers. Once I hit college, not only did I regret procrastination and not caring, but I actually wanted to learn more about *how* to learn. I watched other people studying and learning and realized that my study habits were not the best.

During my first year in college, I thought I knew my learning style; I thought I was a visual learner. But it was not until I studied learning styles in class that I found out I had distinct characteristics in all three styles. This made me a mixed modality learner.

I learned some very interesting things about myself and my study habits. I learned that I needed to be in a very bright place to learn, so I go to the third floor of the library so that I am up high and the study area is by the windows. I also learned that if I studied for two or three hours a day, I was able to remember much more than if I crammed the night before the test. Now, I rewrite my notes after class, highlight areas in the text that the professor stresses in class, and study the handouts. I go to the text and review individual topics that the professor talked about in class and pay very close attention to information that the professor says will be on the test.

The bottom line is this: to be successful in college, you need to learn how to learn, and to be quite honest with you, I'm still in the middle of this. I wonder if the study techniques I am using today will be the best for me in the future. If not, I know how to adjust my learning and study habits to be successful.

Tom Craig, *age 20*
Major: Communication
The University of Idaho,
Moscow, Idaho

Discovering and Polishing Your Talents

This chapter will offer you the opportunity to complete three inventories: one to assess your learning style, one to assess your personality type, and one to help you better understand multiple intelligences. We must say up front that these assessments are in no way intended to label you. They are not a measure of your intelligence. They do not measure your worth or your capacities as a student or citizen. The three assessments are included so that you might gain a better understanding of your multiple intelligences and identify your learning styles and your personality type. There are no right or wrong answers and there is no one best way to learn. We hope that by the end of this chapter, you will have experienced a "Wow" or an "Ah-ha!" as you explore and discover new and exciting components of your education. We also hope that by the end of this chapter, you will have the skills needed to more effectively use your dominant traits and improve your less dominant traits.

Some educators and researchers do not even believe in the theory of learning styles or multiple intelligences. Anita Woolfolk (1998) states that "there has been considerable controversy over the meaning of intelligence. In 1986 at a symposium on intelligence, 24 psychologists offered 24 different views about the nature of intelligence."

However, we approach and include this information because many students have met with great success by identifying and molding their study environments and habits to reflect their learning style and personality type. If you have ever been in a class where you felt lost, inadequate, or simply out of place, it may have been because your professor was not teaching to your learning style. Conversely, if you are doing very well in a class, it may be because the information, professor, or class format matches the way you process information best.

There are many ways to learn how to ski. The learning technique that works best for you depends on many different factors, which may differ from situation to situation.

FROM THE WORLD OF WORK

As a student, I didn't really know what my learning style was. I knew that I had certain strengths and interests, including intelligence for math and naturalistic sciences. I was years into college before I learned that I was an auditory learner.

When I began college, I knew exactly what I wanted to do. I knew that I wanted to use my aptitude for logic, math, and science. I was one of the lucky ones who chose a major, followed the course of study, and graduated into the profession of my dreams. Don't get me wrong, it was not easy and there were many stumbling blocks, but discovering my strengths and weaknesses early on really helped me excel.

One area on which I had to concentrate was interpersonal and verbal communication. I had always loved to talk and converse with my friends, but my profession demanded that I learn how to put all of my science and math talents into verbal and written form. That was not an easy job for me.

Today, my job at Shell is to develop ideas on how to find oil and gas around the world. Communicating those ideas is everything. If I can't communicate to my boss and my boss's boss, then I am useless to the company. Therefore, having identified my strengths early and spent time working on my less dominant areas paid off in my career.

Brian Delph, *Geologist,* Shell Offshore, New Orleans, Louisiana

By taking your time and carefully and honestly completing each assessment instrument, you will be able to better understand and identify your strongest traits and then tailor your individual study process to better understand information that may have been difficult to understand in class.

TAKE THE MIS

The Multiple Intelligences Survey

by Robert M. Sherfield, Ph.D., 1999, 2002

Directions: Read each statement carefully and thoroughly. After reading the statement, rate your response using the scale below. There are no right or wrong answers. This is not a timed survey. The MIS is based, in part, on *Frames of Mind* by Howard Gardner, 1983.

3 = Often Applies

2 = Sometimes Applies

1 = Never or Almost Never Applies

_____ 1. When someone gives me directions, I have to visualize them in my mind in order to understand them.

_____ 2. I enjoy crossword puzzles and word games like Scrabble.

_____ 3. I enjoy dancing and can keep up with the beat of music.

_____ 4. I have little or no trouble conceptualizing information or facts.

_____ 5. I like to repair things that are broken such as toasters, small engines, bicycles, and cars.

_____ 6. I enjoy leadership activities on campus and in the community.

_____ 7. I have the ability to get others to listen to me.

_____ 8. I enjoy working with nature, animals, and plants.

_____ 9. I know where everything is in my home such as supplies, gloves, flashlights, camera, and compact discs.

_____ 10. I am a good speller.

_____ 11. I often sing or hum to myself in the shower or car, or while walking or just sitting.

_____ 12. I am a very logical, orderly thinker.

_____ 13. I use a lot of gestures when I talk to people.

_____ 14. I can recognize and empathize with people's attitudes and emotions.

_____ 15. I prefer to study alone.

_____ 16. I can name many different things in the environment such as clouds, rocks, and plant types.

_____ 17. I like to draw pictures, graphs, or charts to better understand information.

_____ 18. I have a good memory for names and dates.

_____ 19. When I hear music, I "get into it" by moving, humming, tapping, or even singing.

_____ 20. I learn better by asking a lot of questions.

_____ 21. I do enjoy playing competitive sports.

_____ 22. I communicate very well with other people.

_____ 23. I know what I want and I set goals to accomplish it.

_____ 24. I have some interest in herbal remedies and natural medicine.

_____ 25. I enjoy working puzzles or mazes.

_____ 26. I am a good storyteller.

_____ 27. I can easily remember the words and melodies of songs.

_____ 28. I enjoy solving problems in math and chemistry and working with computer programming problems.

_____ 29. I usually touch people or pat them on the back when I talk to them.

_____ 30. I understand my family and friends better than most other people do.

_____ 31. I don't always talk about my accomplishments with others.

_____ 32. I would rather work outside around nature than inside around people and equipment.

_____ 33. I enjoy and learn more when seeing movies, slides, or videos in class.

_____ 34. I am a very good listener and I enjoy listening to others' stories.

_____ 35. I need to study with music.

_____ 36. I enjoy games like Clue, Battleship, chess, and Rubiks Cube.

_____ 37. I enjoy physical activities such as bicycling, jogging, dancing, rollerblading, skateboarding, or swimming.

_____ 38. I am good at solving people's problems and conflicts.

_____ 39. I have to have time alone to think about new information in order to remember it.

_____ 40. I enjoy sorting and organizing information, objects, and collectibles.

Thoughts ● ● ●

Refer to your score on each individual question. Place that score beside the appropriate question number below. Then, tally each line at the side.

SCORE					TOTAL ACROSS	CODE
1 ____	9 ____	17 ____	25 ____	33 ____	_____	Visual/Spatial
2 ____	10 ____	18 ____	26 ____	34 ____	_____	Verbal/Linguistic
3 ____	11 ____	19 ____	27 ____	35 ____	_____	Musical/Rhythm
4 ____	12 ____	20 ____	28 ____	36 ____	_____	Logic/Math
5 ____	13 ____	21 ____	29 ____	37 ____	_____	Body/Kinesthetic
6 ____	14 ____	22 ____	30 ____	38 ____	_____	Interpersonal
7 ____	15 ____	23 ____	31 ____	39 ____	_____	Intrapersonal
8 ____	16 ____	24 ____	32 ____	40 ____	_____	Naturalistic

MIS TALLY

Multiple Intelligences

Look at the scores on the MIS. What are your top three scores? Write them in the space below.

Top Score _____   Code _____

Second Score _____   Code _____

Third Score _____   Code _____

This tally can help you understand where some of your strengths may be. Again, this is not a measure of your worth or capacities, nor is it an indicator of your future successes. Read the following section to better understand multiple intelligences.

Understanding Multiple Intelligences

In 1983, Howard Gardner, a Harvard University professor, developed a theory called Multiple Intelligences. In his book, *Frames of Mind,* he outlines seven intelligences that he feels are possessed by everyone: visual/spatial, verbal/linguistic, musical/rhythm, logic/math, body/kinesthetic, interpersonal, and intrapersonal. In 1996, he added an eighth intelligence: naturalistic. In short, if you have ever done things that came easily for you, you are probably drawing on one of your intelligences that is well developed. On the other hand, if you have tried to do things that are very difficult to master or understand, you may be dealing with material that calls on one of your less developed intelligences. If playing the piano by ear comes easily to you, your musical/rhythm intelligence may be very strong. If you have trouble writing or understanding poetry, your verbal/linguistic intelligence may not be as well developed. This does not mean that you will never be able to write poetry; it simply means that you have not fully developed your skills in this area.

The Eight Intelligences

The "Smart" column was adapted from Thomas Armstrong, 1994.

VISUAL/SPATIAL   *Picture Smart*

Thinks in pictures; knows where things are in the house; loves to create images and work with graphs, charts, pictures, and maps.

VERBAL/LINGUISTIC   *Word Smart*

Communicates well through language, likes to write, is good at spelling, great at telling stories, loves to read books.

MUSICAL/RHYTHM   *Music Smart*

Loves to sing, hum, and whistle; has the ability to comprehend; responds to music immediately; performs music.

LOGIC/MATH   *Number Smart*

Can easily conceptualize and reason, uses logic, has good problem-solving skills, enjoys math and science.

BODY/KINESTHETIC   *Body Smart*

Learns through body sensation, moves around a lot, enjoys work involving the hands, is graced with some athletic ability.

INTERPERSONAL   *People Smart*

Loves to communicate with other people, possesses great leadership skills, has lots of friends, is involved in extracurricular activities.

Some people express themselves outwardly, while others are more reflective. How would you describe yourself? Are there certain situations that cause you to be more or less extroverted than you are normally?

INTRAPERSONAL   *Self-Smart*

Has a deep awareness of own feelings, is very reflective, requires time to be alone, does not get involved with group activities.

NATURALISTIC   *Environment Smart*

Has interest in the environment and in nature; can easily recognize plants, animals, rocks, and cloud formations; may like hiking, camping, and fishing.

Using Multiple Intelligences to Enhance Studying and Learning

Below, you will find some helpful tips to assist you in creating a study environment and study habits using your multiple intelligences.

VISUAL/SPATIAL

- Use visuals in your notes such as timelines, charts, graphs, and geometric shapes.
- Work to create a mental or visual picture of the information at hand.
- Use colored markers to make associations or to group items together.
- Use mapping or webbing so that your main points are easily recognized.
- When taking notes, draw pictures in the margins to illustrate the main points.
- Visualize the information in your mind.

VERBAL/LINGUISTIC

- Establish study groups so that you will have the opportunity to talk about the information.
- Using the information you studied, create a story or a skit.
- Read as much information about related areas as possible.
- As you read chapters, outline them in your own words.
- Summarize and recite your notes aloud.

MUSICAL/RHYTHM

- Listen to music while studying (if it does not distract you).
- Write a song or rap about the chapter or information.
- Take short breaks from studying to listen to music.
- Commit the information being studied to the music from your favorite song.

LOGIC/MATH

- Strive to make connections between subjects.
- Don't just memorize the facts; apply them to real-life situations.
- As you study the information, think of problems in society and how this information could solve those problems.
- Create analyzing charts. Draw a line down the center of the page, put the information at hand in the left column and analyze, discuss, relate, and synthesize it in the right column.
- Allow yourself some time to reflect after studying.

Thoughts

BODY/KINESTHETIC

- Don't confine your study area to a desk or chair; move around, explore, go outside.
- Act out the information.
- Study in a group of people and change groups often.
- Use charts, posters, flash cards, and chalkboards to study.
- When appropriate or possible, build models using the information studied.
- Verbalize the information to others.
- Use games such as chess, Monopoly, Twister, or Clue when studying.
- Trace words as you study them.
- Use repetition to learn facts; write them many times.
- Make study sheets.

INTERPERSONAL

- Study in groups.
- Share the information with other people.
- Teach the information to others.
- Interview outside sources to learn more about the material at hand.
- Have a debate with others about the information.

INTRAPERSONAL

- Study in a quiet area.
- Study by yourself.
- Allow time for reflection and meditation about the subject matter.
- Study in short time blocks and then spend some time absorbing the information.
- Work at your own pace.

NATURALISTIC

- Study outside whenever possible.
- Relate the information to the effect on the environment whenever possible.
- When given the opportunity to choose your own topics or research projects, choose something related to nature.
- Collect your own study data and resources.
- Organize and label your information.
- Keep separate notebooks on individual topics so that you can add new information to each topic as it becomes available to you.

Thoughts

Understanding Learning Styles Theory

Rita Dunn defines learning styles as, "the way in which each learner begins to concentrate on, process, and retain new and difficult information." We must note that there is a difference between a learning *style* and a learning *strategy*. A learning strategy is how you might choose to learn or study, such as by using note cards, flip charts, color slides, or cooperative learning groups. Flip charts and slides are strategies. Learning styles are more sensory. They involve seeing, hearing, and touching.

TAKE THE LEAD

The Learning Evaluation and Assessment Directory

by Robert M. Sherfield, Ph.D., 1999, 2002

Directions: Read each statement carefully and thoroughly. After reading the statement, rate your response using the scale below. There are no right or wrong answers. This is not a timed survey. The LEAD is based, in part, on research conducted by Rita Dunn.

3 = Often Applies

2 = Sometimes Applies

1 = Never or Almost Never Applies

_____ 1. I remember information better if I write it down or draw a picture of it.

_____ 2. I remember things better when I hear them instead of just reading or seeing them.

_____ 3. When I get something that has to be assembled, I just start doing it. I don't read the directions.

_____ 4. If I am taking a test, I can "see" the page of the text or lecture notes where the answer is located.

_____ 5. I would rather the professor explain a graph, chart, or diagram than just show it to me.

_____ 6. When learning new things, I want to "do it" rather than hear about it.

_____ 7. I would rather the instructor write the information on the board or overhead instead of just lecturing.

_____ 8. I would rather listen to a book on tape than read it.

_____ 9. I enjoy making things, putting things together, and working with my hands.

_____ 10. I am able to quickly conceptualize and visualize information.

_____ 11. I learn best by hearing words.

_____ 12. I have been called hyperactive by my parents, spouse, partner, or professor.

_____ 13. I have no trouble reading maps, charts, or diagrams.

_____ 14. I can usually pick up on small sounds like bells, crickets, or frogs, or distant sounds like train whistles.

_____ 15. I use my hands and gesture a lot when I speak to others.

Refer to your score on each individual question. Place that score beside the appropriate question number below. Then, tally each line at the side.

SCORE					TOTAL ACROSS	CODE
1 ____	4 ____	7 ____	10 ____	13 ____	_____	Visual
2 ____	5 ____	8 ____	11 ____	14 ____	_____	Auditory
3 ____	6 ____	9 ____	12 ____	15 ____	_____	Tactile

LEAD SCORES

Learning Styles

Look at the scores on the LEAD. What is your top score?

Top Score _____   Code _____

If you learn best by _seeing_ information, you have a more dominant _visual_ learning style. If you learn best by _hearing_ information, you have a more dominant _auditory_ learning style. If you learn best by _touching or doing_, you have a more dominant _tactile_ learning style. You may also hear the tactile learning style referred to as kinesthetic or hands-on.

Some of the most successful students have learned to use all three styles. If you were learning how to skateboard, you might learn best by hearing someone talk about the different styles or techniques. Others might learn best by watching a video where someone demonstrates the techniques. Still others would learn best by actually getting on the board and trying it. However, the student who involved all of his or her senses might gain the most. They might listen to the instructor tell about skateboarding, watch the video, and then go do it. Therefore, they would have involved all of their learning styles: visual, auditory, and tactile. Here are brief descriptions of the three styles.

VISUAL   _Eye Smart_

Thinks in pictures. Enjoys visual instructions, demonstrations, and descriptions; would rather read a text than listen to a lecture; avid notetaker; needs visual references; enjoys using charts, graphs, and pictures.

Thoughts ● ● ●

AUDITORY   *Ear Smart*

Prefers verbal instructions; would rather listen than read; often tapes lectures and listens to them in the car or at home; recites information out loud; enjoys talking, discussing issues, and verbal stimuli; talks out problems.

TACTILE   *Action Smart*

Prefers hands-on approaches to learning; likes to take notes and uses a great deal of scratch paper; learns best by doing something, by touching it, or manipulating it; learns best while moving or while in action; often does not concentrate well when sitting and reading.

THE SIMILARITIES AND DIFFERENCES BETWEEN MULTIPLE INTELLIGENCES THEORY AND LEARNING STYLES THEORY

As you read over the components of MI theory and LS theory, you begin to see several common elements. Both theories deal with the visual, auditory, and tactile (or kinesthetic). Behind the surface, there are also similarities. According to Silver, Strong, and Perini (1997), "Both, in fact, combine insights from biology, anthropology, psychology, medical case studies, and an examination of art and culture." While several components and some background research of MI theory overlap LS theory, there are vast differences. "Learning styles emphasize the different ways people think and feel as they solve problems, create products, and interact. The theory of multiple intelligence is an effort to understand how cultures and disciplines shape human potential. Learning style models tend to concern themselves with the process of learning: how individuals absorb information, think about information, and evaluate the results" (1997).

MI theory, on the other hand, examines and "shows different levels of aptitude in various content areas. In all cases, we know that no individual is universally intelligent; certain fields of knowledge engage or elude everyone" (1997).

Simply stated, you can be a visual learner (this is a learning style) and yet not have visual/spatial (this is one of the multiple intelligences) be your dominant intelligence. How can this be possible? It may be that you learn best by watching someone paint a picture—watching their brush strokes, their method of mixing paints, and their spatial layout—but it may be that you will not be as engaged or as talented at painting as the person you watched. Your painting may lack feeling, depth, and expression. This is an example of how your visual learning style can be strong but your visual/spatial intelligence may not be your dominant intelligence.

On the other hand, your learning style may be visual and your dominant intelligence may be verbal/linguistic. If that is the case, you would learn how to paint by watching someone go through the process. Then, using your verbal/linguistic intelligence, you would be masterful at describing how to paint and talking about the process you observed.

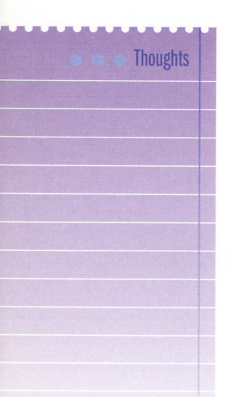
Thoughts

What Can We Learn About Personality?

TAKE THE PAP

The Personality Assessment Profile

by Robert M. Sherfield, Ph.D., 1999, 2002

Directions: Read each statement carefully and thoroughly. After reading the statement, rate your response using the scale below. There are no right or wrong answers. This is not a timed survey. The PAP is based, in part, on the Myers-Briggs Type Indicator® (MBTI) by Katharine Briggs and Isabel Briggs Myers.

3 = Often Applies

2 = Sometimes Applies

1 = Never or Almost Never Applies

_____ 1a. I am a very talkative person.

_____ 1b. I am a more reflective person than a verbal person.

_____ 2a. I am a very factual and literal person.

_____ 2b. I look to the future and I can see possibilities.

_____ 3a. I value truth and justice over tact and emotion.

_____ 3b. I find it easy to empathize with other people.

_____ 4a. I am very ordered and efficient.

_____ 4b. I enjoy having freedom from control.

_____ 5a. I am a very friendly and social person.

_____ 5b. I enjoy listening to others more than talking.

_____ 6a. I enjoy being around and working with people who have a great deal of common sense.

_____ 6b. I enjoy being around and working with people who are dreamers and have a great deal of imagination.

_____ 7a. One of my motivating forces is to do a job very well.

_____ 7b. I like to be recognized for, and I am motivated by, my accomplishments and awards.

_____ 8a. I like to plan out my day before I go to bed.

_____ 8b. When I get up on a non-school or non-work day, I just like to let the day "plan itself."

_____ 9a. I like to express my feelings and thoughts.

_____ 9b. I enjoy a great deal of tranquility and quiet time to myself.

_____ 10a. I am a very pragmatic and realistic person.

_____ 10b. I like to create new ideas, methods, or ways of doing things.

_____ 11a. I make decisions with my brain.

_____ 11b. I make decisions with my heart.

_____ 12a. I am a very disciplined and orderly person.

_____ 12b. I don't make a lot of plans.

_____ 13a. I like to work with a group of people.

_____ 13b. I would rather work independently.

_____ 14a. I learn best if I can see it, touch it, smell it, taste it, or hear it.

_____ 14b. I learn best by relying on my gut feelings or intuition.

_____ 15a. I am quick to criticize others.

_____ 15b. I compliment others very easily and quickly.

_____ 16a. My life is systematic and organized.

_____ 16b. I don't really pay attention to deadlines.

_____ 17a. I can be myself when I am around others.

_____ 17b. I can be myself when I am alone.

_____ 18a. I live in the here and now, in the present.

_____ 18b. I live in the future, planning and dreaming.

_____ 19a. I think that if someone breaks the rules, the person should be punished.

_____ 19b. I think that if someone breaks the rules, we should look at the person who broke the rules, examine the rules, and look at the situation at hand before a decision is made.

_____ 20a. I do my work, then I play.

_____ 20b. I play, then do my work.

Refer to your score on each individual question. Place that score beside the appropriate question number below. Then, tally each line at the side.

SCORE   TOTAL ACROSS   CODE

1a ____	5a ____	9a ____	13a ____	17a ____	_____	**E** Extrovert
1b ____	5b ____	9b ____	13b ____	17b ____	_____	**I** Introvert
2a ____	6a ____	10a ____	14a ____	18a ____	_____	**S** Sensing
2b ____	6b ____	10b ____	14b ____	18b ____	_____	**N** iNtuition
3a ____	7a ____	11a ____	15a ____	19a ____	_____	**T** Thinking
3b ____	7b ____	11b ____	15b ____	19b ____	_____	**F** Feeling
4a ____	8a ____	12a ____	16a ____	20a ____	_____	**J** Judging
4b ____	8b ____	12b ____	16b ____	20b ____	_____	**P** Perceiving

PAP SCORES

Personality Indicator

Look at the scores on your PAP. Is your score higher in the E or I line? Is your score higher in the S or N line? Is your score higher in the T or F line? Is your score higher in the J or P line? Write the code to the side of each section below.

Is your higher score	E or I	Code _____
Is your higher score	S or N	Code _____
Is your higher score	T or F	Code _____
Is your higher score	J or P	Code _____

Understanding Personality Typing (Typology)

The questions on the PAP helped you discover whether you are extroverted or introverted (E or I), sensing or intuitive (S or N), thinking or feeling (T or F), and judging or perceiving (J or P). These questions were based, in part, on work done by Carl Jung, Katharine Briggs, and Isabel Briggs-Myers.

In 1921, Swiss psychologist Carl Jung (1875–1961) published his work *Psychological Types*. In this book, Jung suggested that human behavior is not random. He felt that behavior follows patterns and these patterns are caused by differences in the way people use their minds. In 1942, Isabel Briggs-Myers and her mother, Katharine Briggs, began to put Jung's theory into practice. They developed the Myers- Briggs Type Indicator®, which after more than 50 years of research and refinement has become the most widely used instrument for identifying and studying personality.

As indicated throughout this chapter, we must stress the fact that no part of this assessment measures your worth, your success factors, or your value as a human being. The questions on the PAP assisted you in identifying your type, but neither the PAP nor your authors want you to assume that one personality type is better or worse, more valuable or less valuable, or more likely to be successful. What personality typing can do is to "help us discover what best motivates and energizes each of us as individuals" (Tieger and Tieger, 1992).

Functions of Personality Typology

When all of the combinations of E/I, S/N, T/F, and J/P are combined, there are 16 personality types. Everyone will fit into one of the following categories:

ISTJ	ISFJ	INFJ	INTJ
ISTP	ISFP	INFP	INTP
ESTP	ESFP	ENFP	ENTP
ESTJ	ESFJ	ENFJ	ENTJ

Let's take a look at the four major categories of typing. Notice that the stronger your score in one area, the stronger your personality type is for that area. For instance, if you scored 15 on the E (extroversion) questions, this means that you are a strong extrovert. If you scored 15 on the I (introversion) questions, this means that you are a strong introvert. However, if you scored 7 on the E questions and 8 on the I questions, your score indicates that you possess almost the same amount of extroverted and introverted qualities. The same is true for every category on the PAP.

E Versus I (Extroversion/Introversion)

This category deals with the way we *interact with others and the world around us.*

Extroverts prefer to live in the outside world, drawing their strength from other people. They are outgoing and love interaction. They usually make decisions with others in mind. They enjoy being the center of attention. There are usually few secrets about extroverts.

Introverts draw their strength from the inner world. They need to spend time alone to think and ponder. They are usually quiet and reflective. They usually make decisions by themselves. They do not like being the center of attention. They are private.

● ● ● Thoughts

S Versus N (Sensing/Intuition)

This category deals with the way we *learn and deal with information.*

Sensing types gather information through their five senses. They have a hard time believing something if it cannot be seen, touched, smelled, tasted, or heard. They like concrete facts and details. They do not rely on intuition or gut feelings. They usually have a great deal of common sense.

Intuitive types are not very detail-oriented. They can see possibilities and they rely on their gut feelings. Usually, they are very innovative people. They tend to live in the future and often get bored once they have mastered a task.

T Versus F (Thinking/Feeling)

This category deals with the way we *make decisions.*

Thinkers are very logical people. They do not make decisions based on feelings or emotion. They are analytical and sometimes do not take others' values into consideration when making decisions. They can easily identify the flaws of others. They can be seen as insensitive and lacking compassion.

Feelers make decisions based on what they feel is right and just. They like to have harmony and they value others' opinions and feelings. They are usually very tactful people who like to please others. They are very warm people.

J Versus P (Judging/Perceiving)

This category deals with the way we *live.*

Judgers are very orderly people. They must have a great deal of structure in their lives. They are good at setting goals and sticking to their goals. They are the type of people who would seldom, if ever, play before their work was completed.

Perceivers are just the opposite. They are less structured and more spontaneous. They do not like timelines. Unlike the judger, they will play before their work is done. They will take every chance to delay a decision or judgment. Sometimes, they can become involved in too many things at one time.

After you have studied the chart on the following page and other information in the chapter regarding your personality type, you can make some decisions about your study habits and even your career choices. For instance, if you scored very strong in the extroversion section, it may not serve you well to pursue a career where you would be forced to work alone. It would probably be unwise to try to spend all of your time studying alone. If you are a strong extrovert, you would want to work and study around people.

Thoughts

A Closer Look at Your Personality Type

ISTJ
6% of America

Have great power of concentration; very serious; dependable; logical and realistic; take responsibility for their own actions; they are not easily distracted.

ISFJ
6% of America

Hard workers; detail-oriented; considerate of others' feelings; friendly and warm to others; very conscientious; they are down-to-earth and like to be around the same.

INFJ
5% of America

Enjoy an atmosphere where all get along; they do what is needed of them; they have strong beliefs and principles; enjoy helping others achieve their goals.

INTJ
1% of America

They are very independent; enjoy challenges; inventors; can be skeptical; they are perfectionists; they believe in their own work, sometimes to a fault.

ISTP
6% of America

Very reserved; good at making things clear to others; interested in how and why things work; like to work with their hands; can sometimes be misunderstood as idle.

ISFP
6% of America

Very sensitive and modest; adapt easily to change; they are respectful of others' feelings and values; take criticism personally; don't enjoy leadership roles.

INFP
1% of America

They work well alone; must know others well to interact; faithful to others and their jobs; excellent at communication; open-minded; dreamers; tend to do too much.

INTP
1% of America

Extremely logical; very analytical; good at planning; love to learn; excellent problem-solvers; they don't enjoy needless conversation; hard to understand at times.

ESTP
13% of America

They are usually very happy; they don't let trivial things upset them; they have very good memories; very good at working with things and taking them apart.

ESFP
13% of America

Very good at sports and active exercises; good common sense; easygoing; good at communication; can be impulsive; do not enjoy working alone; have fun and enjoy living and life.

ENFP
5% of America

Creative and industrious; can easily find success in activities and projects that interest them; good at motivating others; organized; do not like routine.

ENTP
5% of America

Great problem-solvers; love to argue either side; can do almost anything; good at speaking/motivating; love challenges; very creative; do not like routine; overconfident.

ESTJ
13% of America

They are "take charge" people; they like to get things done; focus on results; very good at organizing; good at seeing what will not work; responsible; realists.

ESFJ
13% of America

Enjoy many friendly relationships; popular; love to help others; do not take criticism very well; need praise; need to work with people; organized; talkative; active.

ENFJ
5% of America

Very concerned about others' feelings; respect others; good leaders; usually popular; good at public speaking; can make decisions too quickly; trust easily.

ENTJ
5% of America

Excellent leaders; speak very well; hard-working; may be workaholics; may not give enough praise; like to learn; great planners; enjoy helping others reach their goals.

* All percentages taken from Tieger and Tieger, *Do What You Are,* 1992.

Using Your Personality Type to Enhance Learning

Having identified your personality type, use the following suggestions to enhance studying using your present personality type, while improving your study skills using your less dominant type.

TYPE	CURRENT SUGGESTIONS	IMPROVEMENT
Extrovert	Study with groups of people in cooperative learning teams. Seek help from others. Discuss topics with friends. Establish debate or discussion groups. Vary your study habits; meet in different places with different people. Discuss new ideas and plans with your friends.	Work on listening skills. Be sure to let others contribute to the group. Force yourself to develop solutions and answers before you go to the group. Spend some time reflecting. Let others speak before you share your ideas and suggestions. Work to be more patient. Think before acting or speaking.
Introvert	Study in a quiet place, undisturbed by others. When reading and studying, take time for reflection. Use your time alone to read and study support and auxiliary materials. Set aside large blocks of time for study and reflection.	Get involved in a study group from time to time. Allow others inside your world to offer advice and opinions. Share your opinions and advice with others more often. Seek advice from others. Use mnemonics to increase your memory power. Instead of writing responses or questions, speak aloud to friends and peers.
Sensor	Observe the world around you. Experience the information to the fullest degree; feel it and touch it. Explain to your study group or partner the information in complete detail. Apply the information to something in your life that is currently happening. Create a study schedule and stick to it. If the old study habits are not working, stop and invent new ways of studying. Explore what others are doing.	Try to think about the information in an abstract form. Think "What would happen if . . . " Let your imagination run wild. Think about the information in the future tense. Let your gut feelings take over from time to time. Take more chances with the unknown. Trust your feelings and inspirations. Think beyond reality. Don't oversimplify. *(continued)*

TYPE	CURRENT SUGGESTIONS	IMPROVEMENT
Intuitive	After studying the information or data, let your imagination apply this to something abstract. Describe how the information could be used today, right now, in your life at the moment. Describe how this information could help others. View new information as a challenge. Vary your study habits; don't do the same thing all the time. Rely on your gut feelings.	Work on becoming more detail-oriented. Look at information through the senses. Verify your facts. Think in simple terms. Think about the information in a logical and analytical way. Try to explain new information in relation to the senses.
Thinker	Make logical connections between new information and what is already known. Remain focused. Explain the information in detailed terms to a study group. Put things in order. Study with people who do their part for the group.	Try to see information and data in more abstract terms. Look for the "big picture." Develop a passion for acquiring new information. Think before you speak. Strive to be more objective and open.
Feeler	Establish a supportive and open study group. Teach others the information. Continue to be passionate about learning and exploring. Explain the information in a cause/effect scenario. Focus on the "people" factor.	Strive to look at things more logically. Work to stay focused. Praise yourself when others do not. Try to be more organized. Work to stick to policies, rules, and guidelines. Don't give in to opposition just for the sake of harmony. Don't get caught up in the here and now; look ahead.
Judger	Set a schedule and stick to it. Strive to complete projects. Keep your study supplies in one place so that you can locate them easily. Prioritize tasks that need to be completed. Create lists and agendas.	Take your time in making decisions. Complete all tasks. Look at the entire situation before making a judgment. Don't act or make judgments too quickly. Don't beat yourself up if you miss a deadline.

TYPE	CURRENT SUGGESTIONS	IMPROVEMENT
Perceiver	Study in different places with different people.	Become more decisive.
	Since you see all sides of issues, share those with your study group for discussion.	Finish one project before you begin another.
	Obtain as much information as possible so that you can make solid decisions.	Don't put off the harder subjects until later; study them first.
	Create fun and exciting study groups with snacks and maybe music.	Learn to set deadlines.
	Be the leader of the study team.	Create lists and agendas to help you stay on target.
	Allow yourself a great deal of time for study so that you can take well-deserved breaks.	Do your work; then play.

What is an introvert, etc.?
How are you suppose to study?

Refer to the LEAD score sheet. Identify your least dominant learning style. Using this learning style, describe how you could strengthen this learning style and use it in an English class.

Least dominant learning style _____

How could I improve and strengthen and use this learning style in an English class?

_____
_____
_____
_____
_____
_____
_____
_____
_____
_____
_____

Many successful students have learned to use all of their senses. With this theory in mind, describe the color blue using all five senses.

If a person were visually impaired, how could you make them see blue?

_____
_____
_____
_____
_____

If a person were hearing impaired, how would you make them hear blue?

_____
_____
_____

Thinking

How could you help a person understand blue through taste?

_____
_____
_____
_____

How could you help a person understand blue through smell?

_____
_____
_____
_____
_____

How could you help a person understand blue through touch?

_____

Change

LIFE

One Minute *Journal*

In one minute or less, jot down the major ideas that you learned from this chapter.

_____

_____

_____

_____

_____

_____

_____

_____

_____

_____

_____

_____

COMPANION
Website *Journal*

Log on to **www.prenhall.com/montgomery**, choose the version of this book you are using, and then choose Chapter 3 on the menu. Next, choose "Links" on the left side of the page. Explore one of the websites offered and summarize your findings.

_____

_____

_____

_____

_____

_____

_____

_____

_____

_____

at this moment?

Refer to page 62 of Chapter 3.
Review your **GOALS FOR CHANGE**.
Respond in writing as to the progress
you have made toward reaching one
of your three stated goals.

GOAL STATEMENT

PROGRESS

How is your life changing because of this goal?

CORNERSTONES

for learning styles

Surround yourself with people who are very different from you.

Use your less dominant areas more often to *strengthen* them.

Read more about personality typing and learning styles.

Get involved in a *variety* of learning and social situations.

Answer inventories and surveys *thoughtfully.*

Work to *improve* your less dominant areas.

Learning styles *do not* measure your worth.

Try *different ways* of learning and studying.

The road to success is often off the beaten path.   F. Tyger

Think.

CHAPTER 4

Think

POINT:

America is in decline!

There is *no sense of community,* no compassion for others. Road rage takes lives every hour. Violent crime among teens is up 141 percent! Pick up a newspaper and turn to the editorial page. *Almost every word written is negative.* Politicians are taking bribes, *babies are left for dead by teenage mothers and fathers,* auto theft is up, and pornography on the Internet is corrupting our youth.

COUNTERPOINT:

America, the land of waving wheat, purple mountains' majesty, and shining seas. America, the land of plenty. America is back!

Violent crime among adults is down 26 percent. *The economy is better than it has been in over 20 years.* The stock market is booming. Inner-city families are reclaiming their neighborhoods. Cities are cleaning up, and tourism is at an all-time high. Medical advances have helped us prolong life and relieve suffering.

Which viewpoint is correct? Does America need to "get back on track," or is America on track? *How can you decide which point to believe?*

> **Does America need to "get back on track," or is America on track?**

How much thought, critical thought, have you given the issue? As you move through your daily routine, how often do you stop to consider the fate of your country?

If you had one chance to change a social or economic policy in this nation, what would it be? Would you create communities? Would you eliminate prejudice? Would you bring back the "Summer of Love"? Would you create a new social ethic geared toward kindness and compassion? Would you introduce sex or moral education into the school system? Would you create a policy giving all people equal human rights? Would you eliminate the IRS? What is your wish? Have you ever considered it?

Does America need fixing?

Are you part of the problem?

Are you part of the solution?

W hat lies behind us and what lies ahead of us are tiny matters compared to what lies within us.
—*R. W. EMERSON*

STATEMENT	SCORE	Strongly Disagree	Disagree	Don't Know	Agree	Strongly Agree
1. I can identify the root cause of many problems.		1	2	3	4	5
2. I know how to distinguish a fact from an opinion.		1	2	3	4	5
3. I know how to separate emotion from reason.		1	2	3	4	5
4. I use my creative thinking abilities to help me in my classes.		1	2	3	4	5
5. I know how to identify fallacious statements.		1	2	3	4	5
TOTAL		0–5	6–10	11–15	16–20	21–25

FEEDBACK

0 – 5   Extensive changes need to occur to ensure success.

6 – 10   Substantial changes need to occur to ensure success.

11 – 15   Considerable changes need to occur to ensure success.

16 – 20   Moderate changes need to occur to ensure success.

21 – 25   Minor changes need to occur to ensure success.

GOALS FOR CHANGE

Based on this feedback, my goals and objectives for change are . . .

Goal Statement _____

Action Steps 1. _____

2. _____

Goal Statement _____

Action Steps 1. _____

2. _____

Goal Statement _____

Action Steps 1. _____

2. _____

Results

Reading this chapter, completing the exercises, and reflecting on your critical and creative thinking abilities will result in your:

- Defining critical thinking.
- Describing the characteristics of critical thinkers.
- Discussing the value of critical thinking.
- Defining emotional restraint.
- Analyzing problems, ideas, and information.
- Solving problems.
- Differentiating fact from opinion.
- Recognizing fallacious persuasive terminology.
- Identifying faulty tactics in persuasion and argumentation.
- Identifying ways to increase your creative thinking abilities.

Thinking About Thinking

Take a moment to evaluate the two opening questions in your own mind. What are you thinking right now? More importantly, why are you thinking the way you are right now? What is causing you to believe, feel, or think one way or the other about those two questions? What are the facts and/or opinions that have led you to your conclusion? At this moment, are you basing your thoughts about this issue on emotions or facts, fallacies or truths, data or opinions, interviews or hearsay, reason or misjudgment, fear or empathy?

Understanding why and how we formulate thoughts and ideas is the main objective of this chapter. This chapter is about believing and disbelieving, seeking, uncovering, debunking myths, proving the impossible possible. It is about proof, logic, evidence, and developing ideas and opinions based on hard-core facts or credible research. This chapter is about seeking truth and expanding your mind to limits unimaginable. This chapter is about the fundamental aspect of becoming an educated citizen; it is about human thought and reasoning.

Almost any profession you choose to go into will require the ability to think through problems, make decisions, and apply other critical thinking skills.

A Working Definition of Critical Thinking

There are almost as many definitions of critical thinking as there are people who try to define it. According to *The American Heritage Dictionary*, the word *critical* is defined as "careful and exact evaluation and judgment." The word *thinking* is defined as "to reason about or reflect on; to ponder." Critical thinking, then, might be defined as evaluating and judging your reasoning and reflections. This definition is not, however, a complete description. Critical thinking can also mean thinking more deeply, being skeptical, questioning strongly held beliefs, or taking no information or opinion for granted. It is also important to note that critical thinking is not innate; it is a learned skill that every student can acquire and polish.

For the purpose of this chapter, we will use the working definition of critical thinking as defined by Diane Helpern in her book *Thought and Knowledge: An Introduction to Critical Thinking* (1996). She defines critical thinking as "thinking that is purposeful, reasoned, and goal directed—the kind of thinking involved in solving problems, formulating inferences, calculating likelihoods, and making decisions."

The Importance of Critical Thinking

Have you ever made a decision that turned out to be a mistake? Have you ever said to yourself, "If only I could go back . . . "? Have you ever regretted actions you took toward a person or situation? Have you ever planned an event or function that went off flawlessly? Have you ever had to make a hard, painful decision that turned out to be "the best decision of your life"? If the answer to any of these questions is yes, you might be able to trace the consequences back to your thought process at the time of the decision. Let's face it, sometimes good and bad things happen out of luck. More often than not, however, the events in our lives are driven by the thought processes involved when we made the initial decision.

Critical thinking can serve us in many areas as students and citizens in society. As a student, critical thinking can help you focus on issues; gather relevant, accurate information; remember facts; organize thoughts logically; analyze questions and problems; and manage your priorities. It can assist in your problem-solving skills and help you control your emotions so that rational judgments can be made. It can help you produce new knowledge through research and analysis and help you determine the accuracy of printed and spoken words. It can help you in detecting bias and in determining the relevance of arguments and persuasion.

As a citizen, critical thinking can help you get along with others. It can help you realize cause and effect in the world. It can assist you in financial planning, stress reduction, and health issues, and help you make rational, informed decisions in a variety of cultural and civic duties, such as voting, volunteering, or contributing money.

Critical thinking is a skill that is not only valuable in the academic arena, but also invaluable in relationships, neighborhood planning, environmental concerns, and lifelong goal setting, to name a few. It can help you and your family solve problems together. It can help you make decisions that permanently affect the lives of your family members, and it can help you choose alternatives that are best for you, your family, and your friends.

Insider's view

When trying to understand learning opportunities, it is important to understand what type of learner you are and how you think. Critical thinking is one of the most vital skills in our world today. For me, critical thinking helped me learn how to sort out what was important and necessary from what was not important or necessary. You'll need those skills too, because of the immense amount of work in college life.

One of the areas where I needed to draw on my critical thinking skills was a management class. In this class, we were required to do role-playing and solve real-world situations in business and industry. We had to take these situations and ask ourselves, what would an employer or an employee do in this situation? We had to evaluate the procedures that one might take to be successful in the role-playing situation. My critical thinking skills were monumentally important to me during this and many other management and business classes.

As an emerging Business Education teacher, I had to do an internship at a local high school in Florida. During my internship, I had two cooperating and supervising teachers working with me. They had two very diverse personalities and working styles. One was authoritative while the other was more easygoing. I had to learn how to deal with both of them if I was going to be successful in the program. This situation called on my critical thinking skills once again. This time it was not a role-playing exercise or a simulation, it was my future. I had to deal with both teachers, both personalities, both work styles all the while developing my own style and helping my students learn and grow. I had to learn to think, judge, and justify my positions. This was one of the most important times in my life where critical thinking was essential to my success and the success of others.

As you move through your degree, know that your critical thinking abilities will be called on many, many times. Use this opportunity to polish your skills and prepare for the real world of work.

Melissa Sheré Phillips-Mobley, age 22
Major: Business Education
The University of South Florida,
Florida City, Florida

A Plan for Critical Thinking

As you begin to build and expand your critical thinking skills, we should consider the steps involved. Critical thinking skill development involves

- Emotional restraint
- Thinking on a higher level
- Analysis
- Questioning
- Problem solving
- Distinguishing fact from opinion
- Seeking truth in argument and persuasion

The remainder of this chapter will detail, through explanation, exploration, and exercises, how to build a critical thinking plan for your academic and personal success.

FROM THE WORLD OF WORK

Critical thinking is one of the most important aspects of my job. Much of my time is spent communicating with employees, managers, and colleagues from other properties. If I fail to consider the short- and long-term consequences of a remark that I make, a concept that I teach, or an action in which I engage, I could lose a student, or worse, I could lose my credibility. What I say in a training class affects the entire workplace. I have to employ the skills of critical thinking every day.

As I look back on my college years, I realize that higher education gave me the skills to think and to be creative. The traditional workplace evolves so quickly with new technology and new concepts that you must have the creativity and rational thinking skills to research, explore, and solve. These skills are imperative to success.

I think my college education also helped me understand the value of completing tasks on time. Late papers were never accepted and because so much of my experience in college revolved around group work, if I came in late or submitted a paper late, the entire group suffered because of my actions. Today, I use those organizational skills to complete tasks, manage my time, and delegate responsibilities.

College also taught me the importance of lifelong learning. In my first job out of college, I worked seven days a week, nonstop, for four months. I put in the extra hours to learn what I needed to know to help me be successful. I learned five word processing programs and computer applications on my own, after hours. I discovered that putting in extra hours to learn pays off; putting in extra hours just to put in extra hours does not. Those extra hours that I put in to help me upgrade my computer skills certainly paid off. I was able to learn those computer skills because I knew how to think critically and creatively.

Curtis M. Roe, *Manager,* Caesar's Palace at Sea, Park Place Entertainment, Las Vegas, Nevada

STEP ONE: EMOTIONAL RESTRAINT

Did James Earl Ray really kill Martin Luther King, Jr.? Is there life on other planets? Did a member of Tupak's entourage participate in his murder? Should the drinking age be lowered to 18? Should 16-year-olds be allowed to drive a car? What emotions are you feeling right now? Did you immediately formulate answers to these questions in your mind? Are your emotions driving your thinking process?

Emotions play a vital role in our lives. They help us feel compassion, help others, and reach out in times of need, and they help us relate to others. Emotions, on the other hand, can cause some problems in your critical thinking process. You do not have to eliminate emotions from your thoughts, but it is crucial that you know when your emotions are clouding an issue.

Consider the following topics:

What we need is not the will to believe, but the will to find out.

—BERTRAND RUSSELL

- Should drugs and prostitution be legalized?
- Can the theories of evolution and creationism coexist?
- Is affirmative action reverse discrimination?
- Should terminally ill patients have the right to state-assisted and/or privatized-assisted suicide?

As you read these topics, did you immediately form an opinion? Did old arguments surface? Did you feel your emotions coming into play as you thought about the questions? If you had an immediate answer, it is likely that you allowed some past judgments, opinions, and emotions to enter the decision-making process, unless you have just done a comprehensive, unbiased study of one of these issues. As you discussed these in class or with your friends, how did you feel? Did you get angry? Did you find yourself groping for words? Did you find it hard to explain why you held the opinion that you voiced? If so, these are warning signs that you are allowing your emotions to drive your decisions. If we allow our emotions to run rampant (not using restraint) and fail to use research, logic, and evidence (expansive thinking), we will not be able to critically examine the issues or have a logical discussion regarding the statements.

If you feel that your emotions caused you to be less than objective, you might consider the following tips when you are faced with an emotional decision:

- Listen to all sides of the argument or statement before you make a decision or form an opinion.
- Make a conscious effort to identify which emotions are causing you to lose objectivity.
- Do not let your emotions withdraw you or turn you off from the situation.
- Don't let yourself become engaged in "I'm right, you're wrong" situations.

Thoughts ● ● ●

- Work to understand why others feel their side is valid.
- Physiological reactions to emotions, such as increased heart rate and blood pressure and an increase in adrenaline flow, should be recognized as an emotional checklist. If you begin to experience these reactions, relax, take a deep breath, and concentrate on being open-minded.
- Control your negative self-talk or inner voice toward the other person(s) or situation.
- Determine whether your emotions are irrational.

Candid discussions, and sometimes brutal honesty, are useful and necessary when you are addressing complex or difficult issues. However, be careful not to let emotions take over your objectivity.

In the space provided below, develop a step-by-step plan to evaluate one of the controversial topics listed previously. You do not have to answer the question; your task is to devise a plan to critically address the topic without emotional interference. For example: Do violent TV programs and movies cause violent crime? Before you answer yes or no, your first step might be to define violent TV/movies. A second step might be to define violent crime. A third step might be to research the association between the two. A fourth step might be to objectively evaluate the research, asking the following questions: (1) From where does the research originate: the TV or movie industry, a parental guidance group, or a completely detached agency? (2) How old is the research? (3) For how long a period was the research conducted? This type of questioning does not allow your emotions to rule the outcome.

Select one of the topics from those listed on the previous page, or develop your own statement, and devise a plan for critical analysis.

STATEMENT _____

_____

Step 1. _____

_____

Step 2. _____

_____

Step 3. _____

_____

Step 4. _____

_____

Step 5. _____

_____

STEP TWO: THINKING ON A HIGHER LEVEL

Critical thinking involves looking at an issue from many different angles. It encourages you to dig deeper than you have before; get below the surface; struggle, experiment, and expand. It asks you to look at something from an entirely different angle so that you might develop new insights and understand more about the problem, situation, or question. Thinking on a higher level involves looking at something that you may have never seen before or something that you may have seen many times, and trying to think about it more critically than before.

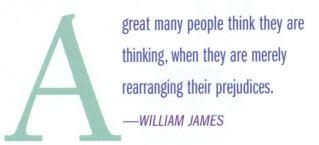

A great many people think they are thinking, when they are merely rearranging their prejudices.

—WILLIAM JAMES

As you begin to look "with different eyes," take a moment to complete the activities below. They are provided to encourage you to look at simple, common situations in a new light. Remember, these exercises do not measure intelligence.

Review the following example of a "brain teaser" and solve the remaining teasers. You will need to break down a few barriers in thought and look at them from a new angle to get them all.

BRAIN TEASERS

Examples:		
	4 W on a C	4 Wheels on a Car
	13 O C	13 Original Colonies

1. SW and the 7 D _____

2. I H a D by MLK _____

3. 2 P's in a P _____

4. HDD (TMRUTC) _____

5. 3 S to a T _____

6. 100 P in a D _____

7. T no PLH _____

8. 4 Q in a G _____

9. I a SWAA _____

10. 50 S in TU _____

How did you do? Was it hard to look at the situation backwards? Most of us are not used to that. As you continue to build your critical-thinking skills, look at the design at the right. You will find nine dots. Your mission is to connect all nine dots with four straight lines without removing your pencil or pen from the paper. Do not retrace your lines. Can you do it?

Finally, as you begin to think beyond the obvious, examine the penny on the following page. You will see the front and back sides of the penny. Pretend that the world has ended and all traces of civilization are

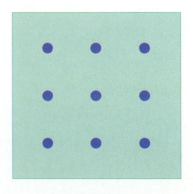

gone. Someone from another planet, who speaks our language, has come to earth and the only thing left from our civilization is one penny. Below, list the things that could be assumed about our civilization from this one small penny. You should find at least ten.

1. _____
2. _____
3. _____
4. _____
5. _____
6. _____
7. _____
8. _____
9. _____
10. _____

While these activities may seem somewhat trivial, they are provided to help you begin to think about and consider information from a different angle. This is a major step in becoming a critical thinker: looking beyond the obvious, thinking outside the box, examining details, and exploring possibilities.

STEP THREE: ANALYZING INFORMATION

Critical thinking goes further than thinking on a different or higher level or using emotional restraint; it also involves analyzing information. To analyze, you break a topic, statement, or problem into parts to understand the nature of the whole. It is a simple, yet crucial, step in critical thinking. An easy way to analyze is to create a chart of the information using a right- and left-hand column.

Example	Why Is Proper Nutrition Important to Humans?
A	**B**
Physical health	Prevents heart disease, high blood pressure, and high cholesterol, and helps control weight.
Dental health	Helps prevent tooth decay; some foods inhibit decay, such as cheese, peanut butter, and protein. Proper nutrition helps prevent gum disease.
Mental health	Self-esteem may increase. You are able to exercise more, thus helping to relieve stress and some types of depression.

As you can see, a question properly analyzed prohibits us from simply answering the nutrition question with "It's good for you." An analysis forces you to ask why it is good or bad, right or wrong, proper or improper.

Now, it's your turn. Analyze the following question: *How can an undeclared student take steps to decide on a career?* Hint: The answer can be found in this edition of *Cornerstone*.

N othing in life is to be feared, it is to be understood.   —*MARIE CURIE*

COLUMN A   COLUMN B

_____   _____
                         _____
                         _____
                         _____
_____   _____
                         _____
                         _____
                         _____
_____   _____
                         _____
                         _____
                         _____
_____   _____
                         _____
                         _____

This method can also be used to formulate new information on a subject. If you read a chapter or article, hear a conversation, or are faced with a problem, you can analyze the situation by creating questions that need to be answered in Column A and providing the answer in Column B. You may have to use more than one source of information to answer the questions you posed in Column A.

STEP FOUR: QUESTIONING ASSUMPTIONS AND COMMON TRUTHS

You've asked questions all of your life. As a child, you asked your parents, "What's that?" a million times. You probably asked them, "Why do I have to do this?" In later years, you've asked questions of your friends, teachers, strangers, store clerks, and significant others. Questioning is not new to you, but it may be a new technique for exploring, developing, and

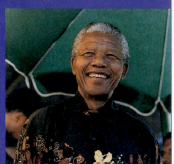

Sometimes you want to ask questions of experts or those whose opinions you value to aid your own thinking. Are there questions you have for any of these people?

acquiring new knowledge. Curiosity may have killed the cat, but it was a smart cat when it died. Your curiosity is one of the most important traits you possess. It helps you grow and learn, and it may sometimes cause you to be uncomfortable. That's OK. This section is provided to assist you in learning how to ask questions to promote knowledge, solve problems, foster strong relationships, and critically analyze difficult situations.

Let's start with a simple questioning exercise. If you could meet anyone on earth and ask five questions, whom would you meet, why would you meet them, and what questions would you ask?

I'd like to meet _____

Because _____

I'd ask the person

1. _____
2. _____
3. _____
4. _____
5. _____

Asking questions can be fun in many situations. They help us gain insight where we may have limited knowledge. They can also challenge us to look at issues from many different angles. Answering properly posed questions can help us expand our knowledge base.

If you were about to embark on writing a college paper dealing with the AIDS epidemic in the United States, what questions would you want to have answered at the end of the paper? Take some time to think about the issue. Write down at least five questions that you will share with the class. At the end of the class brainstorming session, you will have a better idea of the types of questions needed to fully explore this topic.

My five questions are

1. _____
2. _____
3. _____
4. _____
5. _____

Questioning also involves going beyond the obvious. Examine the advertisement below. The car dealership has provided some information, but it is not enough to make an educated decision. What other questions would you ask to make sure that you are getting a good deal?

1. _____
   _____

2. _____
   _____

3. _____
   _____

4. _____
   _____

5. _____
   _____

STEP FIVE: PROBLEM SOLVING

You face problems every day; some are larger and more difficult than others. Some students have transportation problems. Some have child care problems. Some students have academic problems and some have interpersonal problems. Many people don't know how to solve problems at school, home, or work. They simply let the problem go unaddressed until it is too late to reach an amiable solution. There are many ways to address and solve problems. In this section, we will discuss how to identify and narrow the problem, research and develop alternatives, evaluate alternatives, and solve the problem.

It is important to remember that every problem does have a solution, but the solution may not be what we wanted. It is also imperative to remember the words of Mary Hatwood Futrell, President of the NEA. She states that "finding the right answer is important, of course. But more important is developing the ability to see that problems have multiple solutions, that getting from X to Y demands basic skills and mental agility, imagination, persistence, patience."

N ot everything that is faced can be solved. Nothing can be solved until it is faced. —*JAMES BALDWIN*

Identify and narrow the problem. Put your problem in writing. When doing this, be sure to jot down all aspects of the problem, such as why it is a problem, whom it affects, and what type of problem it is. Examine the following situation: You have just failed two tests this week and you are dreadfully behind on an English paper. Now, that's a problem . . . or is it? If you examine and reflect on the problem, you begin to realize that because of your nighttime job, you always get to class late, you are tired and irritable when you get there, and you never have time to study. So, the real problem is not that you have failed tests and are behind; the problem is that your job is interfering with your college work. Now that you have identified and narrowed the problem, you can begin to work toward a solution.

Develop alternatives.   A valuable method of gathering ideas, formulating questions, and solving problems is brainstorming. To brainstorm, you let your ideas flow without any fear of ridicule. A brainstorming session allows all thoughts to be heard. You can brainstorm any matter almost anywhere. You may want to set some guidelines for your sessions to make them more productive.

- Identify the topic, problem, or statement to be discussed.
- Set a time limit for the entire brainstorming session.
- Write all ideas on a board or flip chart.
- Let everyone speak.
- Don't criticize people for their remarks.
- Concentrate on the issue; let all of your ideas flow.
- Suspend judgment until all ideas are produced or the time is up.
- If you're using the session to generate questions rather than solutions, each participant should pose questions rather than statements.

Using the problem identified on the previous page (my nighttime job is causing me to not have enough time for sleep or study), jot down the first few alternatives that come to mind. Don't worry about content, clarity, or quality. Just let your mind flow. Verbalize these ideas when the class brainstorms this problem.

● ● ● **Thoughts**

IDEAS

Evaluate the alternatives.   Some of your ideas or your classmates' ideas may not be logical in solving the problem. After careful study and deliberation, without emotional interference, analyze the ideas and determine if they are appropriate or inappropriate for the solution. To analyze, create Columns A and B. Write the idea in Column A and a comment in Column B. Example:

A	B
Quit the job.	Very hard to do. I need the money for tuition and car.
Cut my hours at work.	Will ask my boss.
Find a new job.	Hard to do because of the job market— but will look into it.
Get a student loan.	Visit financial aid office tomorrow.
Quit school.	No—it is my only chance for a promotion.

With your comments in Column B, you can now begin to eliminate some of the alternatives that are inappropriate at this time.

Solve the problem. Now that you have a few strong alternatives, you have some work to do. You will need to talk to your boss, go to the financial aid office, and possibly begin to search for a new job with flexible hours. After you have researched each alternative, you will be able to make a decision based on solid information and facts.

Pretend that your best friend, Nathan, has just come to you with a problem. He tells you that his parents are really coming down hard on him for going to college. It is a strange problem. They believe that Nathan should be working full time and that he is just wasting his time and money, since he did not do well in high school. They have threatened to take away his car and kick him out of the house if he does not find a full-time job. Nathan is doing well and does not want to leave college.

When solving a problem, it is helpful to look at all possible alternatives and decide on the best one. Sometimes there is one right answer, but often you'll have to settle for the best answer.

In the space provided below, formulate questions to help Nathan solve this problem.

_____

_____

_____

_____

_____

_____

STEP SIX: DISTINGUISHING FACT FROM OPINION

One of the most important aspects of critical thinking is the ability to distinguish fact from opinion. In many situations—real life, TV, radio, friendly conversations, and the professional arena—opinions surface more often than facts. Reread the previous sentence. This is an example of an opinion cloaked as a fact. There is no research supporting this opinion. It sounds as if it could be true, but without evidence and proof, it is just an opinion. A fact is something that can be proved, something that can be objectively verified. An opinion is a statement that is held to be true, but one that has no objective proof. Statements that cannot be proved should always be treated as opinion. Statements that offer valid proof and verification from credible, reliable sources can be treated as factual.

One can't believe impossible things.

—ALICE,

THROUGH THE LOOKING GLASS

Examine the following statements:

Thomas Wolfe was a writer.

FACT

This can be verified by many sources and by the volumes he wrote.

Clara Barton founded the Red Cross.

FACT

This can be verified by reading the history of the Red Cross.

Lincoln was the best president ever.

OPINION

This is only an opinion that can be disputed.

American college students spend more money on pizza than do students from other countries.

OPINION

This is an opinion not based on research or fact.

There are more hotel rooms on the corner of Las Vegas Boulevard and Tropicana Avenue in Las Vegas than are in the entire city of San Francisco.

FACT

This can be verified by using data from the Las Vegas and San Francisco Convention Bureaus.

Gone With the Wind is one of the best movies ever made.

OPINION

This is an opinion, although widely held to be a fact because many movie critics have heralded it as such.

When trying to distinguish between fact and opinion, you should take the following guidelines into consideration:

■ If you are in doubt, ask questions and listen for solid proof and documentation to support the statement.

■ Listen for what is not said in a statement.

■ Don't be led astray by those you assume are trustworthy and loyal.

■ Don't be turned off by those you fear or consider untruthful.

■ Do your own homework on the issue. Read, research, and question.

Again, if you are unsure about the credibility of the source or information, treat the statement as opinion.

Using the spaces provided below, write three facts, three opinions, and three opinions cloaked as facts. Feel free to use professors' comments, comments from friends or family, newspapers, TV stories, or radio reports to complete this activity.

FACT _____

_____

FACT _____

_____

FACT _____

_____

OPINION _____

_____

OPINION _____

_____

OPINION _____

_____

OPINION AS FACT _____

_____

OPINION AS FACT _____

_____

OPINION AS FACT _____

_____

STEP SEVEN: SEEKING TRUTH IN ARGUMENTS AND PERSUASION

Whether or not you realize it, arguments and persuasive efforts are around you daily—hourly, for that matter. They are in newspaper and TV ads, editorials, news commentaries, talk shows, TV magazine shows, political statements, and religious services. It seems at times that almost everyone is trying to persuade us through argument or advice. This section is included to assist you in recognizing faulty arguments and implausible or deceptive persuasion.

There is nothing so powerful as truth, and often nothing so strange.   —*DANIEL WEBSTER*

First, let's start with a list of terms used to describe faulty arguments and deceptive persuasion. As you read through the list, try to identify a situation in which you have heard someone mask an argument in these terms.

Fallacious Persuasive Terminology

Ad baculum	Ad baculum is an argument that tries to persuade based on force. Threats of alienation, disapproval, or even violence may accompany this type of argument.
Ad hominem	Ad hominem is when someone initiates a personal attack on a person rather than listening to and rationally debating his or her ideas. This is also referred to as slander.
Ad populum	An ad populum argument is based on the opinions of the majority of people. It assumes that because the majority says X is right, then Y is not. It uses little logic.
Ad verecundiam	This argument uses quotes and phrases from people in authority or popular people to support one's own views.
Bandwagon	The bandwagon approach tries to convince you to do something just because everyone else is doing it. It is also referred to as "peer pressure."
Scare tactic	A scare tactic is used as a desperate measure to put fear in your life. If you don't do X, then Y is going to happen to you.
Straw argument	The straw argument attacks the opponent's argument to make one's own argument stronger. It does not necessarily make argument A stronger; it simply discounts argument B.
Appeal to tradition	This argument looks only at the past and suggests that we have always done it "this way" and we should continue to do it "this way."
Plain folks	This type of persuasion is used to make you feel that X or Y is just like you. Usually, they are not; they are only using this appeal to connect with your sense of space and time.
Patriotism	This form of persuasion asks you to ignore reason and logic and support what is right for state A or city B or nation C.
Glittering generalities	This type of persuasion or argumentation is an appeal to generalities (Bosak, 1976). It suggests that a person or candidate or professional is for all the right things: justice, low taxes, no inflation, rebates, full employment, low crime, free tuition, progress, privacy, and truth.

Below, you will find statements intended to persuade you or argue for a cause. Beside each statement, identify which type of faulty persuasion is used.

AB	Ad baculum	SA	Straw argument
AH	Ad hominem	AT	Appeal to tradition
AP	Ad populum	PF	Plain folks
AV	Ad verecundiam	PM	Patriotism
BW	Bandwagon	GG	Glittering generalities
ST	Scare tactic		

_____ 1. *This country has never faltered in the face of adversity. Our strong, united military has seen us through many troubled times, and it will see us through our current situation. This is your country; support your military.*

_____ 2. *If I am elected to office, I will personally lobby for lower taxes, a new comprehensive crime bill, a $2500 tax cut on every new home, and better education, and I will personally work to lower the unemployment rate.*

_____ 3. *This is the best college in the region. All of your friends will be attending this fall. You don't want to be left out; you should join us, too.*

_____ 4. *If you really listen to Governor Wise's proposal on health care, you will see that there is no way that we can have a national system. You will not be able to select your doctor, you will not be able to go to the hospital of your choice, and you will not be able to get immediate attention. His proposal is not as comprehensive as our proposal.*

_____ 5. *My father went to Honors College, I went to Honors College, and you will go to Honors College. It is the way things have been for the people in this family. There is no need to break with tradition now.*

_____ 6. *The witness's testimony is useless. He is an alcoholic; he is dishonest and corrupt. To make matters worse, he was a member of the Leftist Party.*

_____ 7. *The gentleman on the witness stand is your neighbor, he is your friend, he is just like you. Sure, he may have more money and drive a Mercedes, but his heart never left the Elm Community.*

_____ 8. *John F. Kennedy once said, "Ask not what your country can do for you; ask what you can do for your country." This is the time to act my fellow citizens. You can give $200 to our cause and you will be fulfilling the wish of President Kennedy.*

_____ 9. *Out of the 7000 people polled, 72 percent believed that there is life beyond our planet. Therefore, there must be life beyond Earth.*

_____ 10. *Without this new medication, you will die.*

_____ 11. *I don't care what anyone says. If you don't come around to our way of thinking, you'd better start watching your back.*

As you develop your critical thinking skills, you will begin to recognize the illogical nature of thoughts, the falsehoods of statements, the deception in some advertisements, and the irrational fears used to persuade. You will also begin to understand the depths to which you should delve to achieve objectivity, the thought and care that should be given to your own decisions and statements, and the methods by which you can build logical, truthful arguments.

Creative Thinking

Creative thinking is much like critical thinking in that you are producing something that is uniquely yours. You are introducing something to the world that is new, innovative, and useful. Creative thinking does not mean that you have to be an artist, a musician, or a writer. Creative thinking means that you have examined a situation and developed a new way of explaining information, delivering a product, or using an item. It can be as simple as discovering that you can use a small rolling suitcase to carry your books around campus instead of the traditional back pack.

Why should we use our creative power? Because there is nothing that makes people so generous, joyful, lively, bold and compassionate. —*BRENDA UELAND*

Creative thinking and critical thinking both require that you "loosen up" your brain and be more flexible in your approaches and tactics. In her book *The Artist's Way: A Spiritual Path to Higher Creativity* (1992), Julia Cameron suggests that there are basic principles of creativity, including the following:

- Creativity is the natural order of life.
- There is an underlying, indwelling creative force infusing all of life.
- We are, ourselves, creations. And we, in turn, are meant to create ourselves.
- The refusal to be creative is counter to our true nature.

So, how do we become more creative in our thought process? It will not be the easiest thing that you have done, but your individual creativity can be revealed if you make a daily effort to hone and use your creative skills. Julia Cameron thinks the first steps to true creativity are

- Stop telling yourself, "It's too late."
- Stop waiting until you have enough money to do what you really love.
- Stop telling yourself that dreams don't matter.

- Stop fearing that your family and friends will think you're crazy.
- Stop telling yourself that creativity is a luxury.

To begin the creative process, consider the following chart. These are some of the characteristics that creative thinkers have in common.

Creative Thinking Involves. . .

Compassion	Creative thinkers have a zest for life and genuinely care for the spirit of others.	**Example:** More than 40 years ago, community members who wanted to feed the elderly created Meals on Wheels, now a national organization feeding the elderly.
Courage	Creative thinkers are unafraid to try new things, to implement new thoughts and actions.	**Example:** An NBC executive moves the *Today Show* out of a closed studio onto the streets of New York, creating the number one morning news show in America.
Truth	Creative thinkers search for the true meaning of things.	**Example:** The astrologer and scientist Copernicus sought to prove that Earth was *not* the center of the universe—an unpopular view at the time.
Dreams	Creative thinkers allow themselves time to dream and ponder the unknown. They can see what is possible, not just what is actual.	**Example:** John F. Kennedy dreamed that space exploration was possible. His dream became reality.
Risk Taking	Creative thinkers take positive risks every day. They are not afraid to go against popular opinion.	**Example:** WWF wrestler Jesse "The Body" Ventura took a risk and ran for mayor in a small Minnesota town, never having had any experience in politics. Later, he became governor of the state.
Innovation	Creative thinkers find new ways to do old things.	**Example:** Instead of continuing to fill the earth with waste such as aluminum, plastic, metal, and old cars, means were developed to recycle these materials for future productive use.

(continued)

Creative Thinking Involves. . .

Competition	Creative thinkers strive to be better, to think bolder thoughts, to do what is good and to be the best at any task.	**Example:** Andre Agassi had a several-year slump in tennis. Most people thought he was a "has-been." He came back to win tournament after tournament because he knew that he could.
Individuality	Creative thinkers are not carbon copies of other people. They strive to be true to themselves.	**Example:** A young man decides to take tap dancing instead of playing baseball. He excels and wins a fine arts dancing scholarship to college.
Thinking	Creative thinkers are always thinking about the world, people, and new ideas.	**Example:** A scientist is not afraid to take time to sit alone with his or her data to study and ponder the results, make connections, and develop ways to use the information.
Curiosity	Creative thinkers are interested in all things; they want to know much about many things.	**Example:** A 65-year-old retired college professor goes back to college to learn more about music appreciation and computer programming to expand her possibilities.
Perseverance	Creative thinkers do not give up. They stick to a project to its logical and reasonable end.	**Example:** Dr. Martin Luther King, Jr., did not give up on his dream in the face of adversity, danger, or death threats.

As you explore your own creativity, you may find yourself at odds with family and friends. Remember the information from Chapter 1. Change takes courage, and the person who initiates change is often times unpopular. Creative thinking may cause some people to be uncomfortable.

When embarking on your creative journey, keep the following tips in mind:

- Don't stop dreaming (Hall, 1995).
- Don't grow up too fast.
- Read books and simulations that promote creative thinking and offer exercises to practice the creative process.
- Do something that you do every day in a different place; for example, study outside.

- Develop a sense of adventure and exploration.
- Force yourself to develop at least five possibilities for each problem you face.
- Force yourself to look at at least five new ways of doing the same old thing.
- Take a class that requires creative thought.
- Don't be afraid to change your environment.
- Understand that in creative thinking there may be more than one or two right answers.
- Play with and fantasize about possibilities.

In his book *Jump Start Your Brain,* Doug Hall (1995) quotes a poster by SARK entitled "How To Be An Artist." We could all learn to be more creative by introducing some of the ideas such as:

Learn to *watch* snails.

Cry during movies.

Do it for *love.*

Take *lots* of naps.

Believe in magic.

Laugh a *lot.*

Take *moonbaths.*

Draw on the walls.

Read *every* day.

Giggle with *children.*

Listen to old people.

Bless *yourself.*

Build a *fort* with blankets.

Write *love* letters.

Choose one topic for which you would be interested in building an argument. It should be something to which you have already given considerable thought. As you research this topic and build your case, keep in mind that your analysis, evaluation, critique, and findings should use research from varied sources and should explore different angles. Also keep in mind the credibility, reliability, and validity of your sources. Your argument should be free of opinions and fallacies.

Sample topics for your consideration:

Is euthanasia ethical?
Is technology ruining our world?
Is genetic engineering ethical?
Is America in decline?
Should all people be allowed free speech?
Is our Constitution outdated?
Should sex education be taught in public schools?
Is the U.S. criminal justice system fair?
Is poverty in America a serious problem?
Should the United States have gun control?
When does life begin?

State the argument or problem.

_____

_____

_____

Why have you chosen this position?

_____

_____

_____

_____

What are the major issues surrounding this topic?

_____

_____

_____

How could this well-designed argument or solution help society?

_____

_____

How could this argument or solution harm society?

_____

_____

What are your opponents saying about the issue?

_____

_____

What are two facts supporting your side?

_____

_____

_____

What is the most surprising thing that you discovered? Why?

_____

_____

What research sources did you use to gather your information?

_____

_____

THE One Minute *Journal*

In one minute or less, jot down the major ideas that you learned from this chapter.

THE COMPANION Website *Journal*

Log on to **www.prenhall.com/montgomery**, choose the version of this book you are using, and then choose Chapter 4 on the menu. Next, choose "Links" on the left side of the page. Explore one of the websites offered and summarize your findings.

at this moment?

Journal

Refer to page 92 of Chapter 4.
Review your **GOALS FOR CHANGE**.
Respond in writing as to the progress
you have made toward reaching one
of your three stated goals.

GOAL STATEMENT

PROGRESS

How is your life changing because of this goal?

CORNERSTONES

for critical thinking

Use only *credible* and *reliable* sources.

Distinguish *fact* from *opinion*.

Be *flexible* in your thinking.

Use emotional *restraint*.

Avoid generalizations.

Strive for *objectivity*.

Reserve judgment.

Do *not* assume.

Ask questions.

Seek *truth*.

Do not squander time, for time is the stuff life is made of.

Prioritize.

Ben Franklin

CHAPTER 5

Prioritize

Yolandra was in my class several years ago. She impressed me as *the most organized person I had ever known.* She always had her calendar with her; she took meticulous notes and transcribed them every day; *and she never missed a deadline.* In her notebook, she had carefully written goals and objectives for every class. Yolandra recognized that she had to prioritize several components in her life: *her time, money, and resources.* She had a regular schedule, which she followed exactly, that detailed on which day she would do laundry, on which day she would shop for groceries, and at what time she would exercise. Yolandra adhered to a carefully organized schedule so she would have plenty of time for studying, reviewing her notes, and meeting with professors. She followed a budget because, as with most college students, resources were tight. Although she was not naturally outstanding academically, *through these efforts Yolandra was able to keep her grades among the highest in the class.*

Her organization and adherence to her priorities also enabled Yolandra to serve on the student council, to be active in a sorority, and to work 15 hours a week. *I have never known a student to be more disciplined about her work.* One of the best things about her self-management style was that *she always took time to have fun and to be with her friends.* Yolandra noted in her calendar "Sacred Day." These were days that were reserved for her to have fun, to renew her spirit, *to do nothing—*days on which work was not on her agenda. Yolandra had learned some of the most important time-management and organizational strategies at a very young age: *make a plan, stick to the plan, work hard, play hard, and reward yourself when you have performed well.*

You may think, "That's great for Yolandra, but it wouldn't work for me." And you may be right. The

> **She impressed me as the most organized person I have ever known.**

important thing to consider as you read this chapter *is how to design a plan that is right for you, a plan based on your schedule, your interests, and your most productive times of day.* You'll want to consider how to manage your time, money, and resources and how to set priorities based on you and your individual needs.

This chapter offers some pointers for getting things accomplished. Some of them will work for you and some of them won't, but when you have finished the chapter, *you should have a better handle on how to get the job done and still have time to play.*

If you can't follow a schedule as rigid as Yolandra's, that's fine. Design a schedule you can follow. You might have heard the old saying, *"All work and no play makes Jack a dull boy."* This statement is true, but so is *"All play and no work will make Jack flunk out of school."* The trick is to find a happy medium.

Life is a grindstone. Whether it grinds a man down or polishes him up depends on what he is made of.
—PROVERB

STATEMENT	SCORE	Strongly Disagree	Disagree	Don't Know	Agree	Strongly Agree
1. I lead a balanced life with a reasonable amount of time devoted to play.		1	2	3	4	5
2. I use a personal calendar that allows me to manage all my school, personal, and work time.		1	2	3	4	5
3. My daily plans are related to my short- and long-term goals.		1	2	3	4	5
4. I know how to prioritize tasks for best results.		1	2	3	4	5
5. I plan projects carefully before plunging in.		1	2	3	4	5
TOTAL		0–5	6–10	11–15	16–20	21–25

FEEDBACK

0 – 5   Extensive changes need to occur to ensure success.

6 – 10   Substantial changes need to occur to ensure success.

11 – 15 Considerable changes need to occur to ensure success.

16 – 20 Moderate changes need to occur to ensure success.

21 – 25 Minor changes need to occur to ensure success.

GOALS FOR CHANGE

Based on this feedback, my goals and objectives for change are . . .

Goal Statement _____

Action Steps 1. _____

2. _____

Goal Statement _____

Action Steps 1. _____

2. _____

Goal Statement _____

Action Steps 1. _____

2. _____

Reading this chapter, completing the exercises, and reflecting on priorities will result in your:

- Identifying your current status of organization.

- Differentiating between *doing* time and *being* time.

- Designing a plan for accomplishing your daily, weekly, and monthly goals.

- Organizing your schedule to include all components of a balanced life.

- Understanding the importance of scheduling the most taxing items on your list for your personal peak performance time.

- Saying "no" if saying "yes" would cause you to be stressed, unhappy, and unable to focus on your own goals and interests.

- Understanding the importance of making and following a budget.

- Including in your plan some time for rest, relaxation, and doing nothing.

- Learning to take fun breaks.

- Putting into practice the cornerstones for using effective organization and time management.

Working Hard and Playing Hard

Developing and perfecting priority-management skills are critical to your success as a college student. You have probably wondered how some people get so much done; how some people always seem to have it together, stay calm and collected, and are able to set goals and accomplish them. At the same time, you are aware of others who are always late with assignments and are unable to complete projects and live up to commitments.

Although college students' abilities vary greatly, most have the intellectual ability to succeed; the difference between success and failure is often the person's ability to organize and manage time and to set priorities. Have you ever thought about the statement "Life is a series of choices"? You can't do everything, so you have to make choices! Making choices is what priority and time management is all about.

This chapter presents guidelines to help you focus on managing your time so that you can devote a sufficient part of your day to your work and studies but still be able to have fun and develop the top line.

Ordinary people think merely how they will *spend* their time; people of intellect try to *use* it.

—*ARTHUR SCHOPENHAUER*

Throughout my college career I have participated in several co-curricular organizations, including my sorority, as well as working and attending classes. It was important for me to be able to work, and I knew my education would not be complete if it only included attending classes. Therefore, I had to work very hard at prioritizing the events in my life to be able to do everything that I wanted and needed to do.

One of the biggest challenges I faced was that of keeping myself organized. If I wasn't studying for class then I was working, and if I wasn't working or in class I usually had a meeting or event that I was supposed to be attending. I found that it was easier to manage my schedule if I kept myself on a schedule.

If I studied at the same time each day, it was easier to maintain my schedule. Using a day planner was also helpful. Being active in my sorority, working, and studying kept me very busy, so I needed to keep things noted in my planner to keep me from being unorganized.

I'm also a visual learner and therefore found it helpful if I made notes for myself and put them in very visible places in and around my home and car. This kept important due dates for classes or important meetings in my thoughts so that I wouldn't miss them.

I know that although I'm very busy right now in school, this won't change once I start my career. Learning to prioritize now will only help me in the future.

Wilisha Moore, *age 22*
Major: Communications
The University of Nevada, Las Vegas

It's That "P" Word: Procrastination

We all procrastinate, and then we worry, and then we promise we'll never do it again. We say things to ourselves like, "If I live through this paper, I will never wait until the last minute again." But someone comes along with a great idea for fun, and off we go. Or there is a great movie on TV, and you reward yourself *before* you have done the work.

Most of us are very skilled at procrastination and at fooling ourselves into thinking we are doing other things that really have to be done. The truth is simple: we all avoid the hard jobs in favor of the easy ones. Most of us put off doing unpleasant tasks until our back is against the wall.

I was fortunate in college; in addition to my academic pursuits, I was also involved in social and cultural activities. I also worked for a professor. I learned that the more I had to do, the more I could get done. The semesters that I was the busiest were the semesters that my grades were the highest. You have to learn how to do what you have to do, and when you have to do it. In college, there can be so many distractions. You have to deal not only with your schedule, but with the schedules of those around you.

As a Financial Advisor, I continually employ many of the *priority management skills* I learned in college. With the amount of information circulating around, you learn that you can't pay attention to everything. You quickly learn to prioritize and do the things that have to be done. I learned in college that you may not be able to do it tomorrow; tomorrow may be worse than today.

Technology has greatly impacted the way I conduct my personal and professional life. Learning to use this technology to help me prioritize has been both a challenge and a blessing. Technology is always changing. We just had to upgrade our entire system in the office to deal with the Y2K problem. This has caused our customer service to suffer somewhat, but in the long run, it will be worth it. It sometimes amazes me that we functioned without email and ATMs. With each new invention, we wonder how we ever survived without it. However, technology can't replace human contact.

Timothy Spencer Rice, *Financial Advisor,* Waddell & Reed, Inc., Shawnee Mission, KS

WHY IS IT SO EASY TO PROCRASTINATE?

Procrastination for most people is a habit that has been formed by years of perfecting the process. There are reasons, however, that cause us to keep doing this to ourselves when we know better.

- Superhuman Expectations—You simply overdo and put more on your calendar than Superman or Superwoman could accomplish.

- Whining—You tell yourself that smart people don't have to study, and everybody is smart but you. Smart people are studying or they have studied in the past and have already mastered the material you are struggling with now. Sooner or later, you must pay the price to gain knowledge. No one is born with calculus formulas totally mastered. So the sooner you quit whining, the sooner you will begin to master procrastination.

- Fear of Failing—You have failed a difficult subject in the past, and you are scared it is going to happen again so you do the natural thing and avoid unpleasant experiences.

- Emotional Blocks—It is time to get started and you have no routine and no past regimen to get you started. You are already feeling guilty because you have wasted so much time. You feel tired, depressed, and beaten.

SO, HOW DO YOU OVERCOME THE "P" WORD?

Not only is it important that you overcome procrastination for the sake of your college career—it is equally crucial to your success at work. Procrastination is a bad habit that will haunt you until you make up your mind to overcome it. Here are some tips that might help:

- Set a regular time for study, and do not vary from it.
- Start studying with positive, realistic thoughts. Push negative thoughts out of your mind. Tell yourself that you are growing and becoming more competent.
- Establish study habits. See Chapter 8 for a thorough discussion of study habits.
- Set a concrete goal that you can reach in about 20–25 minutes.
- Face fear; look it right in the face; and make up your mind you are going to overcome it by studying and preparing every day.
- Get help from your professor. Show the professor what you have done and ask if you are on the right track.
- Avoid whining and people who whine and complain. You have this job to do, and it is not going away.
- Allow yourself more time than you think you need to complete an assignment or to study for a test.
- Practice your new study habits for 21 days. By then, you will have gone a long way toward getting rid of your procrastination habits.

For most college students—whether just leaving home and entering college for the first time, or starting or returning to college after spending time in the workforce or raising a family—learning to manage resources is critically important to successfully completing college. Most college students must learn the important skills needed to prioritize the use of their time, money, and resources. To successfully do this, they must first understand what resources are available to them. In the following space, list all resources available to you to enable you to succeed in college.

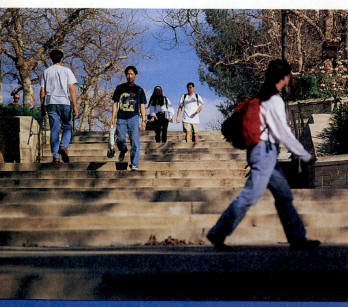

Learning to set priorities and plan your time effectively can eliminate stressful situations like running late to class. How can this skill help you after college?

Financial Resources (Include savings, potential earnings from work you will be doing while in school, parental support, scholarships, and grants.)

_____

_____

_____

_____

Support Resources (Include resources available through your campus or community. Examples include library, free tutoring, counseling, and personal development seminars.)

_____

_____

_____

_____

Time Resources (Include blocks of time in your schedule outside of class that are available for studying and working on class projects.)

_____

_____

_____

_____

Upon careful reflection on their resources, most students are amazed to discover that they possess the raw materials needed to succeed in college, and yet, so many students continue to fail. Failure to succeed in college rarely occurs because students don't have the resources to succeed. Most students fail because they do not use their resources wisely.

Priority Management of Your Time

YOUR BODY'S CYCLES

Priority management and the ability to concentrate are closely linked. Because many people are able to concentrate on visual or auditory stimuli for only about 20 to 30 minutes before they begin to make errors, cramming for tests rarely works. Some people are able to concentrate effectively for longer periods of time, and some people for shorter periods. You'll need to determine your own ability to concentrate and then plan short breaks to avoid making errors.

Other factors affect concentration in different ways.

- Complexity of material. May lead to frustration.
- Time of day. Effect depends on type of task.
- Noise. Improves concentration for some people if it is not too loud.
- Hunger. Makes it difficult to concentrate.
- Environment. Positive or negative feedback and support or lack of support affect concentration.
- Pace. If too fast, may result in errors; if too slow, may result in boredom.

You have a prime time when you are most capable of performing at your peak. For many people, even if they don't like to get up early, the peak performance time is in the morning if they have had enough rest.

You have a prime time when you are most capable of performing at your peak.

Other people function best late at night. Of course you want to work on the most important and demanding jobs at your peak working time. To determine your best working time answer the following questions:

1. Are you lethargic in the morning until you have been up for an hour or so?
2. Did you try to schedule your classes this semester after 10 A.M. so you could sleep later?
3. Do you feel a little down around 5 P.M. but feel ready to go again around 8 P.M.?
4. Have you tended to pull all-nighters in the past?
5. Do you wake up early and spring right out of bed?
6. Do you have a hard time being productive during the late afternoon hours?
7. Is it impossible for you to concentrate after 10 P.M.?
8. Are you one of those rare college students who loves 8 A.M. classes?

If you answered yes to questions 1 through 4, or to most of them, you are a night person; if you answered yes to questions 5 through 8, or to most of them, you are a morning person. Being a morning person does not mean that you can never get anything done at night, but it does mean that your most productive time is morning. If you are a morning person, you should tackle difficult, complex problems early in the morning when you are at your peak. If you are a night person, you should wait a few hours after getting up in the morning before you tackle difficult tasks.

● ● ● Thoughts

PLANNING—THE SECRET TO PRIORITY MANAGEMENT

"I don't have time to plan." "I don't like to be fenced in and tied to a rigid schedule." "I have so many duties that planning never works." No more excuses! To manage your time successfully, you need to spend some time planning. To successfully plan you need a calendar that has a month-at-a-glance section as well as sections for daily notes and appointments.

Planning and Organizing for School

Make a list of your highest priorities for this semester.

- Focus on a few key things that you value the most.
- Include both long-range and short-range tasks.
- Focus on some items that are fun, relaxing, and growth oriented.

Sometimes it helps to put all your tasks in a grid so that you can see them all at once. Many students like to lay out an entire semester or several weeks—and then set their priorities accordingly. You might want to use a month-by-month calendar like the one on the next page to note important due dates for your classes.

- Include long-range projects, such as term papers.
- Include any special events that you really want to attend and that may be rewarding to you.
- Include test dates and study sessions.

Now, utilizing the individual day section of your planner, determine how much preparation time you need for each of the events noted on your monthly calendar. Make sure to take into account other things that are going on in your life at the same time. Once you have determined how long you will need to prepare for the event, note on the days prior to the event the preparation that must take place. For example, if you have a finance exam on January 25 and you determine that you must start studying two weeks in advance for the exam, you would start making notes on your daily to-do lists "study for finance." You would also schedule time on this and any preceding days to study.

> The more time we spend . . . on planning . . . a project, the less total time is required for it. Don't let today's busy work crowd planning time out of your schedule.
>
> —*EDWIN C. BLISS*

Thoughts

January

SUNDAY	MONDAY	TUESDAY	WEDNESDAY	THURSDAY	FRIDAY	SATURDAY
	1	**2** Pick up children	**3**	**4**	**5** 7 pm Lynette's play	**6**
7	**8** 7–9 pm study	**9**	**10** 7–9 pm study	**11** Meet w/ boss	**12**	**13** Football game w/ Tom
14	**15** 7–9 pm study	**16**	**17** 7–9 pm study	**18** *Psy test	**19**	**20**
21	**22** 7–9 pm study	**23** Pick up children	**24** 7–9 pm study	**25** Finance exam	**26** Ski trip! ⎯⎯⎯⎯	**27** ⎯⎯⎯⎯→
28 Ski trip! ⎯⎯→	**29** 7–9 pm study	**30** Pick up children	**31** 7–9 pm study			

First, look over the sample "Today" list on the next page. Then, use the blank "Today" form to make a list of everything you can reasonably do tomorrow and still take some fun breaks and spend some time being instead of just doing. Schedule no more than 60 to 75 percent of your time; leave time for thinking, planning, and interacting.

- Include segments of long-range projects (for example, going to the library to begin research for a paper or project that isn't due for six weeks).
- Build in flexibility, in case a project takes longer than foreseen.

When you have completed your Today list, place a 1, 2, or 3 by each item in the priority code column. Place a 1 by those items that absolutely must be done on this day if you are to avoid a major crisis. For example, you absolutely must finish a paper that is due the following day because the professor will not accept late papers. Place a 2 by those items that should be done today if possible because they are important, and further delay of these items could create a stressful situation and become a major problem. *Preparation relieves stress and improves your confidence.* Place a 3 by those items that could be done today if time permits, but that have no major bearing on overall goals and objectives. For example, shopping for a new pair of shoes would rate a 3. If it is not done today, you will not have a major crisis.

Today	DATE: Jan. 10

LIST OF PRIORITIES		APPOINTMENTS AND CLASSES	
Priority Code		End-of-Day Checklist	
3	Buy Mom's gift	8:00	Math class
3	Wash car	9:00	History class
1	Study—Finance test	10:15	Student. Gvt. Mtg.
1	Ask for Jan. 24 off fm. work	11:30	Canteen w/ John
2	Run 3 miles	12:30	Lunch w/ Rolanda
1	Read Ch. 14	2:00	Study—Finance test
2	Write 2/15 Paper	5—6	Run w/ Rolanda

Expenses for Today

lunch 2.50, gas 5.00

notebook 3.79

Phone Numbers Needed Today

Mary 555-1234

Fun Breaks Canteen @ 11:30 w/ John, run w/ Rolanda

Sacred Day to look forward to: SKI TRIP!! Feb. 18

Now, put your plan to work. As soon as you have any time that is free from class, work, meals, committees, athletic practice, and so on, focus on accomplishing the first priority item on your list. Work hard to discipline yourself to finish this item in a designated amount of time. When you have finished the first task, move to the next one. As you work, occasionally focus on the fact that you will get a reward when you finish this task.

Reward yourself with short, fun breaks—watch a brief TV program, call a friend to talk for a few minutes (but limit your time), drink some juice, or eat an apple. Then go back to work! Work as long as you continue to be productive and don't feel that you are getting stale and performing inadequately. If you are a nontraditional student with a family, a fun break might be to talk with your children or partner about their day, to play a game, to take a walk together, or to ride bikes. Nontraditional students and their family members feel time pressures keenly. Don't expect to put your life and theirs on hold while you go to school. If you do, you all will begin to build resentments, which can damage your family life.

Write appointments and meetings in a calendar that you keep with you at all times. Own only one calendar. It is a mistake to try to keep a big calendar at home and carry a small one with you. *Always* take your calendar to meetings and classes. You might try placing stickers in strategic spots on your calendar to help you focus on important tasks that you

Today

DATE: _____

LIST OF PRIORITIES

Priority Code

APPOINTMENTS AND CLASSES

End-of-Day Checklist

Expenses for Today

Phone Numbers Needed Today

Fun Breaks

might otherwise overlook, such as fun breaks and sacred days. Fun breaks, sacred days, and rewards give you something to look forward to. They are diversions from work that you enjoy *after* you have earned them!

Determine what style of calendar works best for you. There are now several computer pocket calendars that may fit your needs better than a traditional calendar. Because you have to carry it everywhere, you'll probably want to select one that is not too heavy or bulky. Until you find a calendar you like, feel free to duplicate the Today sheet or any other forms in this book as often as you like.

Planning and Organizing for Work

Some supermen and superwomen work full-time and go to school full-time while they juggle families and other responsibilities. *We don't recommend this schedule unless it is for one semester only, when you are pushing to graduate.* If kept up for a long period, you will burn out from the stress that such a pace imposes on your mind and body, and if you have children, they may be adversely affected by your overfull schedule. If you work less and, if necessary, take longer to graduate, you will have more opportunity to savor your college experience.

Use the following questions to help you get organized:

What are your most important responsibilities at work?

_____

_____

_____

_____

Be sure to plan carefully to accomplish these tasks. Your job and your reputation at work depend on their accomplishment, and this job may be the one that gets you your dream job later on.

What measures do your employers use to evaluate your work?

_____

_____

_____

_____

All bosses have pet things they want done—always get these done on time! If you are given a formal evaluation, read it carefully to be sure that you are performing well in all categories.

Must you keep strict hours or can you use flexible scheduling?

_____

_____

_____

_____

If your talents are in great demand, such as graphic arts skills or computer skills, if you can teach a sport or activity, such as swimming, or if you have an academic strength and can tutor, you may be able to set your own hours to a greater extent than if you have to meet an employer's schedule.

IMPORTANT PRINCIPLES FOR PRIORITY MANAGEMENT AT WORK

- Organize your materials at work as they are organized at home. If you have a desk in both places, keep your supplies in the same place in both desks. Simplify your life by following similar patterns at work and at home. Make your office or work space inviting, attractive, and stimulating. If you are a visual thinker and need to see different assignments, be considerate of others who may work close to you. Use clear plastic boxes, colored file folders, and colored file boxes to organize your projects.

Thoughts

- Write directions down! Keep a notebook for repetitive tasks. Keep a calendar, and be on time to meetings.
- Learn to do paperwork immediately rather than let it build up. File—don't pile!
- Never let your work responsibilities slide because you are studying on the job. Employers always notice.
- Leave the office for lunch, breaks, and short walks.
- When you are given projects that require working with others, plan carefully to do your work well and on time.
- Keep a Rolodex file of important phone numbers and addresses that you use frequently.
- Perform difficult, unpleasant tasks as soon as you can so you don't have them hanging over your head.
- When you plan your work schedule, allow for unexpected problems that might interfere with the schedule.
- Practice detached concern—care about your work but avoid taking it home with you.

Use these tips to help generate ideas for managing your time better, performing more effectively, and reducing stress at work. List your ideas in the space provided.

Planning and Organizing at Home

Some people organize effectively at work and school but allow things to fall apart at home. Whether you are a traditional student living in a residence hall or a nontraditional student living in a house with your family, your home should be pleasant and safe. It should be a place where you can study, relax, laugh, invite your friends, and find solitude. The following ideas about home organization will help you maximize your time.

IMPORTANT PRINCIPLES FOR PRIORITY MANAGEMENT AT HOME

For Traditional Students:

- Organize as effectively at home as you do at work.
- If you have roommates, divide the chores. Insist on everyone doing his or her share.

- Plan a rotation schedule for major household chores and stick to it—do laundry on Mondays and Thursdays; clean bathrooms on Saturdays; iron on Wednesdays; and so on.
- Organize your closet and your dresser drawers. Get rid of clothes you don't wear.
- Put a sign by your telephone that reads "TIME" to remind yourself not to waste it on the phone.
- If you can't study in your room because of drop-in visitors or loud roommates, go to the library.
- Pay bills twice monthly. Pay them on time so you don't ruin your credit rating.
- Practice sound money management so you are not stressed by too many bills and too little money.
- If you drive to class or work, fill up your tank ahead of time so you won't be late.
- Keep yourself physically fit with a regular exercise plan and nutritious meals.
- Get out of the house. Take a walk. Visit a friend.

Nontraditional students face special challenges and choices.

For Nontraditional Students:

If you are a nontraditional student and have children, teach them to be organized so they don't waste your time searching for their shoes, books, and assignments. Teach family members responsibility! You can't work, go to school, and hold everybody's hand all the time. Give each of your children a drawer in a filing cabinet. Show them how to organize their work. You will be preparing them to be successful.

- If you are a perfectionist and want everything in your home to be perfect, get over it!
- Get rid of the clutter in your garage, basement, and closets.
- Establish a time for study hall in your home. Children do their homework, and you do yours.
- If you have a family, insist that all of you organize clothes for school or work for several days.
- Put a message board in a convenient place for everyone to use.
- If your children are old enough to drive, have them run errands at the cleaners, post office, and grocery store.
- Carpool with other parents in your neighborhood.
- Delegate, delegate, delegate! You are not Superwoman or Superman. Tell your family you need help. Children can feed pets, make their own beds, fold clothes, vacuum, sweep, iron, and cut the grass if they are old enough.
- Schedule at least one hour alone with each of your children each week. Make this a happy, special time—a fun break!

- Plan special times with your spouse or partner if you have one so that he or she does not get fed up with your going to school.
- Tell your family and friends when you have to study; ask them to respect you by not calling or dropping by at this time.
- Post a family calendar where everyone can see it. Put all special events on it—for example, Janie's recital, Mike's baseball game, Jasmine's company party.
- Put sacred days on this calendar so that your entire family has something to look forward to.

Prioritizing Your Finances

When we talk about finances in our classes we've noticed that most college students do not budget. They have a reasonable idea of what they can spend and how much they require to cover their basic expenses, including tuition, books, housing, car payment, food, and utilities, but basically this is just a guesstimate. They have never sat down and decided to live within their income and to use their money wisely. As a result, many of the students we see are often strapped for money. The information in this section is intended to help you choose how to spend your money more wisely and to instill in you the belief that money management is an everyday process. If you are going to be financially secure, you cannot afford to live day to day and hand to mouth with no plan for accumulating wealth.

To fully maximize your financial resources, you need to establish a budget and learn to live within your means. According to Konowalow in his book *Cornerstones for Money Management* (1997),

> Watching and calculating how much money is coming in each month and how much you spend is important to taking control of your finances. While not having control of your income and expenditures may not be a problem this week or next, it is sure to become one soon if the money you are spending each month exceeds the money coming in.

When budgeting, you must first determine how much income you earn monthly. Complete the following chart.

Source of Income	Estimated Amount
Work	$ 2,000
Spouse Income	$ 3,000
Parental Contributions	$ 0
Scholarships	$ 0
Loans	$ 5,000
Savings	$ 0
Investments	$ 0
Other	$ 0
Total Income	$ 5000

Next you must determine how much money you spend in a month. Complete the following chart.

Tuition	$ 3,500
Books and Supplies	$ 700
Housing	$ 0
Utilities	$ 200
Phone	$ 40
Car Payment	$ 860
Insurance	$ 800
Gas	$ 900
Clothing	$ 0
Food	$ 350
Household Items	$ 800
Personal Hygiene Items	$ 60
Health Care and/or Health Insurance	$ 0
Entertainment/Fun	$ 200
Other	$ 00
Total Expenditures	$

If the amount of your total expenditures is smaller than your monthly income, you are on your way to controlling your finances. If your total expenditures figure is larger than your monthly income (as is the case for many of our students), you are heading for a financial crisis. Often students see credit cards as a way to make up this difference, but we caution you not to do this.

Most college students receive several credit cards as soon as they enter college. By the time they graduate, they may have considerable credit card debt. It is easy to consider credit cards a short-term fix for your cash flow shortage by thinking you are certain you will pay off the credit cards when you get a full-time job. This practice leads to several problems. First, upon graduation you may end up with a sizeable debt with a very high interest rate. Second, making late payments for any reason could lead to a poor credit rating. A poor credit record can keep you from receiving further financial aid or buying a new car or home. Credit card debt is the worst kind of debt that you can have. If you currently are using credit cards, we encourage you to pay off any existing balances and then close all of your accounts, keeping one for emergencies only.

Instead of using credit cards to pay for the expenditures that cause you to go over your budget, modify your expenditures. Almost every line on the expenditure chart can be modified. For example, adding a roommate or moving can lower your housing expense. You can change your car to a less expensive one or consider using public transportation or carpooling with colleagues. In the space below, list five ways you can modify your expenditures.

1. _____

2. _____

3. _____

4. _____

5. _____

Hints for cutting your expenses:

■ Control impulse buying. (Don't buy anything that costs more than $15 until you have waited 72 hours; it is amazing how often you decide you don't need the item that you thought you had to have.)

■ Carpool, take public transportation, or walk to classes.

■ Don't eat out as often. Make your own meals.

■ Use coupons and buy during sales.

■ Live more simply by getting rid of unnecessary items like cell phones, beepers, and cable television.

Maximizing Other Resources

Generally, institutions of higher learning provide a plethora of resources for students. These resources vary from institution to institution but usually include student employment services, student loan services, student psychological services, and other student support services. For a complete listing of all of the resources available to you at your institution, contact your institution's Office for Student Affairs. This office typically serves as a clearinghouse for services to assist students throughout their college career. Don't miss out on services and assistance your college or university provides just because you didn't know they existed.

List two campus resources of interest to you. Research the location and contact numbers.

1. _____

   Location _____ *Phone* _____

2. _____

   Location _____ *Phone* _____

As you have learned in this chapter, correctly identifying the problem is the most important step in setting priorities. If you fail to correctly identify the problem, all the other steps will have no impact.

What are your primary problems in managing your priorities?

Place a 1 (one) beside the most serious priority management problem you have identified in the list at left. Consider the major problem you have identified, brainstorm alternatives, and consider possible solutions. List your alternatives in the space below:

Evaluate each alternative that you have listed above. Realizing that some problems have multiple solutions, what are the best solutions to your major problem? Write the best solution in the space below:

LIFE

Intelligence

Self-Esteem

The One Minute Journal

In one minute or less, jot down the major ideas that you learned from this chapter.

_____

_____

_____

_____

_____

_____

_____

_____

_____

_____

_____

THE COMPANION Website Journal

Log on to **www.prenhall.com/montgomery**, choose the version of this book you are using, and then choose Chapter 5 on the menu. Next, choose "Links" on the left side of the page. Explore one of the websites offered and summarize your findings.

_____

_____

_____

_____

_____

_____

_____

_____

_____

Refer to page 122 of Chapter 5.
Review your **GOALS FOR CHANGE**.
Respond in writing as to the progress
you have made toward reaching one
of your three stated goals.

GOAL STATEMENT

PROGRESS

How is your life changing because of this goal?

CORNERSTONES

of priority management

Manage your time, money, and resources effectively.

Include *fun breaks*, rewards, and sacred days.

List who and what brings you *joy*.

Maximize your abilities.

Focus on quality and joy.

Balance your life.

Keep a *calendar*.

Make *to-do* lists.

Prepare to *work*.

Know how to listen, and you will profit even from those who

Listen.

say nothing. Plutarch

CHAPTER 6

Listen

LaTonya had been through a *rough evening.* She had received a phone call from home to say that *her grandmother was very ill and had been taken to the hospital.* As she sat in math class the next morning, her mind was flooded with images of home. She had lived with her grandmother most of her life. *In her mind's eye, she saw a house filled with people and she could smell the bread baking in the oven.* She saw her grandmother calling her down to eat before the arrival of the school bus. Her daydream was so vivid that for a moment, LaTonya could feel the *gentle kiss of her grandmother on her forehead.*

LaTonya was filled with anxiety, *wondering whether her grandmother would be all right.* Her mind was a million miles away when a deep voice rang through her daydream. *"Do you agree with the solution to this problem, Ms. Griffin?"* LaTonya knew the voice was speaking to

> **LaTonya had no idea whether she agreed or not. She had not heard the problem or the solution.**

her, but *it took her a few seconds to focus on it.* Again the instructor asked, *"Do you agree with the solution to this problem, Ms. Griffin?"* LaTonya had no idea whether she agreed or not. *She had not heard the problem or the solution.* She looked at the instructor and out of embarrassment and intimidation, she answered, *"Yes, I do."*

The situation took a turn for the worse. "Why do you think this is the proper way to solve this problem, Ms. Griffin?" *LaTonya sat, bewildered, at her desk.* She looked down at her notes for help, but she had written only the date and the topic for the day on her notepad. The tension grew as the entire class waited for her answer. "I don't know, Dr. Huggins, I don't know."

A bility is what you are capable of doing. Motivation determines what you do. Attitude determines how well you do it. —*LOU HOLTZ*

STATEMENT	SCORE	Strongly Disagree	Disagree	Don't Know	Agree	Strongly Agree
1. I know how to listen for important clues.		I	2	3	4	5
2. I am always focused on the person speaking.		I	2	3	4	5
3. I know how to listen with my whole body.		I	2	3	4	5
4. I do not allow my feelings for the speaker to interfere with my listening.		I	2	3	4	5
5. I know how to listen for "how" something is said.		I	2	3	4	5
TOTAL		0–5	6–10	II–15	16–20	21–25

FEEDBACK

0 – 5   Extensive changes need to occur to ensure success.

6 – 10   Substantial changes need to occur to ensure success.

11 – 15   Considerable changes need to occur to ensure success.

16 – 20   Moderate changes need to occur to ensure success.

21 – 25   Minor changes need to occur to ensure success.

GOALS FOR CHANGE

Based on this feedback, my goals and objectives for change are . . .

Goal Statement _____

Action Steps 1. _____

2. _____

Goal Statement _____

Action Steps 1. _____

2. _____

Goal Statement _____

Action Steps 1. _____

2. _____

Results

Reading this chapter, completing the exercises, and reflecting on your personal listening qualities will result in your:

- Differentiating between listening and hearing.

- Defining active listening.

- Explaining the benefits of active listening.

- Identifying active and passive listening characteristics.

- Identifying key phrases and words for effective note taking.

- Identifying obstacles to active listening.

- Listening visually.

- Describing and using the cornerstones for effective listening.

The Importance of Listening

Listening is one of the most important and useful skills human beings possess. For all animals, listening is a survival skill needed for hunting and obtaining food; for humans, listening is necessary for establishing relationships, growth, survival, knowledge, entertainment, and even health. It is one of our most widely used tools. How much time do you think you spend listening every day? Research suggests that we spend almost 70 percent of our waking time communicating, and 53 percent of that time is spent in listening situations (Adler, Rosenfeld, and Towne, 1989). Effective listening skills can mean the difference between success or failure, A's or F's, relationships or loneliness.

For students, good listening skills are critical. Over the next two to four years you will be given a lot of information in lectures. Cultivating and improving your active listening skills will help you to understand the lecture material, take accurate notes, participate in class discussions, and communicate with your peers.

College classes demand active critical listening skills.

The Difference Between Listening and Hearing

We usually do not think much about listening until a misunderstanding occurs. You've no doubt been misunderstood or misunderstood someone yourself. Misunderstandings arise because we tend to view listening as an automatic response when it is instead a learned, voluntary activity, like driving a car, painting a picture, or playing the piano. Having ears does not make you a good listener.

After all, having hands does not mean you are capable of painting the Mona Lisa. You may be able to paint the Mona Lisa, but only with practice and guidance. Listening, too, takes practice and guidance. Becoming an active listener requires practice, time, mistakes, guidance, and active participation.

Hearing, however, is not learned; it is automatic and involuntary. If you are within range of a sound you will probably hear it although you may not be listening to it. Hearing a sound does not guarantee that you know what it is, or what made it. Listening actively, though, means making a conscious effort to focus on the sound and to determine what it is.

Listening is a four-step cycle, represented by the mnemonic **ROAR.**

R—Receiving the information
O—Organizing the sounds heard and focusing on them
A—Assigning meaning
R—Reacting

Objective listening can be a difficult skill to learn. Have you encountered people with radically different views than your own? How did you respond?

RECEIVING

Receiving means that you were within the range of the sound when it was made. Receiving a sound is not the same as listening. To become an active listener, when receiving information make an effort to

1. Tune out distractions other than the conversation at hand.
2. Avoid interrupting the speaker.
3. Pay close attention to nonverbal communication, such as gestures, facial expressions, and movements.
4. Concentrate on what is being said at the moment, not on what will be said next.
5. Listen for what is not said. Are important facts omitted?

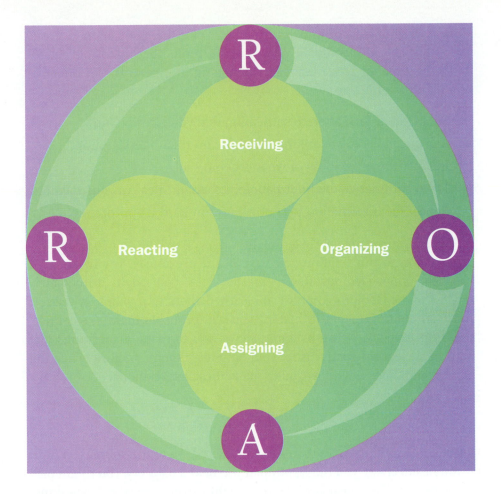

ORGANIZING

Organizing and focusing means choosing to listen actively to the sound, to pay attention to its origin, direction, and intention. To become an active listener, when organizing and focusing on information make an effort to

1. Sit up straight or stand near the person speaking, so that you involve your entire body.
2. Make eye contact with the speaker; listen with your eyes and ears.
3. Try to create a visual picture of what is being said.

ASSIGNING

Assigning refers to mentally assigning a name or meaning to what you have been listening to. Sometimes you may have to pay special attention to sounds in order to assign the correct name or meaning to them. Have you ever been sitting inside and heard a crash? You might have had to hear it again before you could identify the sound as dishes falling, books dropping, or cars colliding. Your brain tries to create a relationship between what you hear and what you have heard before; it tries to associ-

Thoughts

ate one piece of information with another. Once the association is made, you will be able to identify the new sound by remembering the old sound.

To become an active listener, when assigning meaning to information make an effort to:

1. Relate the information to something that you already know.
2. Ask questions to ensure that there are no misunderstandings.
3. Identify the main ideas of what is being said.
4. Try to summarize the information into small "files" in your memory.
5. Repeat the information to yourself (or out loud if appropriate).

When you are actively listening in class, you will be able to relate new information to information you have heard previously. For instance, if you hear about Oedipus Rex in theater class, you might immediately relate it to the Oedipus complex you learned about in psychology class. If you hear about Einstein in history, you will probably make the connection from science. Active listening allows you to make associations that help create learning patterns for your long-term memory. Simply hearing information does not allow you to make these associations.

REACTING

Reacting is nothing more than making a response to the sound you hear. If you hear a crash, you might jump; if you hear a baby cry, you might pick the baby up; if you hear a voice, you might turn to see who is speaking. Reacting can be a barrier to active listening. Tuning out because you are bored or do not agree with the speaker's point of view is a way of reacting to information.

To become an active listener, when reacting to information make an effort to:

1. Leave your emotions behind; do not prejudge.
2. Avoid overreacting.
3. Avoid jumping to conclusions.
4. Ask yourself, "How can this information help me?"

Practical Definitions of Listening

According to Ronald Adler (Adler, Rosenfeld, and Towne, 1989), the drawing of the Chinese verb "to listen" provides the most comprehensive and practical definition of listening. To the Chinese, listening involves the ears, the eyes, undivided attention, and the heart. Do you make it a habit to listen with more than your ears? The Chinese view listening as a

Ear

Eyes

Undivided attention

Heart

聽

whole-body experience. People from Western cultures seem to have lost the ability to involve their whole body in the listening process. We tend to use only our ears and sometimes, we don't even use them—remember LaTonya at the beginning of the chapter.

The American Heritage Dictionary defines listening as follows: "To make an effort to hear something; to pay attention; to give heed." This standard definition is not very concrete nor does it offer much direction. Listening needs to be personalized and internalized. To understand listening as a whole-body experience, we can define it on three levels:

1. Listening with a purpose
2. Listening objectively
3. Listening constructively

Listening with a purpose suggests a need to recognize different types of listening situations— for example, class, worship, entertainment, and relationships. People do not listen the same way in every situation.

Listening objectively means listening with an open mind. You will give yourself few greater gifts than the gift of knowing how to listen without bias and prejudice. This is perhaps the most difficult aspect of listening. If you have been cut off in mid-conversation or mid-sentence by someone who disagreed with you or if someone has left the room while you were giving your opinion of a situation, you have had the experience of talking to people who do not know how to listen objectively.

Listening to people from different cultures, backgrounds, and religions can open many doors.

Listening constructively means listening with the attitude of "How can this be helpful to my life or my education?" This type of listening involves evaluating the information you are hearing and determining whether it has meaning to your life. Sound easy? It is more difficult than it sounds because, again, we all tend to shut out information that we do not see as immediately helpful or useful. To listen constructively, you need to know how to listen and store information for later dates.

Obstacles to Listening

Several major obstacles stand in the way of becoming an effective listener. To begin building active listening skills, you first have to remove some barriers.

OBSTACLE ONE: PREJUDGING

Prejudging means that you automatically shut out what is being said; it is one of the biggest obstacles to active listening. You may prejudge because of the content, because of the person communicating, or because of your environment, culture, social status, or attitude.

The ability to actively listen is a critical component to being successful in the world of work. As a cast member with Disneyland Resorts, I spend a great deal of my day listening to guests and other cast members. My capacity to completely focus on what the individual is saying is key to my ability to provide outstanding service to all those I work with. My position requires that I do a significant amount of entertaining, and learning to listen in the various environments in which I work has been quite a challenge. I've had to learn how to really hear what people are saying and then translate it into information that can be disseminated to the individuals who must act on the information.

One of the most important things that I learned in college was the importance of actively listening. I noticed in your textbook that the authors use the Chinese character to describe what active listening really involves. I've found that I must give the individual with whom I am speaking my undivided attention and utilize not only my ears but also my eyes and heart to truly understand what they are saying. College helped me to hone my listening skills, but I must constantly strive to become a better listener.

Another thing that I have come to realize is that listening is critical to my relationships with others. Call it pixie dust, call it magic, or call it a miracle, but your ability to interact and communicate with other people will get you further than almost any other skill that you have. Take every opportunity to learn social skills and graces, learn to communicate with others, and learn the fine art of give and take. Teamwork is the key to success.

Life is about learning, both through higher education and through daily lessons from living. You never know where life is going to lead you. Be open, think beyond the moment, and all your dreams may come true.

Maritza E. Correa, CMP, *Convention Services/Disneyland Resort Express Director,* Disneyland Resort Hotels, Anaheim, CA

Do You Prejudge Information or Its Source?

Answer yes or no to the following questions:

1. I tune out when something is boring. (YES) (NO)

2. I tune out when I do not agree with the information. (YES) (NO)

3. I argue mentally with the speaker about information. (YES) (NO)

4. I do not listen to people I do not like. (YES) (NO)

5. I make decisions about information before I understand all of its implications or consequences. (YES) (NO)

If you answered yes to two or more of these questions, you tend to prejudge in a listening situation.

Tips for Overcoming Prejudging

1. Listen for information that may be valuable to you as a student. Some material may not be pleasant to hear but may be useful to you later on.

2. Listen to the message, not the messenger. If you do not like the speaker, try to go beyond personality and listen to what is being said, without regard to the person saying it. Conversely, you may like the speaker so much that you automatically accept the material or answers without listening objectively to what is being said.

3. Try to remove cultural, racial, gender, social, and environmental barriers. Just because a person is different from you or holds a different point of view does not make that person wrong; and just because a person is like you and holds a similar point of view does not make that person right. Sometimes you have to cross cultural and environmental barriers to learn new material and see with brighter eyes.

OBSTACLE TWO: TALKING

Not even the best listener in the world can listen while he or she is talking. The next time you are in conversation with a friend, try speaking while your friend is speaking—then see if you know what your friend said. To become an effective listener, you need to learn the power of silence. Silence gives you the opportunity to think about what is being said before you have to respond.

Are You a Talker Rather than a Listener?

Answer yes or no to the following questions:

1. I often interrupt the speaker so that I can say what I want. (YES) (NO)

2. I am thinking of my next statement while others are talking. (YES) (NO)

3. My mind wanders when others talk. (YES) (NO)

4. I answer my own questions. (YES) (NO)

5. I answer questions that are asked of other people. (YES) (NO)

If you answered yes to two or more questions, you tend to talk too much in a listening situation.

1. Force yourself to be silent at parties, family gatherings, and friendly get-togethers. We're not saying you should be unsociable, but force yourself to be silent for 10 minutes. You'll be surprised at what you hear. You may also be surprised how hard it is to do this. Test yourself.

2. Ask someone a question and then allow that person to answer the question.

   Too often we ask questions and answer them ourselves. Force yourself to wait until the person has formulated a response. If you ask questions and wait for answers, you will force yourself to listen.

OBSTACLE THREE: BRINGING YOUR EMOTIONS TO THE TABLE

Emotions can form a strong barrier to active listening. Worries, problems, fears, and anger can keep you from listening to the greatest advantage. Have you ever sat in a lecture, and before you knew what was happening your mind was a million miles away because you were angry or worried about something, like LaTonya in the opening story? If you have, you know what it's like to bring your emotions to the table.

Thoughts ● ● ●

Do You Bring Your Emotions to the Listening Situation?

Answer yes or no to the following questions:

1. I get angry before I hear the whole story. (YES) (NO)

2. I look for underlying or hidden messages in information. (YES) (NO)

3. Sometimes I begin listening on a negative note. (YES) (NO)

4. I base my opinions of information on what others are saying or doing. (YES) (NO)

5. I readily accept information as correct from people whom I like or respect. (YES) (NO)

If you answered yes to two or more of these questions, you tend to bring your emotions to a listening situation.

1. Know how you feel before you begin the listening experience. Take stock of your emotions and feelings ahead of time.

2. Focus on the message; determine how to use the information.

3. Create a positive image about the message you are hearing.

Listening for Key Words, Phrases, and Hints

Learning how to listen for key words, phrases, and hints can help you become an active listener and an effective note-taker. For example, if your English professor begins a lecture saying, "There are ten basic elements to writing poetry," jot down the number 10 under the heading "Poetry" or number your notebook pages 1 through 10, leaving space for notes. If at the end of class you listed six elements to writing poetry, you know that you missed a part of the lecture. At this point, you need to ask the professor some questions.

Here are some key phrases and words to listen for:

in addition	another way	above all
most important	such as	specifically
you'll see this again	therefore	finally
for example	to illustrate	as stated earlier
in contrast	in comparison	nevertheless
the characteristics of	the main issue is	moreover
on the other hand	as a result of	because

Picking up on transition words will help you filter out less important information, and thus listen more carefully to what is most important. There are other indicators of important information, too. You will want to listen carefully when the professor:

Writes something on the board	Uses computer-aided graphics
Uses an overhead	Speaks in a louder tone or changes vocal patterns
Draws on a flip chart	Uses gestures more than usual

Once you have learned how to listen actively, you will reap several key benefits as a student, as an employee, and as a citizen.

How Do I Get Others to Listen to Me?

As a college student, an employee, community leader, spouse, or caregiver there will be times when you want people to listen to your views and opinions. There will be times when you want to speak out at a club meeting, a civic group meeting, or the PTA, and you want people to hear what you are saying. Below, you will find several tips that you can use to help other people listen to you.

Repetition

Make an effort to state your main ideas or points more than once when you're speaking. We need to hear things as many as 14 times to have them placed in our long-term memory. Repetition helps.

Movement

When you are speaking, use some degree of movement with your body, such as gestures and facial expressions. If you are standing in front of a group of people, you might want to move from one side of the room to the other. However, it is important to remember not to pace restlessly.

Energy

When you are speaking and trying to get others to listen to you, be energetic and lively with your words. It is hard to listen to someone who speaks in the same tone all the time. Be excited about what you are saying and people will listen to you more attentively. This is perhaps the single most important way to get people to listen to your views.

Creativity

This simply means that you need to have something to say when you are speaking and you need to say it in a way that is creative, fresh, and new. You know how hard it is to listen to people who never say a thing. They talk all the time, but seldom say anything important. When you speak, make sure that you are making a contribution to the topic.

Clarity

When making a point, try to arrange your thoughts and statements in a logical, reasonable fashion. It is much easier for people to listen to a clear message than one that is jumbled and disorganized.

Credibility

Few things are more important when trying to get others to listen to you than your past record of accuracy. Avoid fabricating or embellishing the truth. Know the facts before you speak. Your opinion is great, but when

In many situations, like cooperative learning teams, other people rely on your information to be accurate, timely, and useful.

conversing with friends or speaking to a group, you should let people know whether you are speaking from opinion or fact.

Cultural Thoughtfulness

The great thing about America is that you can say what you want to say. Freedom of speech is one of our Constitutional rights. However, one should also realize that for every statement made, consequences follow. When speaking to peers, colleagues, or members of a group, show respect for your audience. This does not mean that you have to agree or that you can't have controversial opinions. It is to say, however, that the quickest way to turn others off is to be rude, insensitive to differences, and arrogant in our beliefs that our opinions are the only ones that matter. Think before you speak and others will listen actively.

Top 10 Reasons for Listening Actively

1. You will be exposed to more information and knowledge about the world, your peers, and yourself.

2. You will be able to help others if you listen to their problems and fears, and you will gain a greater sense of empathy.

3. You will avoid problems at school or work that result from not listening.

4. You will be able to participate in life more fully, because you will have a keener sense of what is going on in the world around you.

5. You will gain friends and healthy relationships, because people are drawn to those to whom they can talk and who they feel listen sincerely.

6. You will be able to ask more questions and to gain a deeper understanding about subjects that interest you or ideas you wish to explore.

7. You will be a more effective leader. People follow people who they feel listen to their ideas and give their views a chance.

8. You will be able to understand more about different cultures from around the world.

9. You will be able to make more logical decisions regarding pressing and difficult issues in your life and studies.

10. You will feel better about yourself because you will know in your heart and mind that you gave the situation your best.

LIFE

Music is the universal language. Or is it? Most everyone enjoys some type of music. Your favorite type may be rhythm and blues, rap, jazz, country, or classical. Regardless of the type of music, musicians are trying to communicate a message just as writers do with words. For this critical thinking exercise, choose your least favorite type of music or the music that you listen to least. If you love country, maybe you will choose rap. If you love rap, you may choose classical. Listen to one song at least three times and answer the following questions:

What emotional response did you have to this music?

_____
_____
_____
_____

Was there a difference in your emotional response the three times you listened to the music?

What were the differences?

_____
_____
_____
_____
_____

What is the primary instrument used in the piece?

_____
_____
_____
_____

Why do you think this music appeals to other people?

_____
_____
_____
_____

What is the artist's message?

_____
_____
_____
_____

While listening to this music, did your level of appreciation increase or decrease as a result of listening objectively? Why or why not?

_____
_____
_____
_____
_____

One Minute Journal

In one minute or less, jot down the major ideas that you learned from this chapter.

COMPANION Website Journal

Log on to **www.prenhall.com/montgomery**, choose the version of this book you are using, and then choose Chapter 6 on the menu. Next, choose "Links" on the left side of the page. Explore one of the websites offered and summarize your findings.

Refer to page 148 of Chapter 6.
Review your **GOALS FOR CHANGE**.
Respond in writing as to the progress
you have made toward reaching one
of your three stated goals.

GOAL STATEMENT

PROGRESS

How is your life changing because of this goal?

CORNERSTONES

for listening

Evaluate the *content*, not the delivery.

Leave your *emotions* at the door.

Listening requires an *open mind*.

Listen for *how* something is said.

Listen to the *whole* story.

Eliminate *distractions*.

Listen for what is *not* said.

Listening is *voluntary*.

Don't give up too soon.

Listen for *major* ideas.

Listen for *key* words.

Stop talking.

Whomever neglects learning in their youth, loses the past and

Record.

is dead for the future.   Euripides

CHAPTER 7

Record

William loved to play pool. *Pool was his passion,* his hobby, his job, and his first love. *Few things ever got in the way of William's pool game.* On more than one occasion, *William cut class to go to the pool hall* with his buddies. "I'll just get the notes from Wanda," he would say. "She's always in class."

When class met on Monday morning, *William asked Wanda for her notes.* She told him that her handwriting was not very good and that *she took notes in her own shorthand.* "Oh, that's all right," William said. "I'll be able to get what I need from them." *Wanda agreed to make a copy of her notes* and to bring them to William on Wednesday. Wanda kept her promise and brought a copy of her notes. William put them into his backpack just before class began. The notes stayed in his backpack until the night before the midterm exam. He had not taken them out to look at them or to ask Wanda any questions about them. When he unfolded the notes, *he was shocked at what he found.*

> *On more than one occasion, William cut class to go to the pool hall with his buddies.*

The notes read:

Psy started as a sci. disc. from Phi and Physio. Wihelm Wundt/GERM and Will James/US= fndrs. in lt. 19th cent.

APA est. by Stanely Hall in US.

5 mjr Pers in PSY=

    Biopsy. Per

    Psychodym. Per

    Humanistic. Per

    Cog. Per.

    Beh. Per.

Psy wk in 2 mjr. areas 1. Acad.

2. Practicing

William was in trouble. He could not understand Wanda's shorthand, and it was too late to ask her to translate her notes. To add insult to injury, he had lost his textbook a few weeks earlier. After trying unsuccessfully to make sense of the notes, *he gave up and went to the pool hall* to relax and have fun before the test. *William failed his midterm.*

The only place success comes before work is in the dictionary.
—*DONALD KENDALL*

at this moment?

STATEMENT	SCORE	Strongly Disagree	Disagree	Don't Know	Agree	Strongly Agree
1. I use abbreviations when taking notes.		1	2	3	4	5
2. I rewrite my notes after each class.		1	2	3	4	5
3. I use symbols when taking notes.		1	2	3	4	5
4. I ask questions in class.		1	2	3	4	5
5. I know how to listen for clues from the professor.		1	2	3	4	5
TOTAL		0–5	6–10	11–15	16–20	21–25

FEEDBACK

0 – 5   Extensive changes need to occur to ensure success.

6 – 10   Substantial changes need to occur to ensure success.

11 – 15   Considerable changes need to occur to ensure success.

16 – 20   Moderate changes need to occur to ensure success.

21 – 25   Minor changes need to occur to ensure success.

GOALS FOR CHANGE

Based on this feedback, my goals and objectives for change are . . .

Goal Statement _____

Action Steps 1. _____

2. _____

Goal Statement _____

Action Steps 1. _____

2. _____

Goal Statement _____

Action Steps 1. _____

2. _____

Results • • •

Reading this chapter, completing the exercises, and reflecting on your personal note-taking style will result in your:

- Identifying key phrases and words for effective note taking.

- Understanding why note taking is essential to successful students.

- Using the L-STAR system.

- Developing and using a personalized, shorthand note-taking system.

- Using the outline technique for taking notes.

- Using the mapping (or webbing) technique for taking notes.

- Using the Cornell (T or modified) technique for taking notes.

- Putting into practice the cornerstones of effective note taking.

Why Take Notes?

Sometimes it all seems like a big, crazy chore, doesn't it? Go to class, listen, and write it down. Is note taking really important? Actually, knowing how to take useful, accurate notes can dramatically improve your life as a student. If you are an effective listener and note-taker, you have two of the most valuable skills any student could ever use. There are several reasons why it is important to take notes:

- You become an active part of the listening process.
- You create a history of your course content when you take notes.
- You have written criteria to follow when studying.
- You create a visual aid for your material.
- Studying becomes much easier.

Good note-taking skills help you do more than simply record what you're taught in class or read in a book so that you can recall it. These skills can also help to reinforce that information so that you actually know it.

Preparing to Take Notes

Just as an artist must have materials such as a brush, palette, canvas, and paints in order to create a painting, you must have certain materials to become an effective note-taker.

Insider's View

"What is it that the people in your class who are getting straight A's know that you don't know?" This was one of the most important questions my professor asked. "The answer," he said, "is in your book." This was a wake-up call for me. I was always bothered by the belief that certain people in my classes were better than me. I was about to find out that I was as good as anyone in my class!

My name is Carlos Fernandez, and like you, I had to take the College Orientation/Study Skills course. It was my first semester back in college — two years after high school and one year after I flunked out of college. The previous year, I had registered for an English class and had failed miserably. When I returned, I was required to take this course. I was not happy about that and I didn't mind letting the professor know. But, I knew that if I was going to take other courses, I had to pass this class first.

I began to read—I mean seriously read—the text and listen in class. I was surprised how much difference this made. I had been pretty negative about the whole class, but little by little, I began to understand points that the professor was making and all of the chapters in the text that I thought would not interest me, actually began to make sense and open me up to new ideas.

One important thing I learned to do was to use the Cornell note-taking method. This has made such a difference in my student life. To make a long story short, I began reading, listening, and using the Cornell note-taking method and now I hold a 3.8 grade point average. It is amazing—my classmates look at me and wonder how I do it. It's a blast!

Carlos Fernandez, age 24
Major: Undecided
Miami-Dade Community College,
North Campus, Miami, Florida

TIPS FOR EFFECTIVE NOTE TAKING

- Attend class. This may sound like stating the obvious, but it is surprising how many college students feel they do not need to go to class. "Oh, I'll just get the notes from Wanda," said William in the opening story. The only trouble with getting the notes from Wanda is that they are Wanda's notes. You may be able to copy her words, but you may very well miss the meaning behind them. If she has developed her own note-taking style, you may not be able to read many of her notes. She may have written something like this:

  G/Oke lvd in C/SC for 1yr ely 20c.

  Can you decode this? How would you ever know that these notes mean "Georgia O'Keeffe lived in Columbia, South Carolina, for one year in the early part of the twentieth century"? To be an effective note-taker, class attendance is crucial; there is no substitute for it.

- Come to class prepared. Do you read your assignments nightly? College professors are amazed at the number of students who come to class and then decide they should have read their home-

Good written communication skills are necessary for success in any business organization. Good note-taking skills lay the groundwork for effective written communication skills. Your college experiences will help you develop the ability to be a good listener and to take good notes.

As a college student, you are required to attend classes, listen intently, organize lecture materials, and convert that information into meaningful text for future use. Tomorrow, as a professional in your chosen field, you will be asked to attend meetings, seminars, and conferences; listen intently and analyze the information being disseminated; and then write reports for your organization. Throughout my career as a technical support/training professional, I was called upon to attend meetings with client/user groups, vendors, suppliers, and co-workers and to report to management the outcome of these meetings. The note-taking skills I developed in college enabled me to listen effectively, discern which information is most important, and convert my notes into meaningful reports and summaries.

Today, I am a university instructor and I'm still using the listening and writing skills I developed in college. Not only must I take accurate notes at faculty and committee meetings, but also I must take good notes when listening to students' reports and presentations to fairly assess their progress and learning. I must often meet with community and business leaders concerning various aspects of the Administrative Information Management program at USC and must keep track of who is willing to participate in which program, who will be speaking on which date, etc. This is achieved by taking good notes.

Garcia Mills Tate, *Professor, College of Applied Professions,* The University of South Carolina, Columbia, South Carolina

---

work. Doing your homework—reading your text, handouts, or workbooks or listening to tapes—is one of the most effective ways to become a better note-taker. It is always easier to take notes when you have a preliminary understanding of what is being said. As a student, you will find fewer tasks more difficult than trying to take notes on material that you have never seen or heard before. Coming to class prepared means doing your homework and coming to class ready to listen.

Coming to class prepared also means bringing the proper materials for taking notes: your textbook or lab manual, at least two pens, enough sharpened pencils to make it through the lecture, a notebook, and a highlighter. Some students also use a tape recorder. If you choose to use a tape recorder, be sure to get permission from the instructor before recording.

■ Bring your textbook to class. Although many students think they do not need to bring their textbook to class if they have read the homework, you will find that many professors repeatedly refer to the text while lecturing. Always bring your textbook to class with you. The professor may ask you to highlight, underline, or refer to the text in class, and following along in the text as the professor lectures may also help you organize your notes.

- Ask questions and participate in class. Two of the most critical actions you can perform in class are to ask questions and to participate in the class discussion. If you do not understand a concept or theory, ask questions. Don't leave class without understanding what has happened and assume you'll pick it up on your own. Many professors use students' questions as a way of teaching and reviewing materials. Your questions and participation will definitely help you, but they could also help others who did not understand something!

Beginning the Building Process

You have been exposed to several thoughts about note taking: first, you need to cultivate and build your active listening skills; second, you need to overcome obstacles to effective listening, such as prejudging, talking during a discussion, and bringing emotions to the table; third, you should be familiar with key phrases used by professors; fourth, you need to understand the importance of note taking; fifth, you need to prepare yourself to take effective notes; and finally, you must scan, read, and use your textbook to understand the materials presented.

THE L–STAR SYSTEM

One of the most effective ways to take notes begins with the **L-STAR** system.

L Listening
S Setting It Down
T Translating
A Analyzing
R Remembering

This five-step program will enable you to compile complete, accurate, and visual notes for future reference. Along with improving your note-taking skills, using this system will enhance your ability to participate in class, help other students, study more effectively, and perform well on exams and quizzes.

L—Listening

One of the best ways to become an effective note-taker is to become an active listener. A concrete step you can take toward becoming an active listener in class is to sit near the front of the room where you can hear the professor and see the board and overheads. Choose a spot that allows you to see the professor's mouth and facial expressions. If you see that the professor's face has become animated or expressive, you can bet that you are hearing important information. Write it down. If you sit in the back of the room, you may miss out on these important clues. Listening was discussed in Chapter 6.

S—Setting it down

The actual writing of notes can be a difficult task. Some professors are organized in their delivery of information; others are not. Your listening skills, once again, are going to play an important role in determining what needs to be written down. In most cases, you will not have time to take notes verbatim. You will have to be selective about the information you choose to set down. One of the best ways to keep up with the information being presented is to develop a shorthand system of your own. Many of the symbols you use will be universal, but you may use some symbols, pictures, and markings that are uniquely your own. Some of the more common symbols are:

w/	with	w/o	without
=	equals	≠	does not equal
<	less than	>	greater than
%	percentage	#	number
&	and	^	increase
+	plus or addition	–	minus or subtraction
*	important	etc	and so on
eg	for example	vs	against
esp	especially	"	quote
?	question	. . .	and so on

These symbols can save you valuable time when taking notes. Because you will use them frequently, it might be a good idea to memorize them. As you become more adept at note taking, you will quickly learn how to abbreviate words, phrases, and names.

Using the symbols listed and your own shorthand system, practice reducing the following statements. Be sure that you do not reduce them so much that you will be unable to understand them later.

1. *It is important to remember that a greater percentage of money invested does not necessarily equal greater profits.*

   Reduce. _____

   _____

   _____

   _____

Thoughts

2. *She was quoted as saying, "Money equals success." Without exception, the audience disagreed with her logic.*

Reduce. _____

_____

_____

_____

T—Translating

One of the most valuable activities you can undertake as a student is to translate your notes immediately after each class. Doing so can save you hours of work when you begin to prepare for exams. Many students feel that this step is not important, or too time-consuming, and leave it out. Don't. Often, students take notes so quickly that they make mistakes or use abbreviations that they may not be able to decipher later.

After each class, go to the library or some other quiet place and review your notes. You don't have to do this immediately after class, but before the end of the day, you will need to rewrite and translate your classroom notes. This process gives you the opportunity to put the notes in your own words and to incorporate your text notes into your classroom notes. You can correct spelling, reword key phrases, write out abbreviations, and prepare questions for the next class. Sounds like a lot of work, doesn't it? It is a great deal of work, but if you try this technique for one week, you should see a vast improvement in your comprehension of material. Eventually, you should see an improvement in your grades.

Translating your notes helps you to make connections between previous material discussed, your own personal experiences, and readings and new material presented. Translating aids in recalling and applying new information. Few things are more difficult than trying to reconstruct your notes the night before a test, especially when they were made several weeks earlier. Translating your notes daily will prove a valuable gift to yourself when exam time comes.

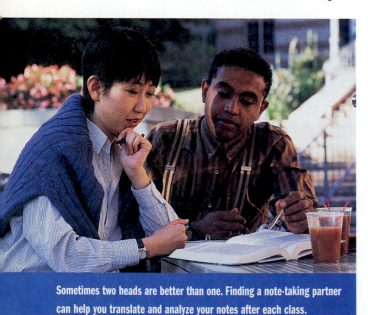

Sometimes two heads are better than one. Finding a note-taking partner can help you translate and analyze your notes after each class.

A—Analyzing

This step takes place while you translate your notes from class. When you analyze your notes, you are asking two basic questions: (1) What does this mean? and (2) Why is it important? If you can answer these two questions about your material, you have almost mastered the information. Though some instructors will want you to spit back the exact same information you were given, others will ask you for a more detailed understanding and a synthesis of the material. When you are translating your notes, begin to answer these two questions using your notes, textbook, supplemental materials, and information gathered from outside research. Once again, this process is not simple or quick, but testing your understanding of the material is important. Remember that many lectures are built on past lectures. If you do not understand what happened in class on September 17, you may not be able to understand what happens on September 19. Analyzing your notes while translating them will give you a more complete understanding of the material.

R—Remembering

Once you have listened to the lecture, set your notes on paper, and translated and analyzed the material, it is time to study, or remember, the information. Some effective ways to remember information include creating a visual picture, speaking the notes out loud, using mnemonic devices, and finding a study partner. Chapter 8 will help you with these techniques and other study aids.

Putting It All Together: Note-Taking Techniques

There are as many systems and methods of note taking as there are people who take notes. Some people write too small, others too large. Some write too much, others not enough. Some write what is really important, others miss key points. The aim of this section is to help you use the L-STAR system with a formalized note-taking technique. The L-STAR system can be used with any of the techniques presented.

Before examining the three most commonly used note-taking systems, let's review a few principles about basic note taking.

- Always date your notes and use a meaningful heading.
- Keep notes from each class separate by using dividers or separate notebooks.
- Use 8 1/2-by-11 inch paper with a three-hole punch.
- Copy any information that is written on the board, used on an overhead, or presented in charts and graphs.
- Organize and review your notes the same day you take them.
- Do not doodle while taking notes.
- Use your own shorthand system.
- Clip related handouts to appropriate notes.

There are three common note-taking systems: (1) the outline technique; (2) the Cornell, or split-page technique (also called the T system); and (3) the mapping technique.

Thoughts

THE OUTLINE TECHNIQUE

The outline system uses a series of major headings and multiple subheadings formatted in hierarchical order. The outline technique is one of the most commonly used note-taking systems, yet it is also one of the most misused systems. It can be difficult to outline notes in class, especially if your professor does not follow an outline while lecturing.

When using the outline system, it is best to get all the information from the lecture and afterward to combine your lecture notes and text notes to create an outline. Most professors would advise against using the outline system of note taking in class, although you may be able to use a modified version in class. The most important thing to remember is not to get bogged down in a system during class; what is critical is getting the ideas down on paper. You can always go back after class and rearrange your notes as needed.

If you are going to use a modified or informal outline while taking notes in class, you may want to consider grouping information together under a heading as a means of outlining. It is easier to

Chances are that sometime in your college career you'll find yourself in a large lecture hall class, where it can be difficult to ask questions or seek clarification.

THE OUTLINE TECHNIQUE

Study Skills 101   Oct. 17
                                                        Wednesday

Topic: Listening
I. The Process of Listening (ROAR)
    A. R = Receiving
        1. W/in range of sound
        2. Hearing the information
    B. O = Organizing & focusing
        1. Choose to listen actively
        2. Observe the origin, direction & intent
    C. A = Assignment
        1. You assign a meaning
        2. May have to hear it more than once
    D. R = Reacting
        l. Our response to what we heard
        2. Reaction can be anything
II. Definitions of Listening (POC)
    A. P = Listening w/ a purpose
    B. O = Listening w/ objectivity
    C. C = Listening constructively

remember information that is logically grouped than to remember information that is scattered across several pages. If your study skills lecture is on listening, you might outline your notes using the headings "The Process of Listening" and "Definitions of Listening."

After you have rewritten your notes using class lecture information and material from your textbook, your notes may look like those on page 178.

THE CORNELL (MODIFIED CORNELL, SPLIT PAGE, OR T) SYSTEM

The basic principle of the Cornell system, developed by Dr. Walter Pauk of Cornell University, is to split the page into two sections, each section to be used for different information. Section A is used for questions that summarize information found in Section B; Section B is used for the actual notes from class. The blank note-taking page should be divided as shown.

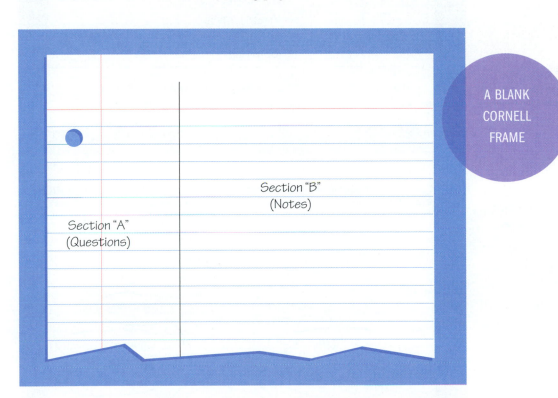

Section "B"
(Notes)

Section "A"
(Questions)

A BLANK CORNELL FRAME

To implement the Cornell system, you will want to choose the technique that is most comfortable and beneficial for you; you might use mapping (discussed later) or outlining on a Cornell page. An example of notes outlined using the Cornell system appears on the following page.

THE MAPPING SYSTEM

If you are a visual learner, this system may be especially useful for you. The mapping system of note taking generates a picture of information. The mapping system creates a map, or web, of information that allows

Study Skills 101   Oct. 19
Topic: Listening   Friday

What is the listening process? (ROAR)	*The Listening Process (ROAR)
	A= Receiving
	   1. Within range of sound
	   2. Hearing the information
	B = Organizing
	   1. Choose to listen actively
	   2. Observe origin

Definition of Listening (POC)	*Listening Defined A. Listening w/ a purpose B. Listening objectively C. Listening constructively
Obstacles (PET)	*What interferes w/ listening A. Prejudging B. Emotions C. Talking

The listening process involves Receiving, Organizing, Assigning & Reacting - Talking, Prejudging & Emotions are obstacles.

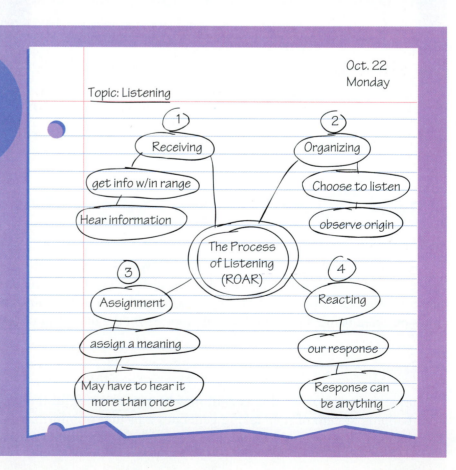

Oct. 22
Monday

Topic: Listening

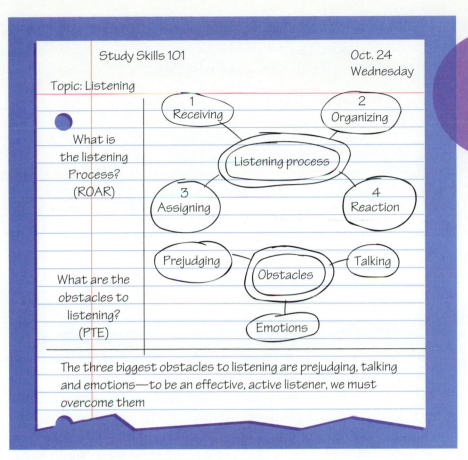

you to see the relationships among facts, names, dates, and places. A mapping system might look something like the notes on page 180.

The most important thing to remember about each note-taking system is that it must work for you. Do not use a system because your friends use it or because you feel that you should use it. Experiment with each system or combination to determine which is best for you.

Always remember to keep your notes organized, dated, and neat. Notes that cannot be read are no good to you or to anyone else.

What to Do When You Get Lost

Have you ever been in a classroom trying to take notes and the professor is speaking so rapidly that you cannot possibly get all of the information? Just when you think you're caught up, you realize that he or she has made an important statement and you missed it. What do you do? How can you handle, or avoid, this difficult note-taking situation? Here are several hints:

- Raise your hand and ask the professor to repeat the information.
- Ask your professor to slow down.

Public Speaking		Oct. 7
Lecture: Types of Research for Speeches		
*Periodicals	- Magazines, trade & professional	
*Newspapers	Local, state & national (some international as well)	
*Reference materials	Specialized . . . (?)	} If you missed it, leave it blank
*Government documents	- Maps, reports, federal proceedings	

- If he or she will do neither, leave a blank space with a question mark at the side margin. You can get this information after class. This can be a difficult task to master. The key is to focus on the information at hand. Focus on what is being said at the exact moment.

- Meet with your professor immediately after class or at the earliest time convenient for both of you.

- Form a note-taking group that meets after each class. This serves two purposes: (1) you can discuss and review the lecture, and (2) you will be able to get the notes from one of your note-taking buddies.

- Never lean over and ask questions of another student during the lecture. This will cause them to lose the information as well.

- Rehearse your note-taking skills at home by taking notes from TV news magazines or channels like the History Channel.

- As a last resort, you can ask the professor's permission to use a tape recorder during the lecture. Do not record a lecture without permission. We suggest that you try to use other avenues, such as the ones listed above, instead of taping your notes. It is a time-consuming task to listen to the lecture for a second time. However, if this system works for you, use it.

Using Your Laptop Computer for Note Taking

In this age of high technology, some students prefer to take notes or transfer their notes onto their computers. Some students bring laptops to class while others immediately type and reorganize their notes after class. If you choose to use a computer for note taking, use the following tips:

IN CLASS

- Come to class early to set up your computer. Don't disturb others by arriving late.
- Try to sit where you can see the professor and overhead, but also be respectful of other students. Tapping on the keyboard can disturb others' concentration.
- Don't worry too much about spelling or grammar. You can run the spelling and grammar checker after class while cleaning up your notes.
- Set your tabs before you begin. You can set them to use an outline format or the Cornell format.

OUT OF CLASS

- If you are going to type your notes into the computer, do so as quickly after class as possible. The information obtained in class needs to be fresh in your mind. Try to reorganize your notes within 24 hours.
- Combine your textbook notes and lecture notes together. This will help you access the big picture of the information.

GENERAL HINTS

- Save your notes on both a disk and your hard drive.
- Always print your notes after each entry. It can be catastrophic if all of your notes are on one disk or one hard drive and the computer crashes or the disk is lost.
- After you have printed your notes, use a three-hole punch and place your notes in a three-ring binder. Arrange computer notes with related handouts.

A last note about copying your notes by hand or into a computer: this technique, while valuable to some students, does not constitute studying. Dr. Walter Pauk (2001), creator of the Cornell note-taking system, suggests that "contrary to what most people think, almost no learning takes place during the keyboarding of scribbled notes." Finally, don't be threatened by those who decide to use the computer in class or those who come to class with typewritten, printed notes. *Cornerstone* in general, and this chapter specifically, is about choices. You have to find and use a system that is convenient, easy, and useful to you.

If you remember the concepts of the L-STAR system (listening, setting it down, translating, analyzing, and remembering) and use this system as a study pattern, and if you find a note-taking system that is comfortable and useful for you, then you will begin to see significant improvement in your ability as a note-taker and in your performance as a student.

Thoughts

Consider your most difficult class. Review your notes from the last lecture from this class. Take a primary topic or statement from the lecture. Using the columns below, write the major lecture headings in Column A, and write a brief summary or explanation for that topic in Column B.

Column A

_____
_____
_____
_____
_____
_____
_____
_____
_____
_____
_____
_____

Column B

Thinking

_____
_____
_____
_____
_____
_____
_____
_____
_____
_____
_____

Take one of the major topics from Column A and develop an essay question.

Question

_____
_____
_____
_____
_____

Answer that question as you would for an exam.

Response

_____
_____
_____

Change

_____
_____

LIFE

The One Minute Journal

In one minute or less, jot down the major ideas that you learned from this chapter.

_____

_____

_____

_____

_____

_____

_____

_____

_____

_____

COMPANION
THE Website _Journal_

Log on to **www.prenhall.com/montgomery**, choose the version of this book you are using, and then choose Chapter 7 on the menu. Next, choose "Links" on the left side of the page. Explore one of the websites offered and summarize your findings.

_____

_____

_____

_____

_____

_____

_____

_____

_____

_____

_____

Refer to page 170 of Chapter 7.
Review your **GOALS FOR CHANGE**.
Respond in writing as to the progress
you have made toward reaching one
of your three stated goals.

GOAL STATEMENT

PROGRESS

How is your life changing because of this goal?

CORNERSTONES

for effective note taking

If it's on the board or on an overhead, *write it down.*

Keep the notes for each course *separate.*

Use *abbreviations* and special notes.

Recopy your notes after each class.

Sit where you can *see* and *hear.*

Develop your listening abilities.

Keep your notes *neat* and clear.

Participate in class.

Use loose-leaf paper.

Be *prepared.*

Ask questions.

Attend class.

If you have knowledge, let others light their fire by it.

Remember.

M. Fuller

CHAPTER 8

Remember

Tyrone walked into class beaming. *He was happy, joking, and smiling,* and he spoke to everyone on the way to his seat. He was always a delightful student, *but today he seemed even happier than usual.* Several classmates asked how he could possibly be so up. They could not understand his jovial attitude because *today was test day.* How could he be happy today of all days? *How could anyone be happy on test day?*

Tyrone told his classmates *that he was happy because he was prepared.* "I'm ready for the world," he said. *"I studied all week and I know this stuff."* Most of his classmates ribbed him and laughed. In the final moments before the test began, all the other students were deeply involved in questioning each other and looking over their notes. Tyrone stood by the window finishing his soda until time was called.

After all was said and done, *Tyrone scored the highest on the exam of all his*

> *How could he be happy today of all days? How could anyone be happy on test day?*

peers—a 98. Several students asked him how he did so well. Intrigued by their curiosity, I asked Tyrone to share his secret to successful test taking.

I found his answer extremely useful, *especially in light of his active life:* Tyrone was on the basketball team, held a part-time job, cared for his elderly grandmother, dated, and worked on the college newspaper.

"You have to do it in steps," Tyrone said. *"You can't wait until the night before, even if you have all evening and night."* He explained that he incorporated study time into his schedule several weeks before the test.

If the test was to cover four chapters, he would review two chapters the first week and two chapters the second week. "I have a study room at the library because my house is so full of people. I make an outline of my notes, review my text, answer sample questions in the book, and many times I find someone to quiz me on the material."

Live as if you were to die tomorrow. Learn as if you were to live forever. —*M. K. GANDHI*

STATEMENT	SCORE	Strongly Disagree	Disagree	Don't Know	Agree	Strongly Agree
1. I am a very organized person.		1	2	3	4	5
2. I know how to transfer information into long-term memory.		1	2	3	4	5
3. I know how to survey a chapter and a textbook.		1	2	3	4	5
4. I understand how my memory works.		1	2	3	4	5
5. I know the best ways to retrieve facts from my memory.		1	2	3	4	5
TOTAL		0–5	6–10	11–15	16–20	21–25

FEEDBACK

0 – 5   Extensive changes need to occur to ensure success.

6 – 10   Substantial changes need to occur to ensure success.

11 – 15   Considerable changes need to occur to ensure success.

16 – 20   Moderate changes need to occur to ensure success.

21 – 25   Minor changes need to occur to ensure success.

GOALS FOR CHANGE

Based on this feedback, my goals and objectives for change are . . .

Goal Statement _____

Action Steps   1. _____

              2. _____

Goal Statement _____

Action Steps   1. _____

              2. _____

Goal Statement _____

Action Steps   1. _____

              2. _____

Results ● ● ●

Reading this chapter, completing the exercises, and reflecting on studying, memory, and recall strategies will result in your:

- Determining the proper study environment for successful studying.

- Identifying new methods of reading, highlighting, and taking notes from texts.

- Using the SQ3R method.

- Using the READ method.

- Creating and using mnemonic devices and jingles.

- Using cooperative learning.

- Identifying and using the Cornerstones of Effective Studying.

- Using strategies for studying with small children in the house.

Why Study? I Can Fake It

"I didn't have to study very hard in high school; why should I do it now?" This thought may have crossed your mind by this point in the semester. Many students feel that there is no real reason to study. They believe that they can glance at their notes a few moments before a test and fake it. Quite truthfully, some students are able to do this. Some tests and professors lend themselves to this type of studying technique. More than you imagine, however, this is not the case. College professors are notorious for thorough exams, lengthy essay questions, tricky true–false statements, and multiple choices that would confuse Einstein. If you want to succeed in your classes in college, you will need to make studying a way of life.

Effective studying requires a great deal of commitment, but learning how to get organized, taking effective notes (see Chapter 7), reading a textbook, listening in class, developing personalized study skills, and building memory techniques will serve you well in becoming a successful graduate. Faking it is now a thing of the past. Take a moment to assess your study skills now.

You may choose a non-traditional study environment, but be sure that you are able to study effectively in it.

The Importance of Your Study Environment

You may wonder why your study place is important. The study environment can determine how well your study time passes. If the room is too hot, too noisy, too dark, or too crowded, your study time may not be productive. In a room that is too hot and dimly lit, you may have a tendency to fall asleep. In a room that is too cold, you may spend time trying to warm yourself. Choose a location that is comfortable for you.

Different students need different study environments. You may need to have a degree of noise in the background, or you may need complete quiet. You have to make this decision. If you always have music in the background while you are studying, try studying in a quiet place one time to see if there is a difference. If you always try to study where it is quiet, try putting soft music in the background to see if it helps you. You may have to try several environments before you find the one that is right for you.

Insider's View

Several years ago, I began to volunteer at my daughter's elementary school as a paraprofessional. I began as a volunteer because I wanted to help my daughters and their school. To my surprise, I loved what I was doing. So, I decided to return to college to major in Elementary Education.

Having been out of school for some time, I found it difficult to juggle two children (ages 12 and 9), activities at work, my homework, the daughters' homework, and trying to keep a neat home. All of this taught me the importance of two things: getting organized and learning how to get the most out of my study time.

One of the hardest things I had to learn was that I had to become more selfish. I had to learn how to say no to some things if I wanted to have quality time with my children and time for my college education. I had to learn, as did my family and friends, that my study time was *my* time. They had to learn that I was not to be interrupted by anyone for anything short of an emergency.

I also had to learn how to get organized. I did not have time to look for things. I learned to keep all the things I needed to study with in one place. With children in the house, that was not easy, but take it from me, it can be done. What a time-saver this turned out to be.

As tests, evaluations, papers, and assignments began to roll in, things began to get very hard. There were classes, children, home life, and even Math Lab hours that were prescribed to me. It was only because I developed a study plan that I was able to make it. I wrote a list of things to do over the weekend, developed a regular study plan for the week, and learned how to prioritize. These are the things that have helped me be successful in college.

Yolanda Agosto, age 31
Major: Elementary Education
Miami-Dade Community College,
Miami, Florida

The key to studying is to become as organized as you possibly can and to work from a study plan. From the beginning of the semester, know what is expected of you. What are the deadlines? How are you going to accomplish the overall task? What is your plan of action?

You have to look at studying, course projects, and exam preparation the same way that you would look at preparing a major project for a job in your chosen career. In the hospitality field of study, our classroom assignments were given with the real world in mind. Professors accepted only the professional quality that would be required by the president of a company or a club.

Gaining a college education for a hospitality major and profession (or any major and profession for that matter) is the *minimum* for a point of entry into any management level. In the past, a person might work his or her way up the ladder from a service position, but that is unlikely today. Higher education is preparation for the world of work. It also puts you into the practice of accepting responsibilities that are going to be similar in the world of work such as accomplishing tasks, meeting deadlines, and working toward excellence.

Had I not learned how to manage my time and resources in college, I would have never been able to make it in the world of hospitality. College taught me to be responsible for my own success. No one else did it for me in college and no one else is going to do it for me now.

Joe Perdue, CCM, CHE, Academic Advisor, Club Managers Association of America, Alexandria, Virginia

Describe your current study environment.

_____
_____
_____
_____
_____
_____

Has this environment served you well? Why or why not?

_____
_____
_____
_____
_____

Choosing the best study environment can be challenging. The best study place may depend on the different accommodations available to you and may vary with the kinds of studying required. What kind of study environment has worked best for you?

How could this environment be improved?

_____

_____

_____

_____

_____

Understanding Memory

What would happen if you typed your English research paper into the computer and did not give it a file name? When you needed to retrieve that paper, you would not know how to find it. You would have to search through every file until you came across the information you needed. Memory works in much the same way. We have to store it properly if we are to retrieve it easily at a later time.

This section will detail how memory works and why it is important to your studying efforts. Below, you will find some basic facts about memory.

- Everyone remembers some information and forgets other information.
- Your senses help you take in information.
- With very little effort, you can remember some information.
- With rehearsal (study), you can remember a great deal of information.
- Without rehearsal or use, information is forgotten.
- Incoming information needs to be filed in the brain if you are to retain it.
- Information stored, or filed, in the brain must have a retrieval method.
- Mnemonic devices, repetition, association, and rehearsal can help you store and retrieve information.

Psychologists have determined that there are three types of memory: sensory memory; short-term, or working, memory; and long-term memory.

Sensory memory stores information gathered from the five senses: taste, touch, smell, hearing, and sight. Sensory memory is usually temporary, lasting about one to three seconds, unless you decide that the information is of ultimate importance to you and make an effort to transfer it to long-term memory. Although your sensory memory bank is *very large,* sensory information does not stay with you very long (Woolfolk, 1998). Sensory memory allows countless stimuli to come into your

Thoughts

brain, which can be a problem when you are trying to concentrate on your professor's lecture. You need to make a conscious effort to remain focused on the words being spoken and not on competing noise. When you make an effort to concentrate on the professor's information, you are then committing this information to short-term memory.

Short-term, or working, memory holds information for a short amount of time. Your working memory bank can hold a limited amount of information, usually about five to nine separate new facts or pieces of information at once (Woolfolk, 1998). Although it is sometimes frustrating to forget information, it is also useful and necessary to do so. If you never forgot anything, you would not be able to function. Educational psychologist Anita Woolfolk suggests that most of us can hear a new phone number, walk across the room, and dial it without much trouble, but that if we heard two or three new numbers, we would not be able to dial them correctly. This is more information than our working memory can handle. If you were asked to give a person's name immediately after being introduced, you would probably be able to do so. If you had met several other new people in the meantime, unless you used some device to transfer the name into long-term memory, you would probably not be able to recall it.

As a student, you would never be able to remember all that your professor said during a 50-minute lecture. You have to take steps to help you to remember information. Taking notes, making associations, drawing pictures, and visualizing information are all techniques that can help you to commit information to your long-term memory bank.

Short-Term Memory Assessment

Theo, Gene, and Suzanne were on their way home from class. As they drove down Highway 415 toward the Greengate subdivision, they saw a 1984 Honda Civic pull out in front of a 1990 Nissan Maxima. There was a crash as the two cars collided. Theo stopped the car. Gene and Suzanne jumped from the car to see if they could help. Suzanne yelled for someone to call 911; Robertina, a bystander, ran to the pay phone at the corner of Mason and Long streets. Within 10 minutes, an ambulance arrived and took Margaret, the driver of the Maxima, to St. Mary's Hospital. Tim, the driver of the Honda, was not badly injured.

Cover this scenario with a piece of paper and answer the following questions.

1. *Who was driving the Honda?* _____

2. *What highway were they driving on?* _____

3. *Who called 911?* _____

4. *What hospital was used?* _____

5. *What year was the Maxima?* _____

How many questions did you answer correctly? If you answered four or five questions correctly, your working memory is strong. If you answered only one or two questions correctly, you will need to discover ways to commit more information to your short-term, or working, memory. Some techniques for doing this are discussed later in this chapter.

Long-term memory stores a lot of information. It is almost like a computer disk. You have to make an effort to put something in your long-term memory, but with effort and memory techniques, such as rehearsal and practice, you can store anything you want to remember there. Long-term memory consists of information that you have heard often, information that you use often, information that you might see often, and information that you have determined necessary. Just as you name a file on a computer disk, you name the files in your long-term memory. Sometimes, you have to wait a moment for the information to come to you. While you are waiting, your brain disk is spinning; if the information you seek is in long-term memory, your brain will eventually find it. You may have to assist your brain in locating the information by using mnemonics and other memory devices.

Long-Term Memory Assessment

Without using any reference materials, quickly answer the following questions using your long-term memory.

1. What is your mother's maiden name? _____

2. Who was the first U.S. president? _____

3. What is the capital of California? _____

4. Who wrote A Christmas Carol? _____

5. What shape is a stop sign? _____

6. What is your social security number? _____

7. Name one star from the movie Titanic. _____

8. What is the title of Dr. Martin Luther King's most famous speech? _____

9. What does the "A" stand for in the L-STAR method? _____

10. What does the acronym "IBM" stand for? _____

Did the answers come to you quickly? If you review your answers, you will probably find that you responded quickly to those questions whose content you deal with fairly frequently, such as your social security number. Although you were probably able to answer all the questions, in some instances your brain had to search longer and harder to find the answer. This is how long-term memory works.

There are countless pieces of information stored in your long-term memory. Some of it is triggered by necessity, some may be triggered by the five senses, and some may be triggered by experiences. The best way to commit information to long-term memory and retrieve it when needed can be expressed by:

V Visualizing

C Concentrating

R Relating

R Repeating

R Reviewing

To **visualize** information, try to create word pictures in your mind as you hear the information. If you are being told about a Civil War battle, try to see the blue against the gray, try to visualize the battlefield, or try to paint a mind picture that will help you to remember the information. You may also want to create visual aids as you read or study information.

Concentrating on the information given will help you commit it to long-term memory. Don't let your mind wander. Stay focused. If you find yourself having trouble concentrating, take a small break (two to five minutes).

Relating the information to something that you already know or understand will assist you in filing or storing the information for easy retrieval. Relating the appearance of the African zebra to the American horse can help you remember what the zebra looks like.

Repeating the information out loud to yourself or to a study partner facilitates its transfer to long-term memory. Some people have to hear information many times before they can commit it to long-term memory.

Reviewing the information is another means of repetition. The more you see and use the information, the easier it will be to remember it when the time comes. As you review, try to remember the main points of the information.

Ready, Set, Go!

In Chapter 5 you got organized and prioritized your tasks. In Chapters 6 and 7, you actively listened and developed a note-taking system. So far in this chapter, you've found the appropriate study environment. Now it's time to study. That's exciting, isn't it? No? Well, it can be. All it takes is a positive attitude and an open mind. Next, you'll learn about several methods of studying that you can use to put yourself in charge of the material. After you've reviewed these methods, you may want to use

Thoughts ● ● ●

Four Studying Strategies			
SQ3R METHOD	**READ METHOD**	**MNEMONICS**	**COOPERATIVE LEARNING**
Best used for surveying and reading textbooks	Best used for lecture notes and personal text notes	Can be used when studying lecture or text notes	Can be used when studying in groups for tests, projects, note sharing, and analysis
Survey	Read	Jingles	Questioning
Question			Comparing
Read	Evaluate	Sentences	Drilling
Recite	Ask questions	Words	Brainstorming
			Sharing
Review	Determine	Story lines	Mapping

some combination of them or you may prefer to use one method exclusively. The only rule for choosing a study plan is that the plan must work for you. You may have to spend a few weeks experimenting with several plans and methods to determine the one with which you are most comfortable. Don't get discouraged if it takes you a while to find what is right for you.

THE SQ3R METHOD

The most basic and often-used studying system is the SQ3R method, developed by Francis P. Robinson in 1941. This simple, yet effective, system has proved to be a successful study tool for millions of students. SQ3R involves five steps: Survey, Question, Read, Recite, and Review. The most important thing to remember about SQ3R is that it should be used on a daily basis, not as a method for cramming.

Survey

The first step of SQ3R is to survey, or pre-read, an assigned chapter. You begin by reading the title of the chapter, the headings, and each subheading. Look carefully at the vocabulary, time lines, graphs, charts, pictures, and drawings included in each chapter. If there is a chapter summary, read it. Surveying also includes reading the first and last sentence in each paragraph. Surveying is not a substitute for reading a chapter. Reading is discussed later. Before going any further, select a chapter from any book, or one assigned by your professor, and survey that chapter.

Chapter Survey

1. *What is the title of the chapter?*

   _____

2. *What is the subheading of the chapter?*

   _____

   _____

3. *How many sections does the chapter have? List them.*

   _____

   _____

4. *What are the chapter objectives?*

   _____

   _____

5. *Does the chapter include vocabulary words? List the words you will need to look up.*

   _____

   _____

6. *If the chapter contains quotations, which one means the most to you? Why?*

   _____

   _____

7. *What is the most important graph or chart in the chapter? Why?*

   _____

   _____

8. *Close your book and list five topics that this chapter will cover.*

   _____

   _____

Question

The second step is to question. There are five common questions you should ask yourself when you are reading a chapter: Who? When? What? Where? and Why? As you survey and read your chapter, try turning the information into questions and see if you can answer them. If you do not know the answers to the questions, you should find them as you read along.

Another way to approach the chapter is to turn the major headings of each section into questions (see an example on the following page). When

Thoughts ● ● ●

SUBCONSCIOUS THINKING

What is subconscious thinking?
Why is it important?

Subconscious thinking: reflects your ability to detect and analyze stimuli that you do not consciously perceive.

Subconscious thinking is based on our ability to detect and analyze stimuli that we do not consciously perceive. The process is sometimes referred to as *peripheral attention*. For example, you are talking to a group of students in a crowded cafeteria. You ignore the other voices and noise until someone mentions your name. Then you pay attention to the other conversation.

UNCONSCIOUS THINKING

What is unconscious thinking?
When do I use it?

Unconscious thinking: involves memories, impulses, and desires that are not available to the conscious mind.

The process of **unconscious thinking** involves memories, impulses, and desires that are not available to the conscious mind. Though outside the stream of awareness, unconscious thoughts can still influence attitudes or behavior. Unconscious thoughts sometimes show up as dreams, "slips of the tongue," and bizarre behavior. A somewhat extreme, but not unusual, example of the latter case is when a man stalks a woman.

PRECONSCIOUS THINKING

What is preconscious thinking?
How can I strengthen it?

Preconscious thinking: involves thoughts that you can access but that are not part of your consciousness at the moment.

Preconscious thinking involves thoughts that you can access but that are not part of your consciousness at the moment. Preconscious thoughts involve a large number of functions. Among them are long-term memory, creativity, and mental stability.

Source: Brown, W. *Reaching Your Full Potential: Success in College*, © 1999. Prentice Hall: Upper Saddle River, NJ. Used with permission.

you get to the end of the section, having carefully read the material, taken notes, and highlighted important information, answer the question that you posed at the beginning of the section.

Read

After you survey the chapter and develop some questions to be answered from the chapter, the next step is to read the chapter. Remember, surveying is not reading. There is no substitute for reading in your success plan. Read slowly and carefully. The SQ3R method requires a substantial amount of time, but if you take each step slowly and completely, you will be amazed at how much you can learn and how much your grades will improve.

Read through each section. It is best not to jump around or move ahead if you do not understand the previous section. Paragraphs are usually built on each other, and so you need to understand the first before you can move on to the next. You may have to read a chapter or section more than once, especially if the information is new, technical, or difficult.

Another important aspect of reading is taking notes, highlighting, and making marginal notes in your textbook. You own your textbook and should personalize it as you would your lecture notes. Highlight areas that you feel are important, underline words and phrases that you did not understand or that you feel are important, and jot down notes in the margins.

"If I mark in my text, I may not get much for it when I sell it back to the bookstore," you might say. Right now you need to be concerned with learning the information in the most beneficial and efficient way possible. Don't worry about selling your textbook after the class is over. You might even want to consider keeping your book until you have completed your degree, especially if it relates to your major field of study.

As you begin to read your chapter, mark the text, and take notes, keep the following in mind:

- Read the entire paragraph before you mark anything.

- Identify the topic or thesis statement of each paragraph and highlight it.

- Highlight key phrases.

- Don't highlight too much; the text will lose its significance.

- Stop and look up words that you do not know or understand.

Thoughts ● ● ●

COMPREHENSION COMPETENCIES

Reading comprehension is one specialized aspect of general language comprehension. As children use oral language to com- municate with others through meaningful speech and perceptive listening, they employ comprehension strategies. When teachers question students in class, encourage discussions, and promote activities involving listening, they facilitate development of these strategies. All that remains is to encourage children to apply the same type of strategies to printed materials.

Reading strategies =

As with the other language arts, students learn to read by practicing their reading strategies with real books. When teachers provide children with the (1) opportunity to read real texts, to (2) use their prior knowledge, and to (3) make predictions and judgments about what they are reading, they are handing their students the keys to reading comprehension.

Types of comprehension =

It is generally recognized that there are several types, or levels, of comprehension for which students need to develop competencies: (1) literal and (2) interpretive as well as the higher levels of (3) critical and (4) creative comprehension (Burns, Roe, & Ross, 1996). However, these levels do not operate in isolation from one another. In successful reading, they most often operate together to help the reader obtain thorough understanding of the text.

Literal Comprehension

Literal comprehension involves getting meaning straight from the text; usually, the information is directly and plainly stated on the page. Students who are competent in this type of comprehension are able to get information from pictures, to find main ideas and details in text, to identify the sequence of events, and to comprehend the vocabulary used in the selection. Literal comprehension is generally considered the most easily achieved level of comprehension and includes the who, what, when, where, why, and how information.

When you have finished marking in your text, it may look something like the example at left.

Source: Yellin, David, et al. *Integrating the Language Arts, 2/e.* © 2000, HH Publishers. Used with permission.

While reading, you will want to take notes that are more elaborate than your highlighting or marginal notes. Taking notes while reading the text will assist you in studying the material and committing it to memory. There are several effective methods of taking notes while reading:

- Charts
- Outlines
- Key words
- Mind maps
- Flash cards
- Summaries
- Time lines

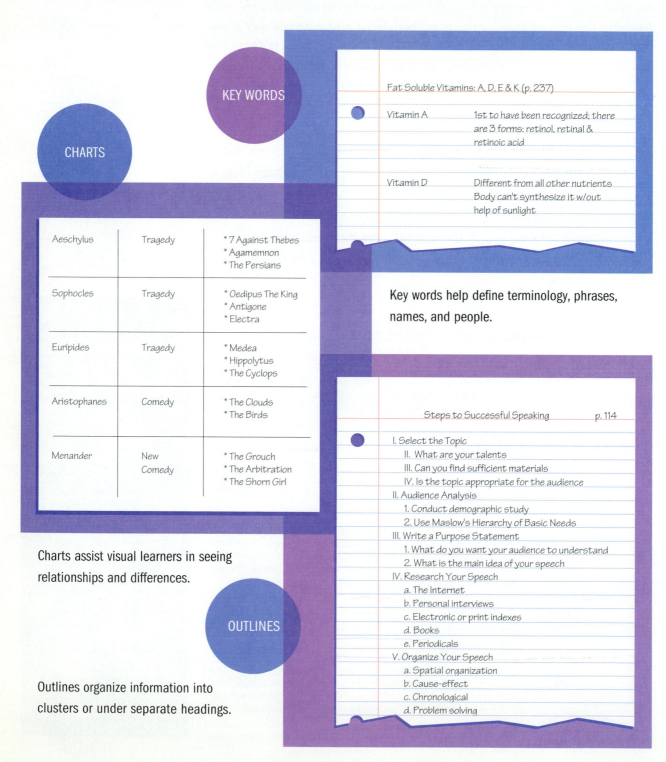

KEY WORDS

Fat Soluble Vitamins: A, D, E & K (p. 237)

Vitamin A   1st to have been recognized; there are 3 forms: retinol, retinal & retinoic acid

Vitamin D   Different from all other nutrients Body can't synthesize it w/out help of sunlight

Key words help define terminology, phrases, names, and people.

CHARTS

Aeschylus	Tragedy	* 7 Against Thebes * Agamemnon * The Persians
Sophocles	Tragedy	* Oedipus The King * Antigone * Electra
Euripides	Tragedy	* Medea * Hippolytus * The Cyclops
Aristophanes	Comedy	* The Clouds * The Birds
Menander	New Comedy	* The Grouch * The Arbitration * The Shorn Girl

Charts assist visual learners in seeing relationships and differences.

OUTLINES

Steps to Successful Speaking   p. 114

I. Select the Topic
  II. What are your talents
  III. Can you find sufficient materials
  IV. Is the topic appropriate for the audience
II. Audience Analysis
  1. Conduct demographic study
  2. Use Maslow's Hierarchy of Basic Needs
III. Write a Purpose Statement
  1. What do you want your audience to understand
  2. What is the main idea of your speech
IV. Research Your Speech
  a. The Internet
  b. Personal interviews
  c. Electronic or print indexes
  d. Books
  e. Periodicals
V. Organize Your Speech
  a. Spatial organization
  b. Cause-effect
  c. Chronological
  d. Problem solving

Outlines organize information into clusters or under separate headings.

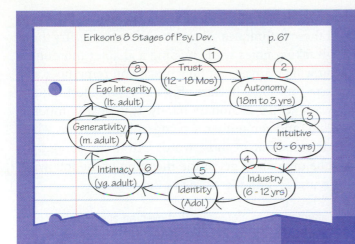

Erikson's 8 Stages of Psy. Dev.   p. 67

⑧ Ego Integrity (lt. adult) ① Trust (12 - 18 Mos) ② Autonomy (18m to 3 yrs) ③ Intuitive (3 - 6 yrs) ⑦ Generativity (m. adult) ⑥ Intimacy (yg. adult) ⑤ Identity (Adol.) ④ Industry (6 - 12 yrs)

MIND MAPS

Mind maps help show relationships among people, places, and things; they can also help show progression and time.

FLASH CARDS

Flash cards are portable and easily accessible. They are useful for remembering key words, phrases, definitions, and procedures. It is best to write the word or phrase on the front and define it on the reverse side.

(Front)

Steps to Improve Listening

(Reverse)

1. Stop talking
2. Leave emotions at home
3. Don't prejudge
4. Actively listen to speaker
5. Know the listening situation
6. Listen for how something is said
7. Don't jump to conclusions

p. 14

The Beginnings of Drama in Greece
(5th C. Athens)

Religious Ritual - The Greeks had religious celebrations
    in honor of the Greek God Dionysus, the god of
    wine & fertility. They worshiped him so much
    because they felt he controlled birth & death -
    the life cycle.
The 1st Contest - The 1st religious theatrical contest
    was held in 534 BC

Summaries are used for very detailed information that cannot be reduced to note cards, outlines, or time lines.

SUMMARIES

Colonization of US   (p. 116)

1620   Pilgrims settle Plymouth
1629   Puritans settle Massachusetts
1632   Maryland given to G. Calvert

1663   Carolina granted to 8
        proprietors
1681   Pennsylvania granted to
        William Penn
1686   Puritan rule ends in Mass.

Time lines are an excellent way to show chronological relationships among events.

TIME LINES

As you read through a chapter in your textbook, you may find that you have to use a variety of these techniques to capture information. Try them for one week. Although taking notes while reading a chapter thoroughly is time consuming, you will be amazed at how much you remember and how much you are able to contribute in class after using these techniques.

While reading, always keep a dictionary handy. It is nearly impossible to read, comprehend, and remember a paragraph or section when you don't know or understand one or more words within the paragraph. For instance, it would be difficult to get at the meaning of the following sentence if you did not understand the words in the sentence.

> It is easier to answer affirmatively to a question that even an anonymous respondent knows would evoke an excruciating response.

When you look up a word, circle it and pull the definition to the margin.

Example:

a person who RESPONDS — It is easier to answer affirmatively to a question that even an anonymous respondent knows would evoke an excruciating response.

TRUE UNKNOWN TO CALL TO MIND PAINFUL

Recite

Recitation is simple, but crucial. Skipping this step may result in less than full mastery of the chapter. Once you have read a section, ask yourself this simple question, "What was that all about?" Find a classmate, sit down together, and ask questions of each other. Discuss with each other the main points of the chapter. Try to explain the information to each other without looking at your notes. If you are at home, sit back in your chair, recite the information, and determine what it means. If you have trouble explaining the information to your friend or reciting it to yourself, you probably did not understand the section and you should go back and re-read it. If you can tell your classmate and yourself exactly what you just read and what it means, you are ready to move on to the next section of the chapter.

Transferring information to your long-term memory involves repetition, concentration, and visualization.

Review

After you have read the chapter, immediately go back and read it again. "What?!! I just read it!" Yes, you did. And the best way to determine whether you have mastered the information is once again to survey the chapter; review marginal notes, highlighted areas, and vocabulary words; and determine whether you have any questions that have not been answered. This step will help you store and retain this information in long-term memory.

THE READ METHOD

The READ method works best for studying notes you have taken from the text or in class. It has four steps:

1. **Read the notes.** Many students take notes and never go back to read them. As we pointed out in Chapter 7, the best way to study your notes is to read them the day you take them. It is important to read your notes as soon after you write them as possible so that you can make corrections. You should also read your notes often. For example, if you took notes on the causes of the Civil War last month, you should read those notes before the lecture on the Battle of Gettysburg tomorrow. Doing so will refresh your memory and prepare you to participate in class discussions. Reading your notes is an important step in your success plan.

2. **Evaluate what you have read.** After you have read your notes, evaluate the information and prioritize what is most important. People often write too much when taking notes. As you read over your notes, you may find that you have included information that is not important or that you have repeated information. Evaluating will help you make your notes more concise and to the point. You may want to highlight your handwritten notes or add marginal notes to your notes.

3. **Ask questions.** As you read and evaluate your notes, ask questions about what you have written: "What was meant by this?" "How does this relate to the textbook information?" "Will I have to use this information on the test or in a paper?" If you have any questions that your notes do not answer, you need to review your text or make yourself a note to ask the professor at the next class meeting. Asking questions of yourself, your notes, your text, and your professors will set you on the road to success as a student.

4. **Determine the main issues.** The last part of the READ method for studying notes is to determine the main issues of what you have written. If you can read your notes and answer the question: "What were the main issues covered?" you have a grasp of the material. If you cannot determine the main issues and recite them to yourself, you will need to review your text, ask questions, and maybe rewrite your notes.

MNEMONIC DEVICES

Mnemonic devices are memory tricks, or techniques, that assist you in putting information into your long-term memory and pulling it out when you need it. I recently gave a test on the basic principles of public speaking. A student asked if she had to know the parts of the communication process in order. When I replied that she should be able to recall them in order, she became nervous and said that she had not learned them in order. Another student overheard the conversation and said, "Some men can read backwards fast." The first student asked, "What do you mean by that?" I laughed and said that the mnemonic was great! The student had created a sentence to remember source, message, channel, receiver, barriers, and feedback. The relationship worked like this:

Some	=	Source
Men	=	Message
Can	=	Channel
Read	=	Receiver
Backwards	=	Barriers
Fast	=	Feedback

The first student caught on fast; she could not believe how easy it was to remember the steps in order using this sentence. This is a perfect example of how using memory tricks can help you retrieve information easily.

The following four types of mnemonic devices may help you with your long-term memory.

Jingles

You can make up rhymes, songs, poems, or sayings to assist you in remembering information; for example, "Columbus sailed the ocean blue in fourteen hundred and ninety-two."

Sentences

You can make up sentences such as "Some men can read backwards fast," to help you remember information. Another example is "Please excuse my dear Aunt Sally," which corresponds to the mathematical operations: **p**arentheses, **e**xponents, **m**ultiplication, **d**ivision, **a**ddition, and **s**ubtraction.

Words

You can create words. For example, Roy G. Biv may help you to remember the colors of the rainbow: **r**ed, **o**range, **y**ellow, **g**reen, **b**lue, **i**ndigo, and **v**iolet.

Story Lines

If you find it easier to remember stories than raw information, you may want to process the information into a story that you can easily tell. Weave the data and facts into a creative story that can be easily retrieved from your long-term memory. This technique can be especially beneficial if your professor gives essay exams, because the "story" that you remember can be what was actually told in class.

COOPERATIVE LEARNING

There is strength in numbers. Many times, groups of people can accomplish what a single individual cannot. This is the idea behind cooperative learning. We form and use groups in our daily lives in situations like work, worship, and hobbies, and we even group our friends together. We develop groups for inspiration, excitement, and reflection, to advance social causes and to grow. Studying in groups can have the same effect. Cooperative learning can benefit you because you have pulled together a group of people who have the same interests and goals as you: to pass the course. Studying and working in groups can help you in ways such as drilling exercises, brainstorming, group sharing, and mapping.

Before we talk about those specific details, we should discuss how to form a study group. The most effective study group will include people with different strengths and weaknesses. It would do little good to involve yourself in an accounting study group with people who are all failing accounting. Here are some tips for forming a cooperative study group:

- Limit the group size to five to seven people.
- Search for students who participate in class.
- Include people who take notes in class.
- Include people who ask questions in class.
- Include people who will work diligently.
- Include people who do their share for the group.
- Invite people who are doing well in a specific area; they may not attend every meeting, but they may be of assistance periodically.

Have you ever studied with a group of people? What were some of the benefits that you experienced? What are some advantages over studying alone?

Appoint members of your team to be responsible for the following jobs:

Timekeeper | This person will let the group know when it is time to move on to another topic.

Note-Taker | This person will keep the notes for the team and will usually assist in getting them copied for everyone in the group.

Facilitator | This person will lead the group and keep the group on task during the meeting.

When the group is formed, you can engage in several different activities to learn, share, and reinforce information.

- Questioning. With this technique, group members bring several questions to the next session. These may be predicted exam questions, questions about methods or formulas, or questions that the member was not able to answer individually.
- Comparing. The study group is a good place to compare notes taken in class or from the text. If you are having problems understanding a concept in your notes, maybe someone in the group can assist you. It is also a good time to compare your notes for accuracy and missing lecture information.
- Drilling. This technique assists you with long-term memory development. Repetition is an important step in transferring information to

long-term memory. Have a group member drill the other members on facts, details, solutions, and dates. A verbal review of the information will help you and other members retain the information.

- Brainstorming. During each session, members can use this technique (discussed in detail in the chapter on critical thinking) to predict exam questions, review information, and develop topic ideas for research, projects, future study sessions, and papers.

- Sharing. The study group is a time when you can give and receive. At the beginning or end of each session, students in the group can share the most important aspect of the lecture or readings. This will assist other members in identifying main points and issues pertaining to the lecture.

- Mapping. This technique can be used in a variety of ways. It is similar to the mapping system discussed in the note-taking chapter. On a board or large sheet of paper, let one member write a word, idea, or concept in the center of the board. The next student will add information, thus creating a map or diagram of information and related facts. This can help the group make connections and associations and assist members in identifying where gaps in knowledge exist.

Using groups can benefit your study efforts tremendously. If you are asked to participate in a group, take advantage of the opportunity. If you feel that a group could help you master the information, take steps to form a cooperative learning group on your campus.

Studying with Small Children in the House

For many college students, finding a place or time to study is the hardest part of studying. Some students live at home with younger siblings; some students have children of their own. If you have young children in the home, you may find the following hints helpful when it comes time to study.

- Study at school. Your schedule may have you running from work to school directly to home. Try to squeeze in even as little as half an hour at school for studying, perhaps immediately before or after class. A half hour of pure study time can prove more valuable than five hours at home with constant interruptions.

- Create crafts and hobbies. Your children need to be occupied while you study. It may help if you have crafts and hobbies available that they can do while you are involved with studying. Choose projects your children can do by themselves, without your help. Depending on their ages, children could make masks from paper plates, color, do pipe cleaner art or papier-mâché, use modeling clay or dough, or build a block city. Explain to your children that you are studying and that they can use this time to be creative; when everyone is finished, you'll share what you've done with each other.

■ Study with your children. One of the best ways to instill the value of education in your children is to let them see you participating in your own education. Set aside one or two hours per night when you and your children study. You may be able to study in one place, or you may have separate study areas. If your children know that you are studying and you have explained to them how you value your education, you are killing two birds with one stone: you are able to study and you are providing a positive role model as your children study with you and watch you.

If you view your studying responsibilities positively, your children will too. Try to separate the time you spend with your family from the time you need to spend on your school work.

■ Rent movies or let your children watch TV. Research has shown that viewing a limited amount of educational television, such as Sesame Street, Reading Rainbow, or Barney and Friends, can be beneficial for children. If you do not like what is on television, you might consider renting or purchasing age-appropriate educational videos for your children. This could keep them busy while you study and it could help them learn as well.

■ Invite your children's friends over. What?! That's right. A child who has a friend to play or study with may create less of a distraction for you. Chances are your children would rather be occupied with someone their own age, and you will gain valuable study time.

■ Hire a sitter or exchange sitting services with another student. Arrange to have a sitter come to your house a couple of times a week. If you have a classmate who also has children at home, you might take turns watching the children for each other. You could each take the children for one day a week, or devise any schedule that suits you both best. Or you could study together, and let your children play together while you study, alternating homes.

■ Ask if your college has an on-site daycare center such as the Boys and Girls Club. Some colleges provide daycare facilities at a reduced cost and some provide daycare at no charge. It is certainly worth checking out.

■ Talk to the Financial Aid Office on your campus. In some instances, there will be grants or aid to assist you in finding affordable daycare for your child.

Studying at any time is hard work. It is even harder when you have to attend to a partner, children, family responsibilities, work, and a social life as well. You will have to be creative in order to complete your degree. You are going to have to do things and make sacrifices that you never thought possible. But if you explore the options, plan ahead, and ask questions of other students with children and with responsibilities outside the classroom, you can and will succeed.

BLUEPRINTS FOR CHANGE

NAME

DATE

C01P22

For this particular critical thinking activity, you will be required to form a team with five or six students from your class. Each student on the Cooperative Learning Team will be required to read Chapter 9 independently. After reading the chapter on testing, use the information presented in the chapter to address each of the following components of Cooperative Learning. You may want to assign each team member a component and make that member responsible for explaining and presenting that information at your next meeting, or you may have each team member prepare one or two statements or questions for each component.

Questioning
_____
_____
_____
_____
_____
_____

Brainstorming
_____
_____
_____
_____
_____
_____

Comparing
_____
_____
_____
_____
_____
_____

Sharing
_____
_____
_____
_____
_____
_____

Drilling
_____
_____
_____
_____
_____
_____

Mapping
_____
_____
_____
_____
_____
_____

One Minute *Journal*

In one minute or less, jot down the major ideas that you learned from this chapter.

_____

_____

_____

_____

_____

_____

_____

_____

_____

_____

COMPANION
Website *Journal*

Log on to **www.prenhall.com/montgomery**, choose the version of this book you are using, and then choose Chapter 8 on the menu. Next, choose "Links" on the left side of the page. Explore one of the websites offered and summarize your findings.

_____

_____

_____

_____

_____

_____

_____

_____

_____

_____

Refer to page 192 of Chapter 8.
Review your **GOALS FOR CHANGE**.
Respond in writing as to the progress
you have made toward reaching one
of your three stated goals.

GOAL STATEMENT

PROGRESS

How is your life changing because of this goal?

CORNERSTONES

for effective studying

Use the *READ* method when studying lecture notes.

Review your classroom and textbook *notes.*

Use the *SQ3R* method when studying texts.

Study your *hardest* material *first.*

Take breaks every half hour.

Don't cram the night before.

Study in a *brightly lit* area.

Have a *healthy snack.*

Use *mnemonic* devices.

Overlearn the material.

Set *rules* for studying.

Turn the *heat down.*

Learning is not attained by chance; it must be attained by

Assess.

CHAPTER 9

Marchia could tell that something was wrong with her roommate, Ellen. Ellen had been quiet and distant for the past two days. That evening, while walking to the dining hall, Marchia asked Ellen if there was something bothering her. Ellen confided that the first test in her nursing class was in one week and that if she failed the test, *she would be asked to leave the nursing program.*

Marchia tried to tell Ellen that she had plenty of time to study the material and prepare for the test. Ellen replied that she was not worried so much about knowing the material, *but that she was worried because she was a poor test-taker.* "I can know it from beginning to end," Ellen said, "but when she puts that test in front of me, *I can't even remember my name!* What am I going to do? *This test is going to determine the rest of my life.*"

Marchia explained to Ellen that she suffered through the same type of anxiety and fear in high school until her math teacher taught the class how to take a test and how to reduce test anxiety. *"It's just a skill, Ellen, like driving a car or typing a research paper. You can learn how to take tests if you're really serious."* Ellen asked if Marchia could give her some hints about test taking.

> *. . . when she puts that test in front of me, I can't even remember my name.*

As they finished eating, Marchia told Ellen that they could begin working for an hour every morning and an hour every evening to learn how to take exams and to reduce anxiety.

The week of the test rolled around, and *Ellen was confident that she knew the material that she was to be tested on.* She still had a degree of anxiety, *but she had learned how to be in control of her emotions during a test.* She had also learned how to prepare herself physically for the exam. She went to bed early the night before the exam. On exam day, she got up early, ate a healthy breakfast, had a brief review session, packed all the supplies needed for the exam, and *headed to class early so that she could relax a little* before the instructor arrived.

When the exam was passed out, *Ellen could feel herself getting somewhat anxious,* but she quickly put things into perspective. She sat back and took several deep breaths, listened carefully to the professor's instruc-tions, read all the test instructions before beginning, *told herself silently that she was going to ace the exam,* and started.

After one hour and five minutes, time was called. Ellen put her pencil down, leaned back in her chair, took a deep breath, rubbed her aching finger, and cracked the biggest smile of her life. Marchia had been right. The strategies worked. *Ellen was going to be a nurse.*

T he splendid achievements of the intellect, like the soul, are everlasting.   *—UNKNOWN*

at this moment?

STATEMENT	SCORE	Strongly Disagree	Disagree	Don't Know	Agree	Strongly Agree
1. I do not get anxious when taking a test.		1	2	3	4	5
2. I can control my anxiety.		1	2	3	4	5
3. I know how to relax before taking a test.		1	2	3	4	5
4. I never "black out" during a test.		1	2	3	4	5
5. I remember information when the test is over.		1	2	3	4	5
TOTAL		0–5	6–10	11–15	16–20	21–25

FEEDBACK

0 – 5   Extensive changes need to occur to ensure success.

6 – 10   Substantial changes need to occur to ensure success.

11 – 15   Considerable changes need to occur to ensure success.

16 – 20   Moderate changes need to occur to ensure success.

21 – 25   Minor changes need to occur to ensure success.

GOALS FOR CHANGE

Based on this feedback, my goals and objectives for change are . . .

Goal Statement _____

Action Steps 1. _____

2. _____

Goal Statement _____

Action Steps 1. _____

2. _____

Goal Statement _____

Action Steps 1. _____

2. _____

Results

Reading this chapter, completing the exercises, and reflecting on test-taking strategies will result in your:

- Recognizing symptoms of extreme test anxiety.

- Putting tests into perspective.

- Determining your test-anxiety level.

- Controlling test anxiety.

- Predicting certain test questions.

- Identifying and using strategies for taking matching tests.

- Identifying and using strategies for taking true–false tests.

- Identifying and using strategies for taking multiple-choice tests.

- Identifying and using strategies for taking short-answer tests.

- Identifying and using strategies for taking essay or discussion tests.

How do you really feel about tests? Some students (most, to be honest) view tests as punishment and cruel treatment by professors. Some students believe that testing is not necessary and that it is a tool of coercion. Successful students, however, realize that testing is necessary and even useful, that it has several positive purposes. Testing serves to provide motivation for learning, provide feedback to the student and to the professor, and determine mastery of material.

Successful people accept testing as a fact of life. You have to be tested to drive a car, to continue in school, to join the armed services, to become a teacher, a lawyer, a doctor, or a nurse, and often to be promoted at work. To pretend that testing is not always going to be a part of your life is to deny yourself many opportunities.

You may dread tests for a variety of reasons. You may be afraid of the test itself and the questions it may pose. Test anxiety can be overcome, however, and this chapter will present several ways you can become a more confident test-taker and get started on the path to success.

Controlling Test Anxiety

A student jokes with a professor, "I have five thousand dollars in my savings account and it is yours if you don't make us take the test!" Well, this may be a bit extreme, but many students would do almost anything to get out of taking exams and tests. Some students have physical reactions to testing, including nausea, headaches, and blackouts. Such physical reactions may be a result of being underprepared or not knowing how to take an exam.

Why do you experience test anxiety?

_____

_____

_____

_____

_____

Your answer to this question is more than likely negative. You may approach tests thinking

I'm going to fail.

I knew I couldn't do this.

There is no way I can do well; the teacher hates me.

I should never have taken this class.

These types of attitudes can cause you to be unsuccessful in testing, but with an attitude adjustment and some basic preparation, you can overcome a good deal of your anxiety about tests. You can reduce anxiety when you are in control of the situation, and you can gain control by convincing yourself that you can and will be successful. If you can honestly tell yourself that you have done everything possible to prepare for a test, then the results are going to be positive.

It is important to realize that a test is not an indication of who you are as a person or a mark of your worth as a human being. Not everyone can be good at all things. You will have areas of strength and of weakness. You will spare yourself a great deal of anxiety and frustration if you understand from the start that you may not score 100 on every test. If you expect absolute perfection on everything, you are setting yourself up to fail. Think positively, prepare well, and do your best, but also be prepared to receive less than a perfect score on occasion.

Complete the checklist on the next page. If you checked off more than five items on this list, you experience test anxiety. If you checked off 10 or more, you have severe test anxiety.

Most test anxiety can be reduced by studying, predicting questions, reviewing, and relaxing.

PREDICTING EXAM QUESTIONS

You can also reduce test anxiety by trying to predict what types of test questions the professor will give. Professors frequently give clues ahead of time about what they will be asking and what types of questions will be given.

Test-Anxiety Scale

Check the items that apply to you when preparing for a test.

- ○ I do not sleep well the night before a test.
- ○ I get sick if I eat anything before a test.
- ○ I am irritable and hard to be around before a test.
- ○ I see the test as a measure of my worth as a student.
- ○ I blank out during the test and am unable to recall information.
- ○ I worry when other students are still testing and I am finished.
- ○ I worry when others finish and I am still testing.
- ○ I am always afraid that I will run out of time.
- ○ I get frustrated during the test.
- ○ I have a negative attitude about testing.
- ○ I think about not taking the test.
- ○ I always average my grades before a test.
- ○ My body reacts negatively to testing (sweats, nervousness, butterflies).

Several classes before the test is scheduled, find out from your professor what type of test you can expect. This information can help you study more effectively. Some questions you might ask are:

1. What type of questions will be on the test?
2. How long is the test?
3. Is there a time limit on the test?
4. Will there be any special instructions, such as use pen only or use a number 2 pencil?
5. Is there a study sheet?
6. Will there be a review session?
7. What is the grade value of the test?

Asking these simple questions will help you know what type of test will be administered, how you should prepare for it, and what supplies you will need.

You will want to begin predicting questions early. Listen to the professor intently. Professors use cue phrases, such as, "You will see this again," and "If I were to ask you this question on the test." Pay close attention to what is written on the board, what questions are asked in class, and what areas the professor seems to be concentrating on more

Helpful Reminders for Reducing Test Anxiety

- Approach the test with an "I can" attitude.
- Prepare yourself emotionally for the test, control your self-talk, and be positive.
- Remind yourself that you studied and that you know the material.
- Overlearn the material—you can't study too much.
- Chew gum or hard candy during the test if allowed; it may help you relax.
- Go to bed early. Do not pull an all-nighter before the test.
- Eat a healthy meal before the test.
- Arrive early for the test (at least 15 minutes early).
- Sit back, relax, breathe, and clear your mind if you become nervous.
- Come to the test with everything you need: pencils, calculator, and so on.
- Read over the entire test first; read all the directions; highlight the directions.
- Listen to the professor before the test begins.
- Keep an eye on the clock.
- Answer what you know first, the questions that are easiest for you.
- Check your answers, but remember, your first response is usually correct.
- Find out about the test before it is given; ask the professor what types of questions will be on the test.
- Find out exactly what the test will cover ahead of time.
- Ask the professor for a study sheet; you may not get one, but it does not hurt to ask!
- Know the rules of the test and of the professor.
- Attend the review session if one is offered.
- Know what grade value the test holds.
- Ask about extra credit or bonus questions on the test.
- When you get the test, jot down any mnemonic you might have developed on the back or at the top of a page.
- Never look at another student's test or let anyone see your test.

than others. You will begin to get a feel for what types of questions the professor might ask on the test.

It may also be beneficial for you to keep a running page of test questions that you have predicted. As you read through a chapter, ask yourself many questions at the end of each section. When it is time to study for the test, you may have already predicted many of the questions your professor will ask.

Save all quizzes and exams that your professor lets you keep (some professors take the exams back after students have had a chance to review them). These are a wonderful resource for studying for the next exam or for predicting questions for the course final.

Take a moment to try to predict two essay test questions from Chapter 8.

Question 1.

_____

_____

Why do you think this question will be asked?

_____

_____

Question 2.

_____

_____

Why do you think this question will be asked?

_____

_____

Three Types of Responses to Test Questions

Almost every test question will elicit one of three types of responses from you as the test-taker:

- *Quick-time response*
- *Lag-time response*
- *No response*

Your response is a quick-time response when you read a question and know the answer immediately. You may need to read only one key word in the test question to know the correct response. Even if you have a quick-time response, however, always read the entire question before answering. The question may be worded in such a way that the correct response is not what you originally expected. By reading the entire question before answering, you can avoid losing points to careless error.

You have a lag-time response when you read a question and the answer does not come to you immediately. You may have to read the question several times or even move on to another question before you think of the correct response. Information in another question will sometimes trigger the response you need. Don't get nervous if you have a lag-time response. Once you've begun to answer other questions, you usually begin to remember more, and the response may come to you. You do not have to answer questions in order on most tests.

No response is the least desirable situation when you are taking a test. You may read a question two or three times and still have no response. At this point, you should move on to another question to try to find some related information. When this happens, you have some options:

Thoughts ● ● ●

1. Leave this question until the very end of the test.
2. Make an intelligent guess.
3. Try to eliminate all unreasonable answers by association.
4. Watch for modifiers within the question.

It is very difficult to use intelligent guessing with essay or fill-in-the-blank questions. Remember these important tips about the three types of responses:

1. Don't be overly anxious if your response is quick; read the entire question and be careful so that you don't make a mistake.
2. Don't get nervous if you have a lag-time response; the answer may come to you later, so just relax and move on.
3. Don't put down just anything if you have no response; take the remaining time and use intelligent guessing.

Test-Taking Strategies and Hints for Success

Wouldn't it be just great if every professor gave the same type of test? Then, you would have to worry about content only, and not about the test itself. Unfortunately, this is not going to happen. Professors will continue to test differently and to have their own style of writing. Successful students have to know the differences among testing techniques and know what to look for when dealing with each type of test question. You may have a preference for one type of question over another. You may prefer multiple-choice to essay questions, whereas someone else may prefer essay to true–false questions. Whatever your preference, you are going to encounter all types of questions. To be successful, you will need to know the techniques for answering each type.

The most common types of questions are:

- Matching
- True–false
- Multiple choice
- Short answer
- Essay

Before you read about the strategies for answering these different types of questions, think about this: There is no substitute for studying! You can know all the tips, ways to reduce anxiety, mnemonics, and strategies on earth, but if you have not studied, they will not help you.

STRATEGIES FOR MATCHING QUESTIONS

Matching questions frequently involve knowledge of people, dates, places, or vocabulary. When answering matching questions, you should:

- Read the directions carefully.
- Read each column before you answer.
- Determine whether there is an equal number of items in each column.
- Match what you know first.
- Cross off information that is already used.
- Use the process of elimination for answers you might not know.
- Look for logical clues.
- Use the longer statement as a question; use the shorter statement as an answer.

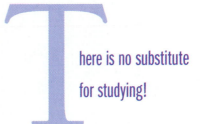
There is no substitute for studying!

Sample Test #1

Directions: Match the information in column A with the correct information in column B. Use uppercase letters.

LISTENING SKILLS

A		B	
_____	They can be long or short, social, academic, religious, or financial	A.	Child within
_____	A step in the change process	B.	Objectivity
_____	Studying cooperatively	C.	Letting go
_____	Your "true self"	D.	Group or team work
_____	Listening with an open mind	E.	Goals

STRATEGIES FOR TRUE–FALSE QUESTIONS

True–false tests ask if a statement is true or not. True–false questions are some of the trickiest questions ever developed. Some students like them; some hate them. There is a 50/50 chance of answering correctly, but you can use the following strategies to increase your odds on true–false tests:

- Read each statement carefully.
- Watch for key words in each statement, for example, negatives.
- Read each statement for double negatives, such as "not untruthful."
- Pay attention to words that may indicate that a statement is true, such as "some," "few," "many," and "often."

Sample Test #2

Place a "T" for true or "F" for false beside each statement.

NOTE-TAKING SKILLS

_____ 1. Note taking creates a history of your course content.

_____ 2. "Most importantly" is not a key phrase.

_____ 3. You should always write down everything the professor says.

_____ 4. You should never ask questions in class.

_____ 5. The L-STAR system is a way of studying.

_____ 6. W/O is not a piece of shorthand.

_____ 7. You should use 4-by-6-inch paper to take classroom notes.

_____ 8. The outline technique is best used with lecture notes.

_____ 9. The Cornell method should never be used with textbook notes.

_____ 10. The mapping system is done with a series of circles.

- Pay attention to words that may indicate that a statement is false, such as "never," "all," "every," and "only."

- Remember that if any part of a statement is false, the entire statement is false.

- Answer every question unless there is a penalty for guessing.

STRATEGIES FOR MULTIPLE-CHOICE QUESTIONS

Many college professors give multiple-choice tests because they are easy to grade and provide quick, precise responses. A multiple-choice question asks you to choose from among usually two to five answers to complete a sentence. Some strategies for increasing your success in answering multiple-choice questions are the following:

- Read the question and try to answer it before you read the answers provided.

- Look for similar answers; one of them is usually the correct response.

- Recognize that answers containing extreme modifiers, such as *always, every,* and *never,* are usually wrong.

- Cross off answers that you know are incorrect.

- Read all the options before selecting your answer. Even if you believe that A is the correct response, read them all.

- Recognize that when the answers are all numbers, the highest and lowest numbers are usually incorrect.
- Recognize that a joke is usually wrong.
- Understand that the most inclusive answer is often correct.
- Understand that the longest answer is often correct.
- If you cannot answer a question, move on to the next one and continue through the test; another question may trigger the answer you missed.
- Make an educated guess if you must.
- Answer every question unless there is a penalty for guessing.

Insider's view

Test taking is an important part of learning. That does not mean, however, that I condone them. To be honest, I think that professors give tests to get a handle on exactly how much we are learning and getting from the class. I think that they are good ways to let professors know if we are having a hard time without us actually having to tell them. The most important thing that I have learned about tests is that they do not measure my worth. They are simply a measure of what I know about a certain thing at a certain point in my life.

As someone who procrastinates more than I should, testing is, and always has been, a fairly stressful experience for me. I have always tried to prepare myself for the "big test" and what was going to be on it, but it was not until I learned a few tricks that I became a better test-taker. I learned that you have to approach the test with a relaxed, calm (yet focused) attitude. You have to learn how to motivate yourself to do your best. If you do this, you will be mentally ready for the test.

I have also learned that you should not overload yourself with information that is not relevant to the test. Listen to the professor, take good notes, read the text, study the handouts, and if necessary, get together with some pals and study together. This will save a lot of worry and stress.

Before starting the test, I try to look over the entire test to get a good feel for what is being asked. From there, I start by answering a question that I know right off the bat. If I don't know the answer to a question, I move to the next one. I try not to get upset or stressed over the fact that I could not answer one question. The best advice that I can give you when testing is to focus on the test only. Focus on the question at hand and nothing else. Everything else will be waiting for you when the test is over. Just concentrate on the material. For me, I have a very short attention span. Focusing is not easy for me, but when I do it, I score better on my tests.

Finally, testing does not have to be fun to be rewarding. When you look back at the test and know that you did your best, there is something motivating in that. It makes you want to "out do" yourself the next time.

Adam Smith, *age 20*
Major: Print Journalism
The University of Kansas,
Lawrence, Kansas

Sample Test #3

Directions: Read each statement and select the best response from the answers given below.

STUDY SKILLS

1. The book *Understanding* reported that men with a master's degree earn:
   A. $12,527 per year
   B. $34,531 per year
   C. $47,192 per year
   D. $57,533 per year

2. According to research from Gardner and Jewler, 40% to 50% of first-year students do not:
   A. have the study habits to "make it" in college.
   B. participate in extracurricular activities.
   C. return for their second year.
   D. write and post their goals.

3. Critical thinking is:
   A. thinking that is motivated by an end result.
   B. thinking that is purposeful, reasoned, and goal-directed.
   C. thinking that is formulated by fallacies.
   D. thinking that is derived from inferences.

4. To be an effective priority manager, you have to:
   A. be very structured and organized.
   B. be very unstructured and disorganized.
   C. be mildly structured and organized.
   D. be sometimes a little of both.
   E. know what type of person you are and work from that point.

5. The listening process involves:
   A. receiving, organizing, assigning, and reacting.
   B. receiving, assigning, transferring, and encoding.
   C. encoding, assigning, organizing, and reacting.
   D. encoding, decoding, organizing, and assigning.

I believe that the primary focus for higher education is to provide society with an intelligent and highly productive workforce. Not only did higher education prepare me for my profession but I know that I have applied the skills learned as a college student to schedule my work and leisure time more reasonably and logically, to make my work time more fruitful and still leave me time for my friends, family, and hobbies.

In my role as a college professor who teaches hospitality accounting and finance, my college experience prepared me to use materials, resources, and technology in the wisest way by focusing on relevant, important, and reliable information sources and disregarding irrelevant, unimportant, and unreliable information.

Of course the information I share in my courses is reinforced through the use of tests. I know students are particularly frightened of quantitative courses and therefore the tests I give create a great deal of stress for my students. I give tests because I believe that they prepare students for the world of work in two ways. They help strengthen the basic knowledge students have learned in or out of class and they sharpen their ability to logically think or reason through the analyzing of data. Without tests, students would have no reason to pull everything together so that they can see the whole picture. Tests, stressful as they may be, encourage students to really get into the material and analyze it so that they can synthesize new information in meaningful ways.

Xheng Gu, College Professor   The University of Nevada, Las Vegas, Nevada

STRATEGIES FOR SHORT-ANSWER QUESTIONS

Short-answer questions, also called fill-in-the-blanks, ask you to supply the answer yourself, not to select it from a list. Although "short answer" sounds easy, these questions are often very difficult. Short-answer questions require you to draw from your long-term memory. The following hints can help you answer this type of question successfully:

- Read each question and be sure that you know what is being asked.
- Be brief in your response.
- Give the same number of answers as there are blanks; for example, _____ and _____ would require two answers.
- Never assume that the length of the blank has anything to do with the length of the answer.
- Remember that your initial response is usually correct.
- Pay close attention to the word immediately preceding the blank; if the word is "an," give a response that begins with a vowel (a, e, i, o, u).
- Look for key words in the sentence that may trigger a response.

Sample Test #4

Directions: Fill in the blanks with the correct response. Write clearly.

LISTENING SKILLS

1. Listening is a _____ act. We choose to do it.

2. The listening process involves receiving, organizing, _____, and reacting.

3. _____ is the same as listening with an open mind.

4. Prejudging is an _____ to listening.

5. Leaning forward, giving eye contact, being patient, and leaving your emotions at home are characteristics of _____ listeners.

STRATEGIES FOR ESSAY QUESTIONS

Most students look at essay questions with dismay because they take more time. Yet essay tests can be one of the easiest tests to take, because they give you a chance to show what you really know. An essay question requires you to supply the information. If you have studied, you will find that once you begin to answer an essay question, your answer will flow easily. Some tips for answering essay questions are the following:

- Sometimes more is not always better, sometimes more is just more. Try to be as concise and informative as possible. A professor would rather see one page of excellent material than five pages of fluff.

- Pay close attention to the action word used in the question and respond with the appropriate type of answer. Key words used in questions include the following:

discuss	illustrate	enumerate	describe
compare	define	relate	list
contrast	summarize	analyze	explain
trace	evaluate	critique	interpret
diagram	argue	justify	prove

- Write a thesis statement for each answer.

- Outline your thoughts before you begin to write.

- Watch your spelling, grammar, and punctuation.
- Use details, such as times, dates, places, and proper names, where appropriate.
- Be sure to answer all parts of the question; some discussion questions have more than one part.
- Summarize your main ideas toward the end of your answer.
- Write neatly.
- Proofread your answer.

Learning how to take a test and learning how to reduce your anxiety are two of the most important gifts you can give yourself as a student. Although there are many tips and hints to help you, don't forget that there is no substitute for studying and knowing the material.

Using proper study techniques and remembering testing tips can increase your chances of success on most tests.

Sample Test #5

Directions: Answer each question completely and thoroughly.

STUDY SKILLS

1. Describe the READ study method.

_____
_____

_____

2. Discuss why it is important to use the SQ3R method.

_____
_____

_____

3. Justify your chosen notebook system.

_____
_____

_____

4. Compare an effective study environment with an ineffective study environment.

_____
_____

_____

Academic Integrity

If you look in your student handbook, you will more than likely find a "Code of Conduct" for student behavior. This code probably outlines the sanctions for cheating, plagiarism, lying, and other forms of misconduct. You may ask yourself, "Who cares if I cheat?" or "OK, I bought a research paper, so what?" or "No one told me that getting a paper from the Internet was wrong." So, who does care, what does it mean, and what are the ramifications for academic dishonesty? Your student handbook will outline the answers for you. Most institutions are intolerant of academic dishonesty. Colleges vary in issuing penalties, but they can range from failing the course to being removed from the campus.

Beyond the college campus, dishonesty affects the community at large. Would you want an accountant who had cheated through the CPA exam investing your money? Would you want a construction engineer to build your office building if she had cheated all the way through electrical engineering classes? Would you want a physician to operate on your child or parent if he had cut corners in medical school?

It is important to know what constitutes dishonesty. Below, you will find what most colleges consider academic misconduct:

● ● ● Thoughts

- Looking on another student's test paper for answers
- Giving another student a test or lab answer
- Using "cheat sheets" on a test or project
- Using a computer, calculator, dictionary, or notes when not approved
- Discussing exam questions with students in classes after yours
- Plagiarism, or using the words or works of others without giving proper credit
- Stealing another student's notes
- Using an annotated instructor's edition of a text
- Having tutors do your homework for you
- Submitting the same paper for more than one class during any semester
- Copying files from lab computers
- Bribing a student for answers or academic work such as papers or projects
- Buying or acquiring papers from individuals or the Internet
- Assisting others with dishonest acts

Using Chapters 1 through 8, predict at least 25 exam questions for a comprehensive exam in this course. You should have:

5 multiple-choice questions

5 true–false questions

5 fill-in-the-blank questions

5 matching questions

5 essay questions

Intelligence

LIFE

Multiple-Choice Questions:

1. _____

2. _____

3. _____

4. _____

5. _____

True–False Questions:

1. _____

2. _____

3. _____

4. _____

5. _____

Fill-in-the-Blank Questions:

1. _____

2. _____

3. _____

4. _____

5. _____

Matching Questions:

1. _____

2. _____

3. _____

4. _____

5. _____

Essay Questions:

1. _____

2. _____

3. _____

4. _____

5. _____

Self-esteem

Answer these questions in your notebook. Share your questions and answers with classmates or your cooperative learning team.

The One Minute Journal

In one minute or less, jot down the major ideas that you learned from this chapter.

THE COMPANION Website Journal

Log on to **www.prenhall.com/montgomery**, choose the version of this book you are using, and then choose Chapter 9 on the menu. Next, choose "Links" on the left side of the page. Explore one of the websites offered and summarize your findings.

at this moment?

Refer to page 220 of Chapter 9.
Review your **GOALS FOR CHANGE**.
Respond in writing as to the progress
you have made toward reaching one
of your three stated goals.

GOAL STATEMENT

PROGRESS

How is your life changing because of this goal?

CORNERSTONES

for test-taking

Use *uppercase* letters for true–false and multiple-choice questions.

Never use drugs or alcohol to get through a test.

Read over the entire test *before* beginning.

Check punctuation, spelling, and grammar.

Write your *name* on every test page.

Ignore the pace of your classmates.

One question may answer *another*.

Ask questions of the professor.

Answer *all* questions.

Don't skip questions.

Watch *time* limits.

Think *positively*.

Write *clearly*.

Let thy speech be better than silence, or be silent. Dionysius

Communicate.

CHAPTER 10

Communicate

I had been teaching Public Speaking for almost 10 years. I had performed in over 30 plays and spoken to groups of business and education leaders numbering in the thousands. I even *majored in Public Speaking* in college. When the phone call came on a Monday morning in December, it should have been a "piece of cake" to accept the opportunity to deliver yet another speech. *It wasn't.* The phone call held a double punch. A wonderful friend had died from cancer and her husband was calling to ask if I would deliver a part of her eulogy. *It wasn't a piece of cake!*

I agreed to speak at Doris' funeral *not realizing how life-altering the event would be.* For the remainder of that day, I reminisced about our time together. I remembered the joy of sharing an office space with her. I remembered *the daily jokes, the sharing of dreams, and the bond we had.* I remembered the time that we took a group of students to Washington, D.C. I remembered that it *was her hand I held as we watched the news of the space shuttle Challenger.*

I honestly believe that *I remembered every moment that we shared together.* So, I spent the day jotting down memories that I wanted to share. *The hardest part still lay ahead.*

After careful consideration and meticulously choosing my words, the speech was ready. That is to say, the written word was ready—*surprisingly, I was not.* On the morning of the funeral, I had never been more nervous, and for the first time in

> **It should have been a piece of cake . . . to deliver another speech. It wasn't.**

my public speaking career, *I was about to deliver a speech that I had never gotten through without becoming emotionally overwhelmed.*

I arrived early so that I could stand behind the lectern, get a feel for the auditorium, and make any last-minute adjustments to my speech. *After all, this is what I would have told any student to do.* I think I really got there early to see if there were any miracles floating around. As I sat on the podium at the front of the auditorium, I watched over 200 people enter the room. I was getting more nervous by the second. *My palms were sweating, my throat was dry, my heart was beating out of my chest, and if I had had a mirror, I know that I could have seen the horror reflected on my own face.*

In the final moments before I was to stand, I remember thinking desperately to myself, *"What would you tell a student to do? What?!"* My mind ran through my public speaking teaching notes that I used on a daily basis. The miracle that I had hoped for happened. In an instant, "it" came to me. *I saw it on the page as clear as crystal.* "This is your moment in the sun." It sounds so simple, so trivial, but the statement I used with my students every semester came to me, and the cloud lifted. *How could I have missed it? How could I not have known that this was the key? The miracle?*

I walked to the lectern, opened my outlined notes, took a breath, and began *to tell the audience how Doris had changed my life.* I was even able to smile as I shared some of the wonderful memories.

You may be asking yourself, "What does 'this is your moment in the sun' mean?" *For me, it meant that this would be the only time in the history of the world that I would ever have the opportunity to tell over 200 people how I felt about Doris.*

It would be the last time in my life that I would ever have this moment. The voice inside my head said, "Shine!" From that day forward, I have approached every speech with that philosophy.

Whether I'm speaking about leadership, change, Generation X, study skills, or camping, I look at the opportunity and say to myself, *"This is my moment and I don't know if it will ever come again . . . so, make the most of it!"*

Wisdom is the one treasure that no thief can touch.
—*JAPANESE PROVERB*

STATEMENT	SCORE	Strongly Disagree	Disagree	Don't Know	Agree	Strongly Agree
1. I know how to select an appropriate topic.		1	2	3	4	5
2. I know how to research a topic thoroughly.		1	2	3	4	5
3. I know how to organize a paper or speech.		1	2	3	4	5
4. I know how to document my research both orally and in writing.		1	2	3	4	5
5. I know how to use visual aids effectively.		1	2	3	4	5
TOTAL		0-5	6-10	11-15	16-20	21-25

FEEDBACK

0 – 5   Extensive changes need to occur to ensure success.

6 – 10   Substantial changes need to occur to ensure success.

11 – 15   Considerable changes need to occur to ensure success.

16 – 20   Moderate changes need to occur to ensure success.

21 – 25   Minor changes need to occur to ensure success.

GOALS FOR CHANGE

Based on this feedback, my goals and objectives for change are . . .

Goal Statement _____

Action Steps   1. _____

               2. _____

Goal Statement _____

Action Steps   1. _____

               2. _____

Goal Statement _____

Action Steps   1. _____

               2. _____

Results

Reading this chapter, completing the exercises, and reflecting on writing and public speaking will result in your:

- Selecting an appropriate topic for a paper or speech.

- Conducting an audience analysis.

- Developing a purpose or thesis statement.

- Conducting research with traditional and electronic methods.

- Organizing and outlining your papers and speeches for clarity.

- Understanding the basic concepts of writing.

- Properly documenting your research in papers and speeches.

- Using audiovisual aids to best advantage.

- Utilizing the techniques of speech rehearsal and delivery.

Your Chance to Shine

"Writing! Research! Public speaking! If I wanted to write papers or speak in front of people, I would have taken a writing class or a public speaking course," you might be saying at this moment. Relax. You are not alone in your anxiety about writing papers or speaking publicly. In fact, according to *The Book of Lists,* 3000 Americans surveyed listed public speaking as their *number one* fear. Public speaking came in ahead of sickness, insects, financial troubles, deep water, and even *death!*

So, why do we include a chapter on writing and public speaking in a first-year orientation text? You probably won't like the answer, but the simple truth is that you are going to be asked to write and speak in many of your classes; from history to chemistry, from engineering to computer programming, writing and speaking are a way of life for today's college students. The more you know about writing papers and speeches and delivering speeches, the more confident you are going to feel in every class.

The language of the heart, which comes from the heart and goes to the heart, is always simple, graceful, and full of power.   —*BOVEE*

Insider's view

I am a coal miner's daughter, and as long as I live, I will remember the exact day that I learned the importance of proper communication. It is etched in my mind as vividly as the scars of a mined hillside.

I was in the second grade and had just moved to a new school in Alabama from the deep hills of Kentucky. We were in the cafeteria when one of the little girls at the table decided that we would be married to the person sitting across from us. As the kids giggled about who was to be married to whom, I saw a boy sitting across from an unoccupied seat. In a loud voice I said, "He's going to marry the chair." However, the word chair came out as "churr" (the same as purr). Another boy yelled, "Did you hear that girl call the chair a 'churr'?" All of my classmates laughed at me, and through my humiliation, I learned a very important lesson about speaking in public.

I considered myself the same as every child at that table, but I felt like an outcast because I spoke differently. I have since learned to be very proud of the attributes that distinguish me from others, but at that moment, I wanted nothing more than to speak like all of the other kids. I vividly remember thinking that I would learn how to speak like the teacher and no one would ever laugh at me again.

Over the course of my life, I have continued to learn the importance of speaking in public. I have seen qualified people passed over for promotions because there was another applicant with better speaking and communication skills. Good communication skills are essential everywhere. A comedian draws a crowd because he or she can speak and touch something inside of people. A professor imparts knowledge by gaining the interest of his or her students. People in relationships make those relationships last because they communicate with each other.

When I first entered the nursing program and took the NLN test, I began to see the importance of communication, writing, and speaking skills. I knew several women who would have been excellent nurses if only they could have passed the test. It was not a very hard test, but speaking, reading, and writing skills were tested. At that time, I thought that it was wrong to block the entrance into a clinical program based on how well one could speak. However, as I progressed in the program, it became clear to me that without advanced communication skills, interactions with patients, families, and physicians could be dangerously hindered.

I now know that our ability to speak and communicate clearly and effectively is one of the most important skills that we can possess. I believe that to whomever we speak, whether it be a packed audience, a child, or an employee, we convey a part of who we are inside.

As students, take every opportunity to learn to speak clearly and effectively. Public speaking can be used as a tool for advancement and knowledge. To be able to communicate our desires, needs, expectations, feelings, and successes is truly an invaluable asset.

Mary M. Cornelius, *age 40*
Major: Nursing
Midlands Technical College,
Columbia, South Carolina

Writing and speaking are two of the most important skills a person can possess at any time, in any profession, anywhere on earth. As a college student, seize the opportunity to take courses and seminars or attend workshops and conferences that promote, teach, and encourage effective writing and speaking skills.

In today's ever-changing world, you must be open to every possibility. Learn computers and electronic communication devices. Keep up with the latest developments and trends, but master the gentle art of conversation. Email has revived the epistolary arts; therefore, study writing! It is not enough to know how to communicate electronically, one must know what to say and how to say it effectively. Computers level the playing fields; anyone can participate who thinks and writes clearly. What to say? How to say it? Ideas, and the effective expression of them, can carry you up the corporate ladder overnight—literally!

As you move through your courses and pursue your career options, remember that higher education gives authority to one's hunches, beliefs, and common sense, so that one works with greater confidence and influence. Higher education gives credibility to life's transformations.

College is a microcosm of future experiences in which one draws heavily upon management skills learned as a student. As a college student, you are forced to budget everything: time, money, emotions, relationships, etc. So, take these experiences seriously.

Finally, in the world of work, you learn that interpersonal skills are simply mandatory. It's all about people. Electronic devices allow us to get the basics out of the way, quickly freeing up more personal time to be "present" for each other. Don't allow email, faxes, and computers to replace the human art of communication.

Steve Brannon, *Executive Director*   Communicorp, Atlanta, Georgia

The Power of Words

The benefits and value of written and oral communication are immeasurable. The power of words has changed nations, built civilizations, preserved traditions, freed masses, and prevented destruction. Think of the words written or spoken by Dr. Martin Luther King, Jr., Lorraine Hansbury, Maya Angelou, Booker T. Washington, Franklin Roosevelt, Frederick Douglass, Spike Lee, Ann Richards, Steven Spielberg, and Princess Diana. Good or bad, right or wrong, appropriate or inappropriate, their words have changed many lives.

The ability to write and speak with confidence and credibility is empowering. "It will give you an edge that other, less skilled communicators lack—even those who may have superior ideas, training, or experience. It will position you for greater things" (Beebe and Beebe,

1997). Whether you are writing a paper for English 101, or speaking to a class of 15 people, a student body of 500, a group of managers at work, or before your child's first grade class, you are gaining skills that will complement your academic knowledge.

If all my talents and powers were to be taken from me, and I had the choice of keeping but one, I would unhesitatingly ask to be allowed to keep the power of speaking, for through it, I would quickly recover the rest. *—DANIEL WEBSTER*

In a 1989 survey by Curtis, Winsor, and Stephens entitled *Top Factors in Helping Graduating College Students Obtain Employment,* oral (speaking) communication was listed as *number one.* Written communication was listed as number four. Note that both writing and speaking ranked above degree held, letters of recommendation, school attended, or grade point average.

As this chapter takes you through the steps of writing and speaking, consider the fact that you are developing skills that will help you not only in your college classes, but for the rest of your life. Not all steps will be used in every situation—as a matter of fact, the last three are exclusive to public speaking. You will also note that the term "audience" is intended to mean a reading or listening audience, the receivers of your written or spoken words.

Getting a Job

Top Factors in Helping Graduating College Students Obtain Employment[1]

RANK	FACTORS/SKILLS EVALUATED
1	Oral (speaking) communication
2	Listening ability
3	Enthusiasm
4	Written communication skills
5	Technical competence
6	Appearance
7	Poise
8	Work experience
9	Resume
10	Specific degree held

[1]Adapted from: Dan B. Curtis, Jerry L. Winsor, and Ronald D. Stephens, "National Preferences in Business and Communication Education," *Communication Education* 38 (January 1989), p. 11.

Ten Steps to Communication Success

Overview of Similarities and Differences Between Writing and Speaking

STEPS	WRITER	SPEAKER
TOPIC	Most likely assigned by the professor Can be very broad to appeal to a mass audience Can be narrative, informative, biographical, technical, analytical, etc.	May be assigned by the professor, most likely chosen by the student Usually narrowed for a specific audience or class Will usually be informative, demonstrative, or persuasive for classroom purposes
AUDIENCE ANALYSIS	Usually written for the professor	Usually written and delivered for the class
PURPOSE STATEMENT	Referred to as a thesis statement, it is usually at the beginning of the paragraph and introduces the topic	Referred to as a purpose or transition statement, it is usually at the end of the introduction and serves as a bridge to the body of the speech
RESEARCH PROCESS	Research based on your topic and thesis statement	Research based on your topic and thesis statement
ORGANIZATIONAL PROCESS	May be assigned by the professor May use a formal outline	Usually determined by the type of speech Will probably use a less formal outline
WRITING PROCESS	Writer can create a draft and revise until polished May be allowed a re-write after a grade is assigned	Speaker can create a draft and rehearse until polished Seldom allowed a second chance for another grade
DOCUMENTATION	Written at the end of the paper as a bibliography or reference page, depending on documentation style	Research and sources usually documented verbally during speech and may be written at the end of the speech as required by the professor
OUTLINING DELIVERY NOTES	Not required for a written paper	Speaker can use a variety of notes such as key word outlines, note cards, or overheads if allowed by the professor
AUDIOVISUAL	Not required for a written paper	Adds strength to the presentation Increases audience attention and retention Speaker must rehearse with the aids used
REHEARSAL AND DELIVERY	Not required for a written paper	Speaker must spend a great deal of time in rehearsal to deliver a polished presentation

Step 1: Topic Selection

Almost every writing and speaking expert will tell you to select a topic on which you are an expert, or a topic on which you have a keen interest and enough preparation time to become an expert. This does not mean that you cannot write or speak on topics that are new or unfamiliar to you, but if you choose such a topic, your preparation time will need to be extended. If you have a choice for your paper or speech, keep the following tips in mind.

W
riting and speaking are two of the most important skills a person can possess at any time.

Tips for Topic Selection

- Know what type of paper or speech you will be writing and/or delivering.
- What are your talents, interests, and experiences?
- Can you find sufficient material and information for your paper or speech?
- Is your topic appropriate to you and your audience?
- Can you adequately discuss the topic within the given time frame or page length?
- Can the topic be narrowed?

As you work your way through this chapter, you will be asked to build a paper or speech as you go through each section. Following your instructor's guidelines, begin to develop your paper or speech by identifying a topic or using the topic given to you in class.

The type of paper or speech for which I am preparing is

_____

_____

My topic is

_____

_____

Why have you chosen this topic?

_____

_____

_____

_____

_____

_____

Step 2: Audience Analysis

Have you ever read a paper that was boring or listened to someone speak about a topic that was so technical that you understood very little of it? It could be because the paper or the speech was poorly written, but it may be that the boring paper or technical speech was inaccessible to you because it was written for a different audience. If you don't understand your audience, it is unlikely that you will be able to maintain their attention, inform or persuade them, or expect them to act on your advice. Although your immediate paper or speech will be written for your professor or class, there will be instances in the future when it will be advantageous to complete an analysis of your audience. This will assist you in learning more about the diversity or homogeneity of your audience. The chart below will assist you in developing a comprehensive audience analysis.

Y ou compose your speech for an audience, and the audience is judge.

—ARISTOTLE

An audience analysis might also consist of customized questions about your topic. If you were writing a paper or delivering a speech on genetic engineering, you might poll your audience to find out how many people believe that we should clone human beings.

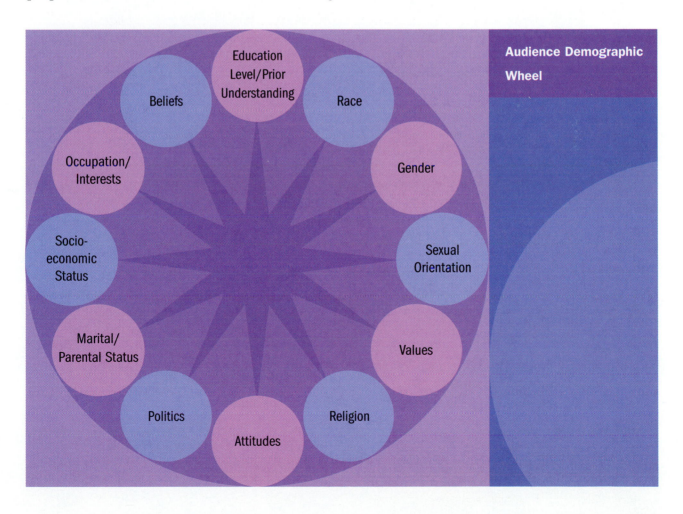

Beliefs · Education Level/Prior Understanding · Race · Gender · Sexual Orientation · Values · Religion · Attitudes · Politics · Marital/Parental Status · Socio-economic Status · Occupation/Interests

Audience Demographic Wheel

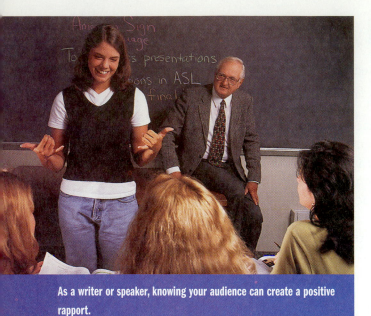
As a writer or speaker, knowing your audience can create a positive rapport.

When you gather this information, you can use it to address the needs of your audience and write a paper or speech that "speaks" to them on a personal level. For instance, if you found out that a majority of your audience members were very concerned about their safety on campus, your paper or speech could detail ways to enhance personal safety. This paper or speech would then have a good chance to gain their attention.

Using your classroom setting as your audience, write a brief analysis about this audience. You may have to make some educated guesses based on observation and keen listening skills, but you may also have to interview them or issue a questionnaire. As a basis for your understanding, you will want to seek answers to the 12 factors in the demographic wheel. You may also need to answer questions such as: "What do I know about them?" "What do I need to find out?" "What do they expect?" and "What does my analysis mean to my paper or speech?"

Brief analysis of your classroom audience:

_____

_____

_____

_____

_____

Step 3: Writing a Thesis Statement

Simply stated, what do you want to accomplish? Are you writing or speaking to entertain, to persuade, or to inform? What do you want your audience to do or feel when you are finished? Do you want them to change their minds, sign a petition, join a cause, give blood, practice

A

nyone who wishes to fulfill a mission in the world must have an overmastering purpose that guides and controls them. —*UNKNOWN*

safer sex, or enjoy a trip down memory lane? If you can answer this question, you are well on your way to writing an effective and engaging paper or speech.

Your thesis statement is one sentence that tells your audience *exactly* what you hope to accomplish. Examples of some thesis statements are the following:

- You will understand the effects of domestic abuse, know how to look for warning signs, and know where to turn for assistance.
- Today, it is my intent to persuade you to complete the organ donor cards that I have brought with me.
- After you have had time to reflect on the research, interviews, and personal testimonials offered, you will stop smoking.

Traditionally, the thesis will come at the end of the first or second paragraph. Placing it earlier in the paper or speech does not serve as an attention-gaining device. More will be discussed about gaining attention in the section on writing an introduction.

Using the topic you selected earlier, write your thesis statement below.

_____

_____

_____

_____

_____

Step 4: Researching Your Speech or Paper

Now that you have selected and narrowed your topic, analyzed your audience, and developed your purpose statement, you are ready to begin accumulating information to support your paper or speech. As you begin to consider resources, you will want to investigate and explore a variety of sources, including the following:

- Personal interviews with experts on your topic
- Electronic and print indexes, such as the *Reader's Guide* and *Humanities Index*
- Books (commonly called stacks in the library)
- Electronic card catalogs and computerized databases
- The Internet (start with Yahoo, Infoseek, Alta Vista, and Netscape Navigator, for example)

Personal interviews with audience members can be an excellent way to take the pulse of the audience or to gain expert viewpoints.

- Periodicals such as *Newsweek, Vital Speeches,* and *American Psychologist*
- Newspapers such as the *New York Times, Chicago Sun Times,* and *Atlanta Constitution*
- Reference materials such as encyclopedias, dictionaries, directories, atlases, almanacs and yearbooks, books of quotations, and bibliographical directories
- Government documents

When collecting your research, you will find that information comes in a variety of forms such as case studies, surveys, polls, statistics, testimonials, and experiment results. You will need to do a variety of research to be able to objectively write your paper or speech. You should also have at least three or more sources supporting your claim or thesis. If you have only one research article supporting your view, you may not have gotten the entire picture.

The success of any argument, short or long, depends in large part on the quantity and quality of the support behind it.   —*ANNETTE ROTTENBERG*

As you begin to collect your data, you may want to consider the following tips to keep your information orderly:

- Collect and keep copies of articles, pages of books, or chapters. You may want to copy them if the copyright laws permit.
- Always keep hard copies of your Internet research. Be sure to write the URL on each article.
- When taking notes from articles, chapters, pages, or the Internet, try to take notes in an organized manner to save you time later in the writing process.

As a researcher, you should know the validity of the sources and research that you plan to use to write your papers and speeches. The credibility of your sources can mean the difference between having a valid argument or thesis and having unsubstantiated opinions. With the Internet becoming an increasingly popular source for information, it is of ultimate importance that you know the validity of your Internet resources.

To critically analyze any information sources, whether Internet or print, use the following guidelines by Ormondroyd, Engle, and Cosgrave (1996b) from Cornell University Libraries:

- Who is the author and what are his or her credentials, educational background, past writings, or experience? Has your instructor mentioned the author? Is he or she cited in other works? Is the author associated with any organizations or institutes?

Thoughts

- When was the source published? If it is a web page, the date is usually found on the last page or the home page. Is the source current or out of date for your topic?

- What edition is the source? Second and third editions suggest that the source has been updated to reflect changes and new knowledge.

- Who is the publisher? If the source is published by a university press, it is likely to be a scholarly publication.

- What is the title of the source? This will help you determine if the source is popular, sensational, or scholarly:

Internet research can be helpful, quick, and timely. But you must watch for false or misleading information.

  - Popular journals are resources such as *Time, Newsweek, Vogue, Ebony,* and *Reader's Digest.* They seldom cite their sources.

  - Sensational resources are often inflammatory, written on an elementary level. They usually have flashy headlines and they cater to popular superstitions. Examples are *The Globe, The National Enquirer,* and *The Star.*

  - Scholarly resources are defined as having a solid base. They are substantial. They always cite their sources and are usually written by scholars in their fields. Usually, they report on original research.

- What is the intended audience of your source? Is the information too simple, too advanced, or too technical for your needs?

- Is the source objective, is it opinionated, or is it propaganda? Objective sources look at all angles and report on each one honestly. Sources of opinion give unfounded information. Propaganda is information that spreads the same message over and over until it is believed by the masses.

- Does the source cover the thesis or question substantially, or does it just gloss over the material? Usually, the more in-depth the source, the more substantial it is going to be to your research.

When using the Internet for resources, use extreme caution. Anyone can create a home page or enter information onto the Internet. This can be good, but it can also create a situation where you have little control over the validity of your resources. Laura Cohen of the University of Albany Libraries suggests "Internet sites change over time according to the commitment and inclination of the creator. Some sites demonstrate an expert's knowledge, while others are amateur efforts. Some may be updated daily, while others may be outdated."

To conduct research on the Internet, you can do several things: (1) join a listserv or Usenet newsgroup; (2) go directly to a site if you have the address; (3) browse the Internet using one of the search engines such as

Infoseek, Yahoo, or AOL; or (4) navigate through a subject directory. When using the Internet, you will need to learn how to narrow your topic search. Again, if your subject is Rape, it may be too broad. You may have to narrow that search to Date Rape, or you could use the words COLLEGE - DATE - RAPE if you wanted to see data pertaining only to rape on college campuses.

To evaluate Internet resources, Laura Cohen suggests the following:

- Consider the intended audience of the Internet piece.
- Many items on the Internet are peripheral or useless.
- Check to see if the piece has an author listed (with the author's address).
- To check the validity of the author, trace back the URL to determine where the document originates.
- Don't take the information presented at face value; conduct additional research using a variety of sources.
- Websites are rarely monitored or reviewed like scholarly journals and books. Therefore, look for point of view, bias, currency, and comprehensiveness.

As a final note, don't hesitate to ask your librarian for assistance. Librarians are trained professionals who devote much of their lives to helping people discover information.

Brainstorm for a moment and jot down what types of research you will need in order to write an informed, objective paper or speech. You may want to visit the library before completing this section.

Source # 1 _____

Source #2 _____

Source #3 _____

Step 5: Organizing Your Paper or Speech

Now that you have gathered enough information from a variety of resources, what are the most effective ways to clearly present your findings and ideas? As you know, every good paper and speech will have an introduction, body, and conclusion. A complete discussion of introductions and conclusions will follow in the next section on writing.

Organizing the body of your paper or speech can be done using one of several proven methods.

Spatial Organization is when you arrange information or items according to their direction or location.

Example: If you were describing the mall in Washington, D.C., you could begin with the Lincoln Memorial and then move on to the reflecting pond, the Washington Monument, and the Smithsonian.

Cause-Effect Organization is when you arrange your information in the cause-and-effect order. You would discuss the causes of a problem and then explore its effects.

Example: If you were speaking about high blood pressure, you would first examine the causes of high blood pressure such as diet, hereditary factors, and weight and then move on to the effects such as heart attack and stroke.

Chronological Organization is presenting information in the order in which it happened. Speeches that deal with historical facts and how-to speeches often use chronological organization.

Example: If you were giving a speech or writing a paper on the history of automobiles in America since 1950, you would begin with the 50s, move to the 60s, 70s, 80s, and 90s. If you were giving a how-to speech on refinishing a table, you would begin with the first process of stripping the old paint or varnish and move forward to the last step of applying a new coat of paint or varnish.

Order and simplification are the first steps toward mastery.

—THOMAS MANN

Problem-Solving Organization is often used in persuasive papers and speeches. Usually, you are trying to get your reader or audience to accept your proposal. You first begin by pointing out the major problem(s) and then move on to revealing the solutions, and the advantages of the solutions.

Example: If you were writing or speaking about crime on college campuses, you would begin by informing the reader or listener about the problems, the crime statistics, and the personal toll on students. You would then propose solutions and tell how the solutions would help all students.

Topical/Categorical Organization is when you group information into subdivisions or cluster information into categories. Some information naturally falls into specific categories, such as the different types of palm trees or the types of rollerblades available.

Example: If you were writing a speech or paper on taxes in the United States, you might categorize your information into local taxes, state taxes, federal taxes, luxury taxes, "sin" taxes, and special taxes.

Compare/Contrast Organization is when you present your information in a fashion that shows its similarities to and differences from other information.

Example: You may be writing a paper or speech that compares the health care system in the United States to that of England or Canada.

Importance/Priority Organization allows you to arrange information from the most important issue to the least or the least important to the most important. You can also arrange your information from the top priority to the lowest priority or vice versa.

Example: If you were writing a paper or delivering a speech to inform readers and listeners about buying diamonds, you might arrange your information so that you speak about the most important aspects of diamond buying, to the least important factor.

Using the topic that you selected at the beginning of the chapter, and referring to the research that you have gathered, which type of organization do you feel would best suit your needs?

_____

_____

_____

Why?

_____

_____

_____

Step 6: Writing Your Paper or Speech

One Sunday morning, the congregation of a local church was surprised to find the following printed in their bulletins, *"Thursday at 5:00 pm, there will be a meeting of the Little Mother's Club. Anyone wishing to become a little mother should meet the minister in his study."* A letter to the San Antonio Veterans' Administration read, *"I am annoyed to find out that you have branded my child as illiterate. It is a dirty, rotten lie. I married his father one week before he was born."* And finally, a sign hanging in a hotel in Mexico reads, *"We are pleased to announce that the manager has personally passed all of the water served here."*

At some point in time, we have all made written or verbal blunders that caused us embarrassment or that even hurt someone. The power of

T

he two most engaging powers of an author are to make new things familiar, and familiar things new.

—JOHNSON

words, as mentioned earlier, is phenomenal. They make us laugh and cry, feel pain and joy, understand and react. When writing your papers and speeches, it is important to remember that you have the power of words at your side. They can be used for good or bad, strengthening or weakening, building or tearing down, love or hatred. The choice is always up to you.

ETHICAL CONSIDERATIONS

As a writer and speaker, you have a personal responsibility to consider the ethics and consequences of your statements.

Gamble and Gamble, in their book *Public Speaking in the Age of Diversity* (1998) suggest that you follow these guidelines when considering the ethical dimensions of writing and speaking:

- Share only what you know to be true.
- Be fully prepared and informed.
- Consider the best interest of your receivers.
- Make it easy for your receivers to understand your message.
- Refrain from using words as weapons.
- Don't wrap information in a positive spin just to succeed.
- Respect the cultural diversity of your receivers.
- Remember: You are accountable for what you say.

USING LANGUAGE

As you begin to write your paper or speech, there are several factors that will assist you in building colorful, meaningful, and memorable work. When writing, consider the following:

- Use colorful, vivid language to evoke images and word pictures.
  Example: Instead of telling the reader or listener about a dog, tell about the six-week-old, black, playful Labrador Retriever. This helps your reader or listener "see" rather than imagine.

- Use unbiased, nonsexist, nonracist, nonageist language.
  Example: Instead of writing or saying, "Everyone should bring his lab kit to class tomorrow," the proper language would be, "Everyone should bring his or her lab kit to class tomorrow."

- Use simple, nontechnical, familiar, layperson terminology (the language should suit the audience).
  Example: Instead of writing or speaking about the absence of monocholorodifloromethane, simply say that the air conditioner was out of Freon. Your audience will appreciate it; so will your spellchecker.

- Use concrete language.
  Example: Instead of saying, "She drove a very expensive car," say, "She drove a Lexus." Instead of saying, "The building was crummy," say, "The building's foundation was crumbling, the walls were dirty, and the roof was in need of repair."

- Use similes and metaphors to enhance your language.
  Example: A simile compares by using the words, "as" or "like": *"Life is like a box of chocolates."* A metaphor uses implied comparisons: *"The winter of our discontent."*

Thoughts

■ Use repetition for understanding and memory.

Example: If you introduce an idea in the introduction, explain it in detail in the body and repeat it in the conclusion. Remember the old public speaking formula: "Tell 'em what you're gonna tell 'em. Tell 'em what you've gotta tell 'em. Then tell 'em what you've told 'em."

■ Use parallelism for balance.

Example: If you open by telling a story about the abuses suffered by Martha and her child, you can mention them in the body and end the story in the conclusion. Martin Luther King, Jr., used parallelism in his "I Have a Dream" speech by repeating throughout the speech, "I have a dream . . ."

SELECTING THE MAIN IDEAS AND ISSUES

At this point, you have carefully selected and narrowed your topic. You have taken a careful look at your audience; you have decided on the basic needs you plan to address; you have written a comprehensive thesis; and you have collected your research. Upon reviewing your research, you have decided on an organizational pattern, and finally, you have examined some interesting and creative ways to add variety and color to your paper or speech. Now, based on your research, you are ready to decide on the main issues and major details that you plan to share with your readers or audience.

The main issues are going to be derived from your research and your thesis statement. Main issues are the major divisions of your paper or speech. David Zarefsky, in his book *Public Speaking: Strategies for Success* (1996), suggests that you can identify main ideas and issues by asking the following questions:

■ What does it mean?
■ What are the facts?
■ What are the reasons?
■ How often does it occur?
■ What is my view?
■ What are the parts?
■ What is the reasoning?

■ What is the cause?
■ How will it happen?
■ Who is involved?
■ What are some examples?
■ What are some objections?
■ What is the effect?
■ What is preventing it?

ORGANIZING THE BODY

One of the most effective ways to begin composing your paper or speech is to create a rough outline of the points you would like to cover. As you begin to outline, remember that your organizational pattern should guide you through this phase. The following is an example of a generic outline:

I. **Point 1 or Major Issue 1**

    a. Who, what, when, where, and why?

Types of   b. Statistics, polls, results

Evidence   c. Personal testimonials, case studies

    d. Causes

    e. Problems and solutions

II. **Point 2 or Major Issue 2**

    a. Who, what, when, where, and why?

Types of   b. Statistics, polls, results

Evidence   c. Personal testimonials, case studies

    d. Causes

    e. Problems and solutions

III. **Point 3 or Major Issue 3**

    a. Who, what, when, where, and why?

Types of   b. Statistics, polls, results

Evidence   c. Personal testimonials, case studies

    d. Causes

    e. Problems and solutions

Once you have developed your outline, you can begin to write your paper or speech. Using the topic you selected earlier, organize the body of your paper or speech by completing an outline of your resources. Use a separate sheet of paper for this exercise.

INTRODUCTIONS

Throughout the day, you are bombarded with ideas, messages, and ads begging for your attention. How do you decide on the messages to which you will direct your attention? Is it the low-key, dull message or idea that grabs you? Is it the idea or message that you have heard countless times? No, it is the message that is vibrant, new, creative, and alive that catches your attention and holds you long enough to hear the information. You are now at the point where you will need to consider the introduction and conclusion to your paper or speech.

The introduction to your work will, in a very large part, determine how the reader or audience perceives you and your work, and it will determine if you are going to obtain and maintain their interest. While the introduction is a very small part of your overall piece, it should never be taken lightly. Oprah Winfrey, noted talk-show hostess and actress, profiles a new book each month on her show. She has said that the first line of the book is the most important to her. If the first line does not grab her or sell her, it is hard for her to be drawn into the message. She gives the example of Toni Morrison's book *Paradise*. The opening line reads, "They

Thoughts

shoot the white girl first." Winfrey said that she was lured in by that line. The very same rule can be applied to papers and speeches. It is the first few lines that will lure your audience to your message or turn them to thoughts of last night's supper.

An introduction serves multiple purposes:

- To gain the attention and interest of the reader or audience
- To indicate the direction of the speech or paper
- To prepare the reader or audience for the thoughts to come
- To establish your credibility and the relevance of your topic
- To reveal the subject matter of the paper or speech
- To build suspense and arouse curiosity

As you study the techniques of introducing that are detailed below, think about the topic you chose earlier. Determine which technique would best suit your individual writing and/or delivery style, which would most greatly appeal to your audience, and which technique you feel would best gain their attention. Introductions are not necessarily written first. Many writers and speakers write their introduction last. Keep this in mind as you begin to compose. Below, you will find a variety of techniques used to create effective introductions:

- Telling a story or creating a vivid, visual illustration
- Using startling facts or statistics
- Referring to an incident with which the audience or reader is familiar
- Asking rhetorical, yet pertinent questions
- Using novel ideas or striking statements
- Using quotations
- Using humor or humorous stories

The following is an example of an introduction using the technique of telling a story. Note the thesis statement at the end of the introduction:

It was a normal Friday, just like every other Friday for the past ten years. Jane had gone to the grocery store, driven home, pulled into her driveway, and had started unloading the groceries from the car. Just as she opened the trunk, she heard a loud scream from inside the house. She threw the groceries back into the trunk and ran toward the house. The front door was slightly ajar. As she entered the front door, her greatest horror was realized. Her 6-year-old son Jeff was sitting in the middle of the floor with blood on the front of his shirt. He was holding his left arm, crying and screaming. Immediately, Jane thought, "Did he fall out of that treehouse again?" "Did he have another accident on his bicycle?" The answer came when she saw her husband coming down the hall with a Ping Pong paddle in his hand and blood on his shirt—drinking again.

What Jane began to realize at this moment was that two years ago when Jeff had a broken arm, he had not fallen out of the treehouse, and last month, when he suffered two cracked ribs, he had not fallen off his bicycle. What she began to realize was that Jeff was suffering from the same thing that she had suffered from for nine years—domestic abuse.

(Thesis or Purpose Statement) This paper will inform you about (or . . . Today, I am going to speak to you about) the causes, effects, and signs of domestic abuse. I will also provide information that will help you gain assistance if you are involved in an abusive relationship or know someone who is.

In the space provided below, choose one technique, or a combination of the techniques we've discussed, to construct an introduction to your topic.

Technique(s) used

_____

_____

Introduction

_____

_____

_____

_____

_____

CONCLUSIONS

Without exception, the conclusion should be one of the most carefully crafted components of your paper or speech. Long after your reader has finished reading or your audience has finished listening, the last part of your work is more than likely going to be the part they remember the most. Some writers and speakers suggest that you write your conclusion *first,* so that your paper or speech is directed toward a specific end result. That decision, of course, is up to you. However, a great piece of advice from writing experts tells us that captivating writers always know how their stories will end long before they begin writing them.

If you have ever read a poor ending or heard a speaker try to deliver an unprepared conclusion, then you know the importance of a well-crafted closing. Don't make the mistake of telling your readers or audience that you are concluding your paper or remarks and then carry on for seven more pages or ten more minutes. A conclusion should be brief, powerful, creative, and memorable. It should refocus attention, reenergize audience members, and redirect the audience toward the desired goals.

The following are some techniques for concluding a paper or speech:

- Summarize and re-emphasize the main points.
- Make a final appeal for action or challenge.
- Refer to the introduction (story, quote, or joke); this is parallelism.

- Complete the opening story.
- Re-emphasize the impact of your topic.
- Use a vivid analogy or simile.

The following is an example of a conclusion using the technique of referring to the introduction (parallelism) and making an appeal for action.

> Jane had denied the abusive situation for so long that she could not see how it was affecting her son. Just as the men and women profiled in this speech (paper) feared retaliation and more violence by leaving the relationship, we saw that there were a variety of resources available for assistance such as the Women's Program for Abuse, Sister Care, Americans for an Abuse Free Nation, and local police departments. I call on you today, if you are in an abusive relationship or know someone who is, to act deliberately and immediately. Tomorrow may be one day too late.

In the space provided below and using your topic from the beginning of the chapter, write a memorable, creative conclusion.

Technique(s) used

_____

_____

Conclusion

_____

_____

_____

_____

_____

_____

Step 7: Documenting Your Paper or Speech

When writing your paper or speech, and certainly once it has been written, you should take careful precautions to document all research and infor-

The telling of a falsehood is like the cut of a knife; though the wound may heal, the scar of it will remain.

—*SAADI*

mation that is not your own. If you have written a paper, you will need to document and cite all statistics, quotes, and excerpts from works that you referenced. The most common means of doing this is by quoting within the paper and then compiling a reference or bibliography sheet at the end. If you have written a speech, you can verbally document researched facts, statistics, quotes, and excerpts. The following is an example of verbal documentation:

> Jane and her son Jeff are not alone in their abusive situation. According to Ronald Cohen in his book *Psychology and Adjustment,* over 1.5 million cases of abuse occur in the United States every year.

This allows the listener to focus on the research and lets them know where the facts, statistics, or excerpts came from.

When writers or speakers fail to give credit where credit is due, this is called plagiarism. "Plagiarism is presenting another person's words or ideas as if they are your own. By not acknowledging a source, you mislead readers into thinking that the material you are presenting is yours, when, in fact, it is the result of someone else's time and effort" (Kirszner & Mandell, 1995). The previous statement was taken from another book; thus, it is cited as not being an original passage written for *Cornerstone.*

According to Kirszner and Mandell, there are four types of unintentional plagiarism:

- Borrowed words not enclosed in quotation marks
- Paraphrasing too close to its source
- Statistics not attributed to a source
- Writer's words and ideas not differentiated from those in the source

Although the above words are borrowed and not in quotation marks, they are cited in the preceding sentence. Therefore, the reader knows that the list was not written by *Cornerstone* authors.

Kirszner and Mandell have also compiled a list of "What to Document":

- Direct quotations
- Opinions, judgments, and insights of others that you summarize or paraphrase
- Information that is not widely known
- Information that is open to dispute
- Information that is not commonly accepted
- Tables, charts, graphs, and statistics taken from a source

There are several popular documentation styles used today. They include, but are not limited to: *The Modern Language Association (MLA), The American Psychological Association (APA),* and *The Chicago Manual of Style (CMS).*

Using your topic, choose two of your research sources, choose a documentation style, and properly document them in the space below.

Style chosen: _____
_____

Source #1 _____
_____
_____

Source #2 _____
_____
_____

Step 8: Outlining Your Notes for Delivery

The techniques for outlining a speech are exclusive to delivery only. If you have used this chapter as a guideline for writing papers, this section and the last two sections on audiovisual aids and rehearsal will not be relevant to you at this time.

If you have ever watched and heard a disorganized speaker, or had to endure a speaker *read* an entire presentation, then you know the value of well-designed speaking notes.

After your speech has been formally written, it is time to outline your speaking notes. It is the mark of an unprofessional, unprepared

Speeches cannot be made long enough for the speakers, nor short enough for the hearers. —*PERRY*

speaker to read verbatim from pages and pages of typed notes. Instead, with rehearsal and a comprehensive keyword outline, you can use surprisingly few notes.

An outline should be used to keep you organized and to assist you should you get lost or blank out during your presentation. It should not be used for reading your speech to the audience. Some speakers prefer to use note cards (3 x 5 or 5 x 7) while others prefer to use several sheets of paper in outline form. The choice is yours unless specified otherwise by your professor.

When outlining, you will want to choose the most important words, names, numbers, or dates to assist you in delivery. Don't waste space writing words like "a," "an," or "the" and don't use complete sentences. Again, these are written cues, not notes to be read verbatim. An example of a note card and a note outline are provided on the next page.

In the space provided below, outline the introduction that you wrote earlier in the chapter. Remember, use only key words. Do not write it out verbatim.

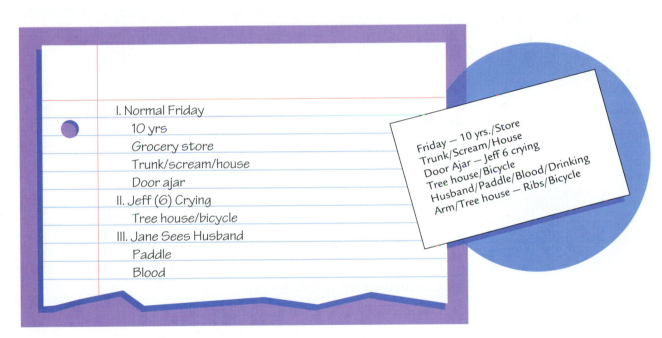

I. Normal Friday
   10 yrs
   Grocery store
   Trunk/scream/house
   Door ajar
II. Jeff (6) Crying
   Tree house/bicycle
III. Jane Sees Husband
   Paddle
   Blood

Friday — 10 yrs./Store
Trunk/Scream/House
Door Ajar — Jeff 6 crying
Tree house/Bicycle
Husband/Paddle/Blood/Drinking
Arm/Tree house — Ribs/Bicycle

Step 9: Using Audiovisual Aids

You have heard it said, "A picture is worth a thousand words." Nowhere is that more true than in public speaking. Visual aids can assist your audience in retaining the information for longer amounts of time. If you simply tell an audience a fact, three days later, they will remember only 10 percent of what you said. If you tell them and show them, three days later, they will remember 65 percent of what you said (Gamble and Gamble, 1998).

Several important factors should be considered when developing your visual aids. First, an audiovisual aid is a supplement to, not a substitute for, a presentation. Simply stated, even the most wonderfully creative visual aid will not support a poorly written and delivered speech. When choosing your aid, consider your audience, the location, and your time limits. You should also consider your comfort level with the aid that you have chosen. There are many types of aids available to you:

- Physical objects
- Models
- Drawings
- Maps
- Videotapes
- Audio recordings
- Real people

- Overhead transparencies
- Graphs, tables, and charts
- Photographs and slides
- Slick boards and chalkboards
- Yourself (probably the most important)
- Posters and flip charts
- Computer-generated presentations (such as PowerPoint slides) and CD-ROMs

Eighty percent of all information comes to us through sight. *—BEEBE AND BEEBE*

For a smooth, clean, polished presentation, consider the following guidelines when using your visual aids:

- *Always* rehearse with your audiovisual (AV) aids.
- Make sure your AV is visible to all audience members.
- Make sure all equipment works before you begin your speech.
- Bring any item that you might need to make your AV work (such as extension cords, tape, push pins, and magic markers).
- Reveal each AV when you are ready to use it, not all at once.
- Explain each AV as it is revealed.
- Do not pass any AV around the room.
- Remove the AV when you have finished using it.
- Use any living AV with caution.
- Don't speak to the AV; speak to your audience.
- Use handouts with extreme caution. They should be issued only at the very end of your speech.

Consider the information and research that you plan to share. What type of audiovisual aid would best suit you, your presentation, and your audience?

Type of AV _____

Why? _____

_____

Thoughts

Step 10: Rehearsal and Delivery

The time has come! All of your hard work, creativity, and energy will culminate in this one moment in the sun. You have taken all of the necessary steps for a successful presentation. Now, you only need to consider a few more details before taking the lectern.

Public speaking is an unfair beast. If you study for an exam and do well or fail to study and do poorly, the results are known only to you and the professor. However, the results of your public speaking performance are known to all present. You are evaluated immediately. That is just an accepted fact in the art of speaking. In order to do your very best, consider the following anxiety-reducing and delivery tips.

Speech is power: Speech is to persuade, to convert, to compel.

—RALPH WALDO EMERSON

REDUCING ANXIETY

We mentioned earlier in the chapter, the fear of public speaking is rated as the number one fear among Americans. According to Gamble and Gamble (1998), there are several reasons why we fear public speaking:

- Fear of failure
- Fear of the unknown
- Fear of evaluation
- Fear of being the center of attention
- Fear of difference
- Fear imposed by culture

These fears are real, but they are also manageable. When faced with anxiety over public speaking, keep the following tips in mind:

- A certain degree of anxiety is good for you. Use it to create energy.
- Choose a topic about which you know a great deal and one about which you care deeply.
- Prepare for your speech thoroughly!
- When rehearsing, try to re-create the speaking environment, or if possible, rehearse in the room where the speech will be delivered.
- Approach the speech with an "I can" attitude. The more confident you act, the more confident you will eventually become.
- After your first speech, jot down what happened to you physically; that is, did your heart beat faster, did you sweat, did your breathing become erratic? Keep a running tab of these reactions so that you can recognize them and begin to control them.

Thoughts ● ● ●

- Realize that your small mistakes will not be seen and will rarely be heard by the audience; they are magnified in your own mind.

- Remember that listeners want you to succeed; most audiences are supportive.

- Instead of looking at the entire audience as a "room full of people," choose one person and look at him or her for a brief moment. Then, move on to the next person, and so on. This creates the feeling of speaking to only one person at a time.

- Don't try to be something that you are not. Just be yourself, use your own voice, your own gestures, and your own style.

- Don't concentrate on the evaluation. If you have prepared and do your best, you will be evaluated fairly.

- Visualize your success; the power of positive thinking is vastly underrated.

REHEARSAL AND DELIVERY

The moment is close at hand. Your topic is sterling, you have all of the information that you need to succeed, and you have prepared and rehearsed. To achieve a polished and professional touch, keep these final tips in mind:

- Always practice aloud so that you can practice your volume, tone, pace, and articulation.

- Rehearse from beginning to end without stopping.

- Rehearse using minimal notes.

- Rehearse using a tape recorder so that you may evaluate your own performance.

- When rehearsing, use a timer so that you can adjust your speech accordingly.

- Never, ever, under any circumstances, apologize for your speech or presentation.

- Watch your nonverbal communication (body language, facial expressions, and gestures).

- Remove temptations to fidget with things such as keys, change in your pocket, pens, and clips.

- Always maintain eye contact with your audience.

- The occasion should dictate your dress, so dress for the occasion.

- Don't stand in front of an audience and read; know your topic and simply talk to them.

The steps outlined in this chapter will assist you in writing and delivering a paper and public speech. However, without a positive "I can" attitude, much of your preparation will be fruitless. Public speaking is an exciting, rewarding experience that will assist you in almost every endeavor of your collegiate and professional life. This is your moment in the sun—SHINE!

LIFE

Identify and list the emotions that you felt when you were given the assignment to write a major paper or speak in public.

1.

2.

3.

4.

Intelligence

How did these emotions help or hinder you and your writing or performance?

Emotion
1.

Emotion
2.

Emotion
3.

Emotion
4.

How do you plan to address these emotions the next time you are asked to write a paper or speak in public?

Emotion
1.

Emotion
2.

Emotion
3.

Emotion
4.

Self-Esteem

What are the ethical consequences of your paper or presentation?

What steps will you take to avoid plagiarism?

1.

2.

3.

4.

The One Minute Journal

In one minute or less, jot down the major ideas that you learned from this chapter.

_____
_____
_____
_____
_____
_____
_____
_____
_____
_____
_____
_____

THE COMPANION Website Journal

Log on to **www.prenhall.com/montgomery**, choose the version of this book you are using, and then choose Chapter 10 on the menu. Next, choose "Links" on the left side of the page. Explore one of the websites offered and summarize your findings.

_____
_____
_____
_____
_____
_____
_____
_____
_____
_____
_____
_____

Refer to page 244 of Chapter 10.
Review your **GOALS FOR CHANGE**.
Respond in writing as to the progress
you have made toward reaching one
of your three stated goals.

GOAL STATEMENT

PROGRESS

How is your life changing because of this goal?

CORNERSTONES

for research, writing, & speaking

Develop a *comprehensive* thesis statement.

Always rehearse *aloud*. Rehearse *often*.

Use a *logical* organizational pattern.

Use a *variety* of research sources.

Always document your research.

"This is your moment in the *sun!*"

Develop an *"I can"* attitude.

Speak on what you *know*.

Use a *keyword* outline.

Analyze the audience.

Use *credible* research.

Use *vivid* language.

Friendship is the only cement that will ever hold the world

Understand.

together.   Woodrow Wilson

CHAPTER 11

Understand

I n the year 1800, one of the most fascinating cases of human identity and social relationships came to light. Early one morning, a man working in his vegetable garden in Aveyron, France, heard something making a sound. He looked for the origin of the sound and found a boy. This "wild" boy "showed no signs of behaviors one would expect in a social human" (Adler, 1989). *Apparently, he had spent his early childhood without any human contact.*

The boy could not speak a single word, *but uttered only cries and moans as one would expect from an animal.* Ronald Adler (1989) suggests that more significant than his lack of social skills was his total lack of identity as a social human. *"He had no sense of being in the world. He had no sense of himself as a*

> **The boy could not speak a single word, but uttered only cries and moans as one would expect from an animal.**

person related to other persons." Only after years of contact with a "mother" did the wild boy of Aveyron begin to behave as a human being.

This true story, referenced in the 1995 movie *Nell,* is important to us today because *it proves that we learn who and what we are from our relationships with other people. It is only through contact with other humans that we know we are human.* Alder says that we gain an idea of who we are from the way others define us. Our development as human beings in a social world continues throughout our lives.

Everyone has the power for greatness,
not fame, but greatness because greatness is determined by service.
—*MARTIN LUTHER KING, JR.*

at this moment?

STATEMENT	SCORE	Strongly Disagree	Disagree	Don't Know	Agree	Strongly Agree
1. I rarely have problems with relationships.		1	2	3	4	5
2. I understand how to be a good friend.		1	2	3	4	5
3. I know what effect drugs have on my body.		1	2	3	4	5
4. I recognize the signs of drug abuse.		1	2	3	4	5
5. I understand the importance of communication in relationships.		1	2	3	4	5
TOTAL		0-5	6-10	11-15	16-20	21-25

FEEDBACK

0 – 5   Extensive changes need to occur to ensure success.

6 – 10   Substantial changes need to occur to ensure success.

11 – 15   Considerable changes need to occur to ensure success.

16 – 20   Moderate changes need to occur to ensure success.

21 – 25   Minor changes need to occur to ensure success.

GOALS FOR CHANGE

Based on this feedback, my goals and objectives for change are . . .

Goal Statement _____

Action Steps 1. _____

2. _____

Goal Statement _____

Action Steps 1. _____

2. _____

Goal Statement _____

Action Steps 1. _____

2. _____

Results

Reading this chapter, completing the exercises, and reflecting on relationships and personal responsibility will result in your:

- Understanding the importance of relationships.

- Discussing the importance of friendships.

- Differentiating among the different stages of relationships.

- Identifying the major legal and illegal drugs.

- Developing a healthy approach to relationships.

- Discussing the qualities of a true friend.

- Understanding more about your own sexuality.

- Discussing sexually transmitted diseases.

Relationships

Life is about relationships. Relationships between people, between people and nature, and between people and the environment. The statement "No man is an island" is true. You would literally have to be shipwrecked on an island to be free of relationships with other humans, but you would still have relationships with nature, the animals, birds, and reptiles on the island. People do not live in a vacuum. We are the sum total of all of our relationships.

You are entering a new time in your life; you may be starting college for the first time, returning to college after taking some time off, or transferring from one institution to another. Whatever the circumstances, you are in a state of transition. The relationships in which you have been involved are going to change. If you are a parent going to school, your relationship with your children will change because of your school commitments. If you are a first-year student who left home to go to college, your relationships with your parents, family, and friends at home will change. If you are still living in your community, perhaps even living at home while attending college, your relationships also will change because of college. As we noted in Chapter 1, your involvement in higher education will provoke some of the most significant changes you will experience in your life. This idea may be exciting or scary to you, but knowing how to deal with the changes in old relationships and how to build new relationships will be essential to your success in college.

Why Are Relationships Important?

To function in a happy and healthy manner, human beings need one another. Everything we learn in this life comes through and from our relationships with others. As illustrated by the story about the wild boy from Aveyron, the very essence of our humanness depends on our interaction with other humans. We need each other to help us laugh, help us cry, help us work, help us provide for the survival of the species, and help us die when the time comes.

Insider's View

Before graduating from high school, I remember being told how difficult college was going to be. Teachers, counselors, and my parents said so. It kept boiling down to one thing: in college, you are on your own!

I remember my first day on campus thinking that everyone had been right. Registration took place in this huge auditorium full of people running in every direction. I did not know anybody. All that I knew was that by the end of the day, I needed to have found five classes if I wanted to keep my scholarship. I went from table to table being told time after time that classes were full. By the end of the day, I did have five classes, but as it turned out, only two of them counted toward my degree. I know that this sounds crazy, but it was exactly as I had been told: "In college, you have to work out your own problems."

By the end of the first semester, I got to know people, and being on a soccer scholarship, I ended up with a built-in circle of friends. When registration time came around, I noted that many of my teammates were meeting with advisors. I did not know that I even had an advisor, so, I went to the Advisement Center and lucked out. I still work with that advisor today.

What does this have to do with social responsibility? Well, that advisor helped me choose classes that would count toward my degree. He offered advice that helped me be a better student and, as corny as it sounds, knowing an actual employee of the university made such a difference to me. Finally, there was someone who smiled at me and said hello when we met in the hall. This made me less nervous about a lot of things. He actually remembered my name. Finally, the university had a face and it was no longer a bureaucratic machine.

What all of this means to me is that I have someone on campus to whom I can turn when things get rough. I don't have to run from problems, I don't have to struggle on my own, and I don't have to make uninformed decisions. I have someone who can help me. My advice to you would be to seek out one or two people at your college and get to know them so that when difficult times or questions arise, you will have someone to turn to. You don't have to turn to drugs or alcohol if you get frightened. Basically, I think that in some sense, you are "on your own" in college only if you choose to be.

Arnoldo Gonzalez, age 23
Major: Secondary Education/Spanish
Northeastern Illinois University,
Chicago, Illinois

Throughout our lives we experience a myriad of relationships. We are someone's son or daughter, we may be someone's brother or sister, we probably will be someone's friend and someone's lover, as well as someone's helpmate through life. Each of these relationships has its own individual dynamics, but all successful relationships have some similarities.

In a recent focus group of college students at the University of South Carolina, participants were asked, "What is the most important component of any relationship?" What do you think the answer was? Overwhelmingly, the group agreed that honesty was the most important component in any relationship. Loyalty, which is closely related to honesty, ranked second.

Do you agree with this focus group's emphasis on honesty? Why or why not?

_____

_____

_____

College offers many opportunities for developing relationships with people from backgrounds different than your own.

Communities

Most, if not all, of our relationships take place within a community. Carolyn Shaffer and Kristin Amundsen, in their book *Creating Community Anywhere* (1994), define a community as a dynamic whole that emerges when a group of people:

- Participate in common practices.
- Depend on one another.
- Make decisions together.
- Identify themselves as part of something larger than the sum of their individual relationships.
- Commit themselves for the long term to their own, to one another's, and to the group's well-being.

You may find yourself involved in several separate communities: a home community, a school community, a work community. There is nothing wrong with this; to the contrary, it can be rewarding. You may also find that your communities overlap at times, adding more balance to your life.

What is your current community like? Your community has most likely changed recently because of your entry into higher education. In the past, your community may have been dictated by your physical surroundings, your parents and extended family, or the school you attended. Now you have many more choices in how your community looks and feels and you also have more say about who will be a part of your community.

One of the most important aspects of my profession is that of relationships with other people. I think that relationships can be viewed in two ways, internally and externally. In my agency, we have a very collegial office where we work well together. I think that this is very important for the success of the office and the success of our clients.

Externally, relationships are just as important. If you are in a very unproductive or adversarial relationship with another lawyer or agency, this would be counterproductive to your client. Because of the poor relationship, you, your agency, or your client may suffer.

One of the things that I learned in college was the importance of positive relationships and developing communication and interpersonal skills. The interpersonal skills that I learned have helped me advance in my career. I learned early that If you can't get along with people, you're going to have a very hard time in this world.

In the office of the Assistant Attorney General, it would be very hard to learn from other people or share ideas with other people if we did not have relationships that promote open, honest communication and interpersonal skills. I think that we must learn to be open to others. Externally, if you have good interpersonal skills and know how to communicate, you may be able to work out a problem for your client much more easily than if you did not possess these skills. If you're a jerk, it may be harder to get things done.

Lucinda Moyano, JD, *Assistant Attorney General*   The State of Oregon, Salem, Oregon

---

Describe what you think your ideal community (while you're in school) would look like.

_____

_____

_____

_____

_____

Friendship

It has been said that a very lucky person has three to four good friends at any given time in his or her life. True friends are hard to find, and even harder to keep! Many of us approach friendship as if it just happens, and, in some cases, it does. Think about your best friend. How did you meet? Probably by chance. Fate placed you together. Unfortunately, fate can also cause you to drift apart.

List the qualities you look for in a friend.

_____

_____

_____

_____

_____

_____

Discuss whether you possess any, some, or all of these characteristics.

_____

_____

_____

_____

_____

_____

You can probably tell by looking at these lists that being a good friend takes work. Remember, to have a good friend you need first to be a good friend.

PEER PRESSURE AND DRUG USE

Friendships in college sometimes take on dimensions that you may not have experienced in previous relationships. Your new friends may be roommates, classmates, sorority sisters, or fraternity brothers. They may have backgrounds very different from yours. In your new environment you are likely to encounter all kinds of new situations.

In college you may very well encounter people and behaviors that were not previously a part of your social group. Some of these behaviors may include indiscriminate alcohol and drug abuse. According to the book *Understanding*, "74 million, or 35% of Americans age 12 and older, reported use of an illicit drug at least once in their lifetime" (Werner, 1999). Although drug use was most certainly an issue in your high school, it may not have been as accessible or as acceptable as many of you might find in your new situations.

Finding friendships with new people may require stepping out of your comfort zone.

In the following charts we have detailed the most common legal and illegal drugs you are likely to encounter during college.

Legal Drugs

NAME	USE	SOURCES	NEGATIVE EFFECTS	
Caffeine	Alertness Pleasure Energy Reduce fatigue	Coffee Tea Chocolate Some soft drinks Medications	A stimulant Increased anxiety Highly addictive Increased urination	Irregular heartbeat Indigestion
Alcohol	Relaxation Mood enhancer Overcome depression Overcome shyness Social acceptance Relieve tension Celebrate Bonding	Beer Wine Liquor Medications Some foods	Liver disease Memory loss Blackouts False euphoria Depression Hangovers	Birth defects Loss of balance Mental impairment Increased suicide rate Death

Tobacco	Stimulant
	Relaxation
	Social acceptance
	To curb appetite
	Alertness
		Cigarettes
		Cigars
		Pipes
		Snuff
		Chewing tobacco
			Highly addictive
			Increased heart and
			  respiratory rate
			Increased blood pressure
			Decreased taste
			  sensations
			Increased risk of cancer
				Decreased hunger
				Lung disease
				Gum disease
				Birth defects
				Strokes
				Cardiovascular disease

Over-the-Counter Drugs	Weight loss Alertness Sleeping Body building Depression Pain relief	Laxatives Diet medications Sleep enhancers Stimulants Herbal medications Nasal sprays Cough medications Pain relievers	Addiction Organ damage Nausea Vomiting Reduced absorption of vitamins and minerals Liver damage	
Prescription Drugs	Weight loss Alertness Sleeping Depression Pain relief Mood enhancers Muscle relaxers	Found in many forms prescribed by medical professionals from every area of medical science	Addiction Impaired judgment Loss of memory Weight loss/gain Blackouts Death	

Commonly Abused Drugs

From the National Institute of Drug Abuse

SUBSTANCE	STREET NAME	ADMINISTRATION	PERIOD OF DETECTION
Amphetamine	Black Beauties, Crosses, Hearts	Injected, oral, smoked, sniffed	1–2 days
Cocaine	Coke, Crack, Flake, Rocks, Snow	Injected, smoked, sniffed	1–4 days
Methamphetamine	Crank, Crystal, Glass, Ice, Speed	Injected, oral, smoked, sniffed	1–2 days
Nicotine	Cigars, Cigarettes, Smokeless Tobacco, Snuff, Spit Tobacco	Smoked, sniffed, oral, transdermal	1–2 days
LSD	Acid, Microdot	Oral	8 hours
Phencyclidine & Analogs	PCP, Angel Dust, Boat, Hog, Love Boat	Injected, oral, smoked	2–8 days
Psilocybin	Magic Mushroom, Purple Passion, Shrooms	Oral	8 hours
Amphetamine Variants	Adam, Ecstasy, STP	Oral	1–2 days
Marijuana	Blunt, Grass, Herb, Pot, Reefer, Sinsemilla, Smoke, Weed, Mary Jane	Oral, smoked	1 day–5 weeks
Hashish	Hash	Oral, smoked	1 day–5 weeks
Anabolic Steroids	Testosterone, Nandrolene	Oral, injected	Oral up to 3 weeks Injected up to 3 mo. Nandrolene up to 9 mo.
Heroin	Horse, Smack	Injected, smoked, sniffed	1–2 days
Opium	Dover's Powder	Oral, smoked	1–2 days
Alcohol	Beer, Wine, Liquor	Oral	6–10 hours
Barbiturates	Barbs	Injected, oral	2–10 days
Methaqualone	Quaalude, Ludes	Oral	2 weeks

Loneliness

Developing friends helps you to develop your sense of community and allows you to minimize the feelings of loneliness that so many college students experience. Having friends does not mean that you will not be lonely,

The worst solitude is to be destitute of sincere friendship. —FRANCIS BACON

but friends can help you to deal with loneliness. Loneliness is especially common among first-year college students. Here are some suggestions for how to get through the periods of loneliness you may experience:

1. Join a campus club or activity that involves one of your hobbies or interests.
2. Go to the new-student mixers that most colleges sponsor.
3. Volunteer in one of the organizations sponsored by your department or school, or get a part-time job in the field you are studying.
4. Ask one of your classmates to be a study partner. You could suggest meeting after each class to discuss the day's lecture, readings, and activities.
5. Offer to serve on one of your residence hall's committees.

If these activities don't seem to work for you, if your feelings of loneliness are intensifying and causing you to feel depressed, consider making an appointment with one of the counselors on campus. You can check the campus directory for names and numbers or ask the student health center to direct you to the appropriate person. These feelings are normal; the key is not to stay in this state of loneliness, but to be proactive and deal with the situation. Counselors are trained to help students do just that.

Love Relationships

There are many types and degrees of love relationships. The love between two old friends differs tremendously from the passion of two lovers. Love can be as relaxing and comfortable as an easy chair or as tumultuous and

Love is patient, love is kind. It does not envy, it does not boast, it is not proud. It is not rude, it is not self-seeking, it is not easily angered, it keeps no record of wrongs. Love does not delight in evil but rejoices with the truth. It always protects, always trusts, always hopes, and always perseveres. —1 CORINTHIANS 13:4-7

exhilarating as any rollercoaster ride. The way love is manifested in a relationship does not necessarily attest to the degree or intensity of the love.

For example, Charles and Harriet have been married 63 years. On the surface their relationship resembles that of the odd couple; they bicker and disagree about everything from religion to politics. Yet, if you were to take a closer look at the relationship, you would notice the way Charles' eyes follow Harriet whenever she is in the same room with him, and the way Harriet never passes within arm's reach of Charles without lightly brushing him. Asked about their lives together, they share that they have managed to stay together for so long because they have allowed their love to change, and as their love has changed over the years, they have not felt challenged or threatened or less loved. They accepted the fact that as they changed individually, they also needed to change as a couple.

Regardless of the kind of love relationship we are in, we need to allow that relationship to change. Change is the only constant in our world and therefore the only constant in love.

Most of you have experienced love in a relationship. Some of you have felt the strong love of a close friendship; others have experienced the dizzy exhilaration of first love; still others may have experienced the deep love that comes only after spending a great deal of time with a partner. You may have experienced many of the peaks and valleys associated with marriage. Or you may have had a very close and loving relationship with parents or siblings. All the love relationships you have experienced or hope to experience have a few things in common. Loving someone means caring about that person's happiness, trying to understand and to be understood by that person, and giving as well as receiving emotional support. Most love relationships involve intimacy to some degree. Intimacy is not synonymous with sex; it may or may not involve sexual relations. Intimacy refers to the emotional openness that usually develops over time between two people who love each other. Intimacy allows people to share hopes and dreams as well as pain and sorrows.

Some of you will meet and fall in love with your lifelong partner in college, and the ritual you will most likely use to become acquainted is dating. Keep the following tips in mind when you begin dating a person:

- Don't go out alone with a stranger; go out in a group until you are better acquainted with your date.

- Make sure someone knows with whom you are going out, where you are going, and the approximate time you'll return; call that person if your plans change.

- Have your own transportation, so that you can leave if you are uncomfortable.

- Don't go to someone's home unless you know that person very well.

- Establish a friendship before you try a relationship.

Sexuality

Today you are faced with a profusion of questions concerning human sexuality. In this section we will discuss sexual behavior, sexual harassment, rape, sexually transmitted diseases, and birth control. These discussions will lay a foundation from which you can make your own decisions regarding sexual activity. An important component of responsible decision making is your own feelings. No one can tell you what or how to feel. No one can make decisions about sexual activity for you. You have to make them yourself. In a world that is becoming more and more sexually permissive, it's still okay to say no to something that makes you uncomfortable. It's still okay to be a virgin. Your sexual behavior is not dictated by societal beliefs, preferences of your family and friends, or what the media present as normal sexual behavior. It is governed by your own heartfelt beliefs and attitudes.

Sexual Behavior

When a relationship is based on romantic interest, sexual activity generally becomes an issue (sexual activity can be an issue when romance is not involved, also). The degree of sexual activity within a relationship spans the spectrum from total abstinence to intercourse. You may face situations in college that require you to make decisions about your sexual behavior. It is important to evaluate where you stand on this important issue so that when you are in a situation, your course of action will be based on a solid understanding of what you believe and how you feel. You want to avoid having a situation or set of circumstances dictate your actions. Making good decisions about your sexual behavior is critical not only to your college career but also to your life.

Students in a focus group at the University of South Carolina cited increasing awareness of sexually transmitted diseases (STDs) and AIDS as well as a sense of spirituality or adherence to religious beliefs as reasons for abstaining from intercourse. However, according to recent studies, some degree of sexual activity is almost universal among college students (Rathus, Nevid, and Fichner-Rathus, 1998). The form of sexual activity varies. Some students who want to abstain from sexual intercourse masturbate. Once associated with a terrible stigma and myths connecting it to blindness, sterility, and mental disease, masturbation is now considered a normal response to normal sexual urges. Other college students who choose to abstain from intercourse use petting (touching or massaging another's genitals) as a means of obtaining sexual pleasure without engaging in intercourse. Some people consider oral-genital manipulation a form of petting.

Thoughts

Although many students abstain from sexual intercourse, a large percentage of college students do engage in intercourse. If you are one of the many who are currently engaging in sexual intercourse or are planning to do so, you will need to be responsible for your own protection from unwanted pregnancy and sexually transmitted diseases. Don't assume that your partner will be prepared—that assumption could be dangerous. The most common methods of birth control are presented in the chart on the following page. For more information on birth control, contact your health center, a family practitioner, or a gynecologist.

Healthy relationships offer the opportunity for sharing, companionship, conversation, and different levels of intimacy.

Sexually Transmitted Diseases

Sexually transmitted diseases (STDs) are diseases that are generally transmitted through vaginal or anal intercourse or oral sex. Although they are most commonly spread through sexual contact, some can be transmitted through related nonsexual activities. (For example, human immunodeficiency virus, HIV, can be contracted by using contaminated needles and crabs can be contracted through contact with contaminated bed linens or towels.)

It is estimated that one in every four Americans will contract an STD during his or her lifetime. The majority of these cases occur in people under the age of 25. Seven common STDs are described in the chart that begins on page 293.

NEW WORRIES ABOUT HIV AND AIDS TRANSMISSION

There is good news and bad news. The good news, actually great news, is that there have been tremendous strides in the treatment of HIV and AIDS. In the past several years, a new generation of drugs called *protease inhibitors* have had a remarkable effect. They block reproduction of the HIV particles (Rathus, Nevid, and Fichner-Rathus, 1998). Used in connection with AZT and 3TC, these inhibitors have reduced HIV to below detectable levels in many people. Bruce Shenitz writing for *The Advocate* states that "the National Center for Health Statistics at the federal Centers for Disease Control and Prevention reported in October (1998) that HIV-related deaths fell 47% from 1996 to 1997" (January 19, 1999).

This is the great news. *However,* the cocktail is not a cure. One of the most dangerous aspects of the new protease inhibitors is that people begin to think that HIV and AIDS are cured and that there is no longer a need to think about safe sex. **Nothing could be further from the truth.**

Birth Control

TYPE	USAGE	PREVENTION OF STDs		
		Yes*	No	Not necessarily
Abstinence	Abstention from *ALL sexual activity,* vaginal, anal, and oral. One hundred percent effective.	X		
Outercourse	Oral genital sex and mutual masturbation.			X
The Pill	Also called oral contraceptive. The most widely used form of birth control.		X	
The Male Pill	Also called oral contraceptive. Newly developed for male usage.		X	
Diaphragm	Round, flexible disk inserted into the vagina to cover the cervix.			X
IUD	Also called intrauterine device. Must be inserted into the uterus by a physician.		X	
Male Condom	A sheath, generally latex, worn over the penis to prevent sperm from entering the vagina.	X		
Female Condom	A loose-fitting sheath inserted into the vagina to prevent sperm from entering the uterus.	X		
Spermicides	Inserted into the vagina to kill sperm. Comes in foams, jellies, suppositories, and creams.		X	
Withdrawal	Also called coitus interruptus. The penis is withdrawn from the vagina before ejaculation.		X	
Rhythm Method	Abstaining from sexual intercourse during the menstrual cycle when ovulation occurs.		X	
Norplant	Silicone tubes surgically embedded in a woman's upper arm to suppress fertilization.		X	
Sterilization	Male and female surgery. Male version is called vasectomy, and female versions are called tubal sterilization, tubal ligation, and hysterectomy.		X	
Cervical Cap	Much like the diaphragm, it is fitted into the vagina by a doctor. It is meant to be used with a spermicide and can provide up to 48 hours of protection.		X	
Vaginal Ring	Rings 2–3 inches in diameter and placed by a woman in the vagina to prevent ovulation. They may be left in place continually or removed every three weeks for regular menstruation. Still in developmental stages.		X	

Only total abstinence is 100% effective in preventing sexually transmitted diseases.

Seven Sexually Transmitted Diseases

STD	TRANSMISSION	SYMPTOMS	DIAGNOSIS	CONSEQUENCES
AIDS/HIV	Sexual contact (vaginal, oral, and anal) Infusion with contaminated blood (sharing needles, etc.) From mother to fetus Breast feeding	People may go years without symptoms. When symptoms appear they may include flu-like symptoms, fever, weight loss, fatigue, diarrhea, and cancer.	Bodily fluids such as blood, urine, or saliva reveal HIV antibodies. Two tests include the Western Blot and the ELISA.	Transmission to sexual partners Rapid progression if undiagnosed or untreated Cancer Pneumonia Death
CHLAMYDIA	Sexual contact (vaginal, oral, and anal) By touching one's eye after touching infected genitals From mother to child	Women: Sometimes no symptoms; painful urination, occasional vaginal discharge, bleeding between periods Men: Discharge from penis, painful urination	A cervical smear for women Extract of fluid from the penis for men	Transmission to sexual partners Various inflammations Possible sterility in men and women
GONORRHEA	Sexual contact (vaginal, oral, and anal) From mother to child	Women: Vaginal discharge, painful urination, bleeding between periods Men: Discharge from penis, painful urination	Medical examination from discharge or culture	Transmission to sexual partners Pelvic inflammatory disease Sterility in men and women
GENITAL WARTS	Sexual contact (vaginal, oral, and anal) Other types of contact such as infected towels or clothing	Women: Single or multiple soft, fleshy growths around anus, vulva, vagina, or urethra; itching or burning sensation around sexual organs Men: Burning around sexual organs; single or multiple soft, fleshy growths around anus or penis	Medical examination	Transmission to sexual and non-sexual partners Precancerous conditions Cannot be cured
HERPES (Simplex Virus Types I and II)	Sexual contact (vaginal, oral, and anal) Touching Kissing Sharing towels, toilet seats	Women: Single or multiple blisters or sores on genitals; generally painful, but disappears without scarring, reappears Men: Same as for women	Medical examination Culture and fluid inspections	Transmission to sexual and non-sexual partners Cannot be cured

(continued)

Seven Sexually Transmitted Diseases, continued

STD	TRANSMISSION	SYMPTOMS	DIAGNOSIS	CONSEQUENCES
HEPATITIS (Viral A, B, C, and D types)	Sexual contact, especially involving the anus Contact with infected fecal matter Transfusion of contaminated blood Severe alcoholism Exposure to toxic materials	Women and Men: Can be asymptomatic; mild flu-like symptoms, fever, abdominal pain, vomiting, and yellowish skin or eyes; loss of appetite; whitish bowel movements; brown urine	Medical examination of blood for herpes antibody; liver biopsy	Transmission to sexual and non-sexual partners Severe liver problems or failure Cancer of the liver Death
SYPHILIS	Sexual contact (vaginal, oral, and anal) Touching an infected chancre	Women and Men: Four stages: (1) painless red spots later forming a sore; (2) skin rash or mucous patches; (3) latent stage, no symptoms; (4) complications leading to possible death	Primary stages by medical examination of fluid from a chancre Secondary stage by blood test, VDRL	Transmission to sexual and non-sexual partners Death (although seldom advances this far today)

Adapted from: *Sex on Your Terms* by Elizabeth Powell, Allyn and Bacon, 1996, and *Access to Health, Fourth Edition* by Rebecca J. Donatelle and Lorraine G. Davis, Allyn and Bacon, 1996.

While fantastic results have been shown in many people with HIV and AIDS, the cocktail is very expensive and some people's bodies cannot tolerate the mixture.

David Kirby in his article "The Worst Is Yet to Come" (*The Advocate*, January 19, 1999), states: "Since the introduction of better AIDS treatments, researchers have been worried that safer-sex messages would lose their urgency. This year, those fears came true. One study after another, with depressing consistence, showed . . . alarming spikes in rates of HIV infection and ominously, of other sexually transmitted diseases as well."

Therefore, it is imperative that you know that HIV and AIDS have not been cured, and without considering your conduct and personal responsibility, you are as much at risk as you ever have been.

Sexual Harassment

Those of us in higher education would like to believe that we are immune to problems of sexual harassment, that we foster an atmosphere in which such behavior is not tolerated. But the cold, hard facts prove otherwise. On many campuses, sexual harassment takes place among students, between students and faculty, among faculty, and between faculty and administration. The federal government defines sexual harassment as deliberate or repeated unsolicited verbal comments, gestures, or physical contact of a sexual nature that is considered to be unwelcome by the recipient, male *or* female. It includes:

- Verbal abuse or harassment
- Unwelcome sexual overtures or advances
- Pressure to engage in sexual activity
- Remarks about a person's body, clothing, or sexual activities
- Leering at, or ogling, somebody's body
- Telling unwanted dirty jokes
- Unnecessarily touching, patting, or pinching someone
- Unwanted letters, telephone calls, or written materials
- Pressure for dates
- Personal questions of a sexual nature
- Sexual innuendoes or stories
- Touching of any kind
- Referring to people as babes, hunks, dolls, honey, boy toy, and so forth

If you are faced with a situation that you believe is sexual harassment, you can take several steps to protect yourself.

1. Make a conscious effort to keep interactions between you and the person harassing you as impersonal as possible.
2. Avoid being alone with the person harassing you. If that person is your professor, bring a friend with you to meetings and arrange to meet in a classroom either right before or right after class.
3. Keep a record of the harassment in case you have to bring formal charges.
4. Tell the harasser that you believe he or she is harassing you and you want the behavior to stop. Be very specific, so that the person knows what you perceive as harassment.
5. Tell your academic advisor or a campus counselor about the events. Seek their counsel.
6. See a lawyer. Sexual harassment is against the law, and you may need to bring formal charges.

Rape

The most severe form of sexual harassment is rape. The term *rape* refers to sexual penetration by means of intimidation, force, or fraud for aggressive and/or sexual reasons. Rape is a cause of fear and concern

Thoughts ● ● ●

among college students, and date, or acquaintance, rape has become as much a concern as rape by strangers. You can take steps to lessen the possibility of rape.

TO DECREASE THE CHANCES OF RAPE BY A STRANGER:

1. Know where campus security is located and be familiar with campus security; keep emergency phone numbers handy.
2. Use campus transportation services.
3. Set up signals with other students in your residence hall to alert one another in case of a problem.
4. List only your first initials in the campus directory or on your mailbox.
5. Be aware of yourself and of your surroundings.
6. Vary your route and walk in groups whenever possible.
7. Stay on well-lighted paths, sidewalks, and streets.
8. If a car pulls up beside you, stay at least an arm's length away; never get into the car.
9. If you are afraid, yell "No!" or "Call 911."
10. Use dead-bolt locks on your doors and keep windows locked.
11. Have your keys ready when you approach your car door or home.
12. Drive with your doors locked.
13. Always check the identification of people such as utility workers, security officers, or salespeople who come to your door.
14. Check the back seat of your car before getting in.

TO DECREASE THE CHANCES OF ACQUAINTANCE OR DATE RAPE:

1. Until you are very familiar with your date, avoid being alone together or going to secluded places.
2. Stay sober.
3. Be very clear about your sexual intentions.
4. Understand that when your partner says no, it means no!
5. Tell a friend whom you are out with, where you are going, and when you expect to return home.
6. Use your own transportation.

College is an environment fraught with new experiences, new relationships, and new behaviors. It is our hope that this chapter will help you think about the situations you may find yourself in and prompt you to make responsible decisions.

There is a 45% chance that you or one of your associates in college will contract a sexually transmitted disease (STD) during your college career, and yet most college students are reticent about discussing STDs. What emotions are elicited when someone brings up STDs in a conversation?

_____

_____

_____

How would you feel if someone with whom you had sexual relations in the past called you to tell you that he or she had an STD?

_____

_____

_____

What steps would you take to ensure your well-being after this person contacted you? Where would you start your research and what questions would you need answered?

_____

_____

_____

_____

_____

_____

_____

_____

In Column A, identify four reasons why practicing safer sex is important. In Column B, discuss those reasons.

Column A	Column B

LIFE

One Minute *Journal*

In one minute or less, jot down the major ideas that you learned from this chapter.

_____

_____

_____

_____

_____

_____

_____

_____

_____

_____

COMPANION Website *Journal*

Log on to **www.prenhall.com/montgomery**, choose the version of this book you are using, and then choose Chapter 11 on the menu. Next, choose "Links" on the left side of the page. Explore one of the websites offered and summarize your findings.

_____

_____

_____

_____

_____

_____

_____

_____

_____

_____

_____

_____

Refer to page 280 of Chapter 11.
Review your **GOALS FOR CHANGE**.
Respond in writing as to the progress
you have made toward reaching one
of your three stated goals.

GOAL STATEMENT

PROGRESS

How is your life changing because of this goal?

CORNERSTONES

for relationships & personal responsibility

Tobacco use is the most serious *addiction* in the world.

Alcoholism presents itself in many different forms.

Legal drugs can be as *dangerous* as illegal drugs.

Protect yourself from rape and sexual assault.

Your *personal* behavior means life and death.

Recognize and *stop* sexual harassment.

Develop important *relationships.*

Combat feelings of *loneliness.*

Maintain *close* friendships.

Learn about *STDs.*

Everyone has a purpose in life . . . a unique gift or special

Celebrate.

talent to give others.   Deepak Chopra

CHAPTER 12

Celebrate

The professor called him Jimmie, but the class would later learn that his name was Jhi' Ming. He was a small, quiet man who sat in the front row of the communication class. During the fifth week of class, four team leaders were asked to choose members to form groups that would work together to solve a problem.

The first leader chose Shawanda, the second leader chose Phillip, the third leader chose Clifford, and the fourth leader chose Carolyn. *The selection process continued until everyone had been chosen except Jimmie.* The first leader, Nanette, was forced to include Jimmie in her group by the process of elimination. There were no audible sounds of dismay, but everyone in the class knew that Jimmie had not been chosen because he was "different." Jimmie was considered different because *he was older than the others, because he was married, because he had children, and because he was Vietnamese.*

The groups began working right away. Nanette asked for advice on solving her group's problem. *Several times, Jimmie suggested solutions, but his opinions were ignored and others were sought.* Jimmie finally stopped contributing to the conver-

sation and sat quietly with his group until time was called.

After class, Nanette told another group leader that she was disappointed that she had to *"get stuck with that oddball!"* They laughed and continued down the hall to another class. *Fortunately, Jimmie did not hear the conversation because he had already left.*

Little did Nanette, the other members of her group, or their classmates know what they were to learn from Jimmie during the remaining weeks of the semester. *This shy, quiet man had a remarkable history, which would change the lives of every student who had the privilege of being in his class.* This man called Jimmie, whose opinions were shut out by his group, *would send shock waves through the hearts of 24 students during his presentation the next week.* Those students would never again call him an "oddball."

"My name is Jhi' Ming Yen," he began. "Today, I will share with you the history of my life and the triumph of my family." The class was somewhat

> ... she was disappointed that she had to "get stuck with that oddball!"

uninterested at first, but within a minute, Jhi' Ming's story had begun to affect every person in the class. *"When I was 15, I saw my mother die in front of my eyes.* She, my father, my sister, and I were running toward the American embassy in Saigon when she was shot in the back by a sniper's bullet. She was carrying my eight-year-old sister when she fell to her death. *My father, sister, and I were able to make it aboard one of the last evacuation helicopters before my country fell."* The class was completely silent.

"When we finally arrived in the United States, I found work in New York City as a dishwasher. *My father cleaned kitchens in hotels—menial work for a man who had served in the medical profession in Vietnam for over 15 years.* My father's degree meant nothing in this country. We had to begin our lives all over again . . . *'from scratch,'* as you would say."

His story unfolded *like a book of horrors and triumphs as the class listened,* for the first time, to the quiet man who sat in the front row. He continued, describing what had happened in the years since he left his country, his mother, and the only life and world he knew. *Jhi' Ming was no longer a stranger.* When the class was over,

Nanette and her classmates finally understood how important it is to give people who are different a chance. *They began to realize what a wealth of information, history, and honor each of us carries in our souls.* As others shared their lives and histories, the class began to see that people of a different culture, age, marital status, sexual orientation, ethnicity, race, religion, and educational level can add monumental dimensions to another's life. *They began to learn how to celebrate diversity, because they allowed Jhi' Ming to share the priceless gift of his life's story.*

Diversity is the acknowledgment of humanity within ourselves.

—D. THORESON

at this moment?

STATEMENT	SCORE	Strongly Disagree	Disagree	Don't Know	Agree	Strongly Agree
1. I readily accept people from different regions of the country.		1	2	3	4	5
2. I am interested in knowing people whose nationality is different from mine.		1	2	3	4	5
3. I am open to relationships with people who are of a different race from mine.		1	2	3	4	5
4. I am accepting of the attitudes, values, and beliefs of people of generations other than mine.		1	2	3	4	5
5. I am comfortable around people who are physically, emotionally, or mentally challenged.		1	2	3	4	5
TOTAL		0-5	6-10	11-15	16-20	21-25

FEEDBACK

0 – 5   Extensive changes need to occur to ensure success.

6 – 10   Substantial changes need to occur to ensure success.

11 – 15   Considerable changes need to occur to ensure success.

16 – 20   Moderate changes need to occur to ensure success.

21 – 25   Minor changes need to occur to ensure success.

GOALS FOR CHANGE

Based on this feedback, my goals and objectives for change are . . .

Goal Statement _____

Action Steps   1. _____

                2. _____

Goal Statement _____

Action Steps   1. _____

                2. _____

Goal Statement _____

Action Steps   1. _____

                2. _____

Results

Reading this chapter, competing the exercises, and reflecting on diversity will result in your:

- Discussing different types of prejudices, including racial, religious, sexual, gender, regional, and international.

- Developing communication skills for relating to people from different cultures and backgrounds.

- Identifying your own biases, attitudes, and expectations.

- Learning to examine critically your own thinking and actions relative to people from different cultures.

- Planning ways in which you can eliminate your personal prejudices and biases.

- Discussing strategies for interacting more effectively with people from a variety of cultures.

You Are a Culture of One

During our formative years, each of us develops a unique set of values, beliefs, and customs. We are virtually programmed, based on who raises us, our race, our nationality, where we live, where we go to school, our religion or lack of religion, our friends, our relatives, and our experiences and opportunities. Like fingerprints, no two people with their beliefs, customs, and experiences are exactly alike. This amazing phenomenon is what makes human beings interesting and makes the differences we see in people from cultures other than our own especially interesting as well as personally educational.

Culture is learned. People are born into a culture, but their culture is not a physical trait, such as eye color or hair texture. You probably developed, or absorbed, most of your personal culture from your family. The process is almost like osmosis in plants; it is as though culture seeps gradually through your skin. Many of the beliefs and values you embrace have been passed from one generation to another.

In college, you are likely to find your values, beliefs, and actions changing as you meet new people and become involved in new situations and as your horizons broaden. Quite simply, your college experience enhances your understanding, and your cultural beliefs change as a result. This change is known as cultural adjustment. You can, and should, expect to have your beliefs greatly tested—and perhaps adjusted—before you graduate.

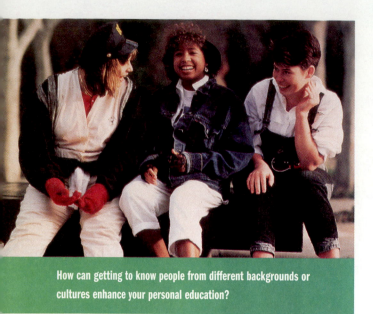

How can getting to know people from different backgrounds or cultures enhance your personal education?

Cultural adjustment doesn't mean that you must abandon your family, church, basic values, and friends. It may mean, however, that you need to re-evaluate why you feel the way you do about certain situations and certain groups. You may have been taught that people belonging to a certain group are bad. As you learn and grow, you may find that they are not bad at all, just different from you, and, like Nanette and her classmates, you will probably discover that this different culture is one to be celebrated.

In this chapter you will be given an opportunity, through a series of scenarios, to put yourself in other people's shoes and thereby gain a better understanding of how someone different from you may feel.

The Components of Culture

Sometimes we can tell that people are from a different culture or ethnic group because of the way they look and dress or by the way they speak— dress and speech are two visible signs of culture. Other components of culture are not so visible. Sociologist David Popenoe (1993) identifies five components of culture:

- Symbols
- Language
- Values

- Norms
- Sanctions

Symbols are items that stand for something, such as the American flag. Most Americans respect the flag and know that it stands for honor, duty, patriotism, service, and freedom. People of other nationalities might not understand that the stars and stripes on the American flag are significant symbols in American culture. The key to relating to people from any culture is understanding. Some common symbols and what they stand for are as follows:

Purple signifies royalty in some cultures.

A *pineapple* is a sign of welcome and hospitality in the southern United States.

Red is associated with anger in some cultures.

An *octagon sign* indicates "Stop!" in several countries.

Name a symbol from your culture:

_____

_____

What does this symbol mean?

_____

_____

Language is another important component of culture; the meaning of a word can vary across cultures. For example, if you were to ask for a biscuit in England, you would get a cookie. How many different words can you think of for that nonalcoholic, carbonated beverage many of us like to drink? Pop? Soda? Soft drink? Coke?

The African American culture in the United States has given some words meanings that are specific to that culture. For example, a "shade and fade" haircut is typical of language used by African American college students. Other cultures within the United States have done the same.

What is a phrase specific to your culture?

_____

_____

What does it mean?

_____

_____

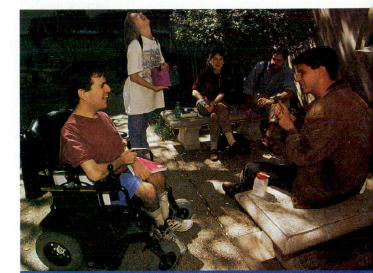

If you know someone with a disability, have you ever talked about or compared your experiences?

Values are typically based on family traditions and religious beliefs. What is unacceptable in one society may be acceptable in another. Most young people in the United States would be unwilling to allow their parents to choose their future spouse, yet in many countries this practice is still common. Some religious services are joyous celebrations; others are formal and solemn. The African American AME church is usually filled with soulful, joyous singing, while the Primitive Baptist Church may include songs not accompanied by musical instruments and may be more solemn—there is no one proper way to conduct a religious ceremony. Like so much else, what is correct depends on the culture.

Name a value of the culture in which you were raised.

_____

_____

Why is this value important to you?

_____

_____

Norms relate directly to the values of a culture or society—they are how we expect people to act based on those values. In an elegant restaurant, for example, you expect people to conduct themselves with more dignity than you might expect in a fast-food restaurant.

What is a norm in your culture?

_____

_____

Why do you think it is a norm? Why is it important?

_____

_____

Sanctions are the ways in which a society enforces its norms. When a society adopts a set of norms that are upheld as valuable, it typically seeks a way to enforce these norms through formal laws. In every society there are people who do not abide by the rules, people who break the law. A person in the United States who breaks the law may be sent to jail or may be required to perform community service. In some cultures punishment is much more severe. For example, the punishment for stealing in some Middle Eastern cultures may be to sever the thief's hand. In the United States this punishment would not be acceptable, but elsewhere it is.

Give an example of a sanction in your culture.

_____

_____

Why do you think it is a sanction?

_____

_____

If you have a desire to understand and appreciate others, you can learn to celebrate diversity and gain valuable lessons from almost everyone you meet.

The Power of an Open Mind

To experience other people and to receive the benefits of knowing someone, you need to enter all relationships with an open mind. If you have a derogatory mind-set toward a race, an ethnic group, a sexual orientation, or a religion, for example, you have internal barriers that can keep you from getting to know who a person really is.

Everyone you meet is a game player to a certain extent. Most people do not allow you to see who they are until they know they can trust you. We protect ourselves and our egos by holding back, covering up, and otherwise shielding ourselves from possible hurt and pain until we know a person will accept us for who we are. Regardless of background, all people want to be accepted for themselves; they want to be able to act naturally and to be comfortable just being themselves.

Learning to interact with people from different cultures is a matter of keeping an open mind and looking at each person as an individual, not as a race, a class, or a religion. We cannot help but be influenced by what we have been taught and what we have experienced, but we can overcome prejudices and biases if we view people as individuals. If you intend to grow as an educated person and as a human being, you will need to expand your capacity to accept and understand people from different cultures within and outside your country.

Have you ever made a connection with someone from a different age group than yours? How might getting to know someone much older or younger than you enhance your college experience?

MY CULTURE OF ONE

Take some time now to identify exactly who you are as a culture of one.

Describe the place(s) where you grew up—the people, the size of the city or town, the schools you attended.

_____

_____

_____

_____

Discuss some of the basic beliefs you learned from your family.

_____

_____

_____

_____

Do you think some of the beliefs you learned from your family might not be right for you today? Why or why not?

_____

_____

_____

_____

Discuss some of the basic beliefs you learned from your teachers.

_____

_____

_____

_____

Name some ways in which your background is reflected in your culture of one, for example, what you wear, your hairstyle, some of the slang phrases you use.

_____

_____

_____

_____

Discuss how you may have been influenced by extracurricular activities, sports, friends, or travel.

_____

_____

_____

_____

Discuss how religious teachings or the absence of religious training has influenced your beliefs.

_____

_____

_____

_____

If you are in a relationship, describe how your partner has influenced your beliefs, actions, or values.

_____

_____

_____

_____

If you have children, discuss how your values, ideas, and associations have changed since you became a parent.

_____

_____

_____

_____

You Are the Center of Your Own Universe

Make use of your responses to the "Culture of One" exercise together with other pieces of information from your personal background to complete the next exercise. The figure on page 314, when completed, will represent you as you are today. The boxes inside the figure represent all aspects of your cultural background that have shaped your beliefs, customs, and habits. In each box, list one source of your personal cultural development. On the lines below, write the basic beliefs, rules, or values you learned from that source. For example, your religious background (source) may have prohibited attending movies (rule). Looking very carefully at your personal background, try now to identify those unique beliefs and experiences that make you who you are. (See the examples provided.)

Y ou are not educated as long as you have prejudices against anyone for any reason other than his or her character.

—*MARTIN LUTHER KING, JR.*

The Colors of My Life

1.
PARENTS
Hard workers
Work ethic
Strict

2.
FAMILY
8 brothers
1 sister
Loving

3.
ENVIRONMENT
Small town
Few neighbors
Country living

4.
EDUCATION
Rural
Small
Homogeneity

1

2

3

4

5

6

Changing Demographics
of the United States

The demographics of the United States are radically different from what they were 50 years ago. Projections point to an increasingly diverse mixture of people with whom you will work and interact; therefore, it is increasingly important for you to learn to understand, work effectively with, and accept that you live in a global community with people from a variety of cultures. According to Carol Kleiman, author of *The 100 Best Jobs for the 90's and Beyond,* "Only fifteen percent of the net new entrants to the workforce will be white men, as the nation's demographics shift and present-day minorities and women become the majority of entry-level workers" (1992).

Perhaps the best opportunity for you to experience multiculturalism will be at college, particularly if you are attending a large or metropolitan university. When you graduate you will have a great advantage if you have become cross-culturally oriented and learned to communicate effectively with people who embrace values, beliefs, and customs that are different from yours.

Researchers Gardenswartz and Rowe (1993) suggest that one cultural mindset determines our behavior and attitudes, from when to smile and with whom to make eye contact, to how to deal with conflict and talk to a supervisor. For example, a teenager's not looking an adult in the eye during a conversation may be considered disrespectful by Anglos, but is a sign of respect for Hispanics. One of the great problems we all face in dealing with cultural diversity is that we typically interpret other people's behavior through our own cultural mindset. Americans may find it strange that in some cultures parents arrange their children's marriages. People from Asian cultures may have difficulty understanding the relative lack of respect Americans show toward elders compared with the reverance for older people in their culture. You can greatly enhance your education this term if you make up your mind to look beyond your own cultural mindset when you encounter people from other cultures.

Other Components of Culture

In addition to the five major components discussed previously, there are several other facets of culture. Each of these facets influences your personal beliefs and shapes the beliefs and actions of people around you. One gift education should provide for you is the appreciation of all kinds of people, many of whom differ greatly from you and come from varying backgrounds.

The cultural mix of the United States' population is undergoing dramatic change. This country is experiencing a rapid growth of people who are categorized as Asian-American (people from India, Laos, China, and the Philippines). Likewise, the number of people categorized as Hispanic (Mexicans, Puerto Ricans, Cubans, and other groups from South and Central America) is exploding. The African American segment of the population has increased almost 20 percent in the last two decades. Simultaneously, the Euro-American population is shrinking. This changing mix of people requires that you and your classmates learn to appreciate and value all kinds of diversity, and further, that you learn to function effectively as a global citizen.

Clearly, the American ethnic mosaic is being fundamentally altered at a rapid pace, making it necessary for this society to find a balance between who we were and who we are becoming. In many American neighborhoods, we are seeing the results of businesses trying to balance the global cultures with the local ones. Most American airports now have signs posted in several languages. Grocery stores have entire sections devoted to foods likely to be purchased by one ethnic group or another, as they try to cater to a changing population base. Businesses, schools, and individuals cannot afford to concentrate on one group and ignore the others. Nor can you!

Because of the ease of travel, the exponential growth of technology, and the overwhelming power of the Internet, a global lifestyle is emerging. For example, in this country we have a large number of restaurants featuring Mexican, Chinese, and French cuisine. Automobiles manufacturers in Japan and Germany now own a major sector of the American market. Michael Jackson's records sell better in Africa than those of the local musicians. American movies, books, and music are known the world over.

The American workplace is changing right along with the neighborhoods, schools, airports, and shops. Large numbers of women have entered the workforce and have permanently changed the internal processes of many organizations. As women become more wealthy and powerful, they are having a dramatic impact on fashions, movies, and children's services and products. Large numbers of women are now managers, causing many people to adjust to having a female boss.

Culture is the primary force in molding human behavior; therefore, the more you learn about different cultures and the major components that shape culture, the more effective you will become in your personal relationships and in your career. The best tools to use as you embark on expanding your cultural understanding are a willingness to be open-minded, to refrain from judgmental opinions, to become an excellent listener, to ask provocative questions, and to practice an objective, accepting behavior toward people who are different from you.

Learning to effectively communicate and function in a global community filled with so many facets of diversity is similar to juggling. Beliefs, symbols, language, and values are only a few of the many components and facets of culture that you should consider when dealing with people from cultures different from your own.

Thoughts

Who Are You?

In _Managing Diversity_, Gardenswartz and Rowe (1993) refer to "individuals as being like the proverbial onion with layer upon layer of cultural teaching." They suggest that cultural identity is shaped by the following factors:

- Ethnicity—the ethnic group with which a person identifies and the person's native language
- Race—the racial group or groups with which a person identifies
- Religion—the organized denomination or sect to which a person subscribes, if any
- Education—the level and type of learning a person receives
- Profession/field of work—the type of work a person is trained to do
- Organizations—groups or associations to which a person belongs or has belonged, such as the military, a scouting group, a labor union, or a fraternal organization
- Parents—the messages, verbal and nonverbal, given by a person's parents about ethnicity, religion, values, and cultural identity

In addition to these powerful cultural influences, gender, family, peers, and place of birth also significantly determine a person's cultural identity.

The Golden Rule for Celebrating Diversity

At one time or another, most of us have been exposed to the Golden Rule: "Do unto others as you would have them do unto you." As you work to improve and expand your knowledge of cultural diversity, it may help you to look at this rule from a different angle. In considering the following scenarios, first by yourself and then with a group, see if you can apply a new version of the Golden Rule: "Do unto others as they would have you do unto them."

I THINK I WOULD . . . AN EXERCISE IN CULTURAL UNDERSTANDING

Respond to each scenario in the space provided. Discuss how the situation makes you feel, how you would feel if you were the person in the cultural minority depicted, and what you might do or say to improve this situation for everyone involved.

Your class may be asked by the instructor to discuss your responses to these scenarios in an open discussion. If so, be aware that these scenarios contain information sensitive to some of your classmates, perhaps to you. While the purpose of the discussion will be to help everyone

Thoughts

understand how their classmates feel, each person in the class should be mindful of others' feelings. Think before you speak. Speak your mind openly, but carefully, to avoid damaging others' self-esteem. Remember, we all take in "messages" about ourselves from others.

Y**ou have to move to another level of thinking, which is true of me and everybody else. Everybody has to learn to think differently, think bigger, to be open to possibilities.** *—OPRAH WINFREY*

You may find that some of your beliefs change slightly—or maybe even dramatically—as you work on these exercises. Growth that allows you to open up your mind, to move beyond biases and prejudices, and to seek to understand people who are different from you is positive growth.

Scenario #1

You and Jack, a friend from high school, are attending the same college. Jack has a physical disability that requires him to use a wheelchair. He was an outstanding basketball player and swimmer prior to a diving accident, which left him a paraplegic. Jack is an honor roll student. He is an avid basketball fan, attends all the games, and plays on a wheelchair team. He has a great sense of humor. He long ago dealt with his personal situation and now he even jokes about it. Jack is one of your favorite people.

Since you and Jack have been in class together, you have been noticing that people tend to treat him differently from others. Sometimes people talk loudly when talking to Jack, as if he couldn't hear. Because getting to and from classes is difficult, Jack has someone to help him maneuver around campus. One day you overhear a student talking to the person who is helping Jack as if Jack weren't there. "What happened to him?" "Can he use his arms?" Although Jack is handsome, friendly, and personable, he is usually left out of the many social activities in which other classmates participate. You know that your classmates would like and admire Jack if they got to know him.

How do you think Jack feels when people treat him as though he doesn't exist?

_____

_____

_____

Why do you think some people have difficulty relating to people who have physical disabilities?

_____

_____

_____

● ● ● Thoughts

What could you do to help Jack become accepted just like any other student?

_____

_____

_____

_____

What could you say to classmates that might help them understand how to relate to Jack better and might make them and him feel more comfortable?

_____

_____

_____

_____

Scenario #2

Douglas met Andy on the first day of class. Douglas struck up a conversation with Andy because he saw a tennis racket in Andy's gym bag—a welcome sight. Douglas had not found anyone to play tennis with since his arrival on campus. The two decided to get together later in the afternoon to play a game. When the game was over, each knew that he had found a friend. They discovered that they lived in the same residence hall, had the same professor for English, only at different times, and both loved to play tennis. As the semester progressed, Douglas and Andy became very close friends; they studied history together, went to hall parties together, ate together when their schedules permitted, and double-dated once or twice.

Douglas and Andy enjoyed many of the same sports and movies and had similar tastes in music. Douglas felt that he had met a true soulmate, and Andy could not have been happier to have Douglas to talk to and hang around with. Andy knew, however, that things could soon change. He had made a serious decision; before the Christmas break he would tell Douglas that he was gay.

Exams ended on Wednesday. Andy decided to break the news to Douglas on Tuesday night. They talked and laughed sitting on a bench outside the athletic center; then the conversation grew still, and Andy chose his words carefully. He told Douglas that he was gay and that he had been involved with someone at home for almost a year.

> I am a citizen, not of Athens or Greece, but of the world.
>
> —*SOCRATES*

If you were Douglas, what would your reaction have been?

_____

_____

_____

_____

Insider's View

I feel that being in a diverse environment is essential to help assist one's learning process. When I first came to the University of South Carolina I knew I was going to have to keep an open mind when dealing with people from different ethnic backgrounds and races. At first, I was a little timid in getting to know other people who were "different" from what I was used to and who grew up in different environments than I had. But as time went on, I looked past the outer appearances of others. Instead, I looked at our similarities and learned from our differences.

When I stepped on campus for the first time, I believe the culture shock is what hit me most. There were so many people from different areas of the United States, different races, and different cultures. But my initial shock when I walked on campus did not stop me from being my friendly self that I had always been around people with whom I am comfortable. I have learned from being on this campus that being around people that you are "comfortable" with is important, but they are not always the people from whom you learn the most. Sometimes you do the most learning from "uncomfortable" situations. I knew that in order to receive the "full" college experience I had to always keep an open mind about individuals I meet both on and off campus.

I have to say it was not hard for me to meet people from different backgrounds because I am a member of the football team. The team in itself was a "melting pot" that included various individuals from different ethnic backgrounds and different areas of the United States. I had to learn how to interact with these individuals in order for us to be a team. But most importantly, I wanted to get to know them on a personal level as well. By being a member of the football team I have made lifelong friendships and met people whom I will never forget. This is all because of my open mind and willingness to get to know others who are outwardly different from me. I have learned from our differences, and it has helped to make me a better person. My advice to all incoming freshmen is to interact with individuals with whom you would not normally interact and get involved in campus activities.

Most importantly, I have learned the importance of being a part of a diverse environment. Being part of a diverse environment helps you as a person to look at a person not based on outward appearance but on what's inside. This environment has helped me to learn about other cultures and how other people grew up. Diversity on campus helps to prepare students for the "real" world, which consists of people from many different ethnic backgrounds. So, my challenge to you is to get out of your comfort zone, get involved on campus, and get to know your fellow classmates. Do not be afraid to enter into a level of discomfort because this is where part of your learning takes place.

Jermale Kelly, *age 23*
Major: Retail
The University of South Carolina,
Columbia, South Carolina

Was Andy right to risk their friendship by telling Douglas about his sexual orientation?

_____

_____

_____

Should Andy have told Douglas sooner?

_____

_____

_____

If Douglas were to walk away from the friendship, how do you think Andy would feel?

_____

_____

_____

Imagine that Douglas, a heterosexual, accepted Andy's orientation, but that Andy went on to say that he was interested in having a relationship with Douglas. How do you think Douglas would have reacted?

_____

_____

_____

Does being gay carry a cultural or social stigma? Why or why not?

_____

_____

_____

Thoughts • • •

Scenario #3

Jerry, an 18-year-old black student, was walking to his residence hall one evening after a fraternity meeting. A pickup truck slowed to match his pace as he walked along the side of the road. One of the two men in the

As a college student who will be entering the world of work soon, you need to know that many situations you will face will be vastly different from the college arena or place where your parents began their careers. Diversity is a frequently discussed issue and impacts every aspect of the workplace, from employment practices to promotion opportunities, from management styles to employee relations, from domestic relationships to global interaction. I can tell you without reservation that learning to celebrate diversity is an absolute must for success in your career.

As an African American, I have experienced some "not too pleasant" people along the way, but I have learned to stay focused on my career goals and to be absolutely sure that I am being fair and consistent in my own workplace habits where diversity is concerned. I am responsible for my actions. I really can't do anything about other people's prejudices and biases, but I can be sure that I give every person a fair chance and that I judge them only on character and work performance.

As a corporate executive for the world's largest corporation, I have had unlimited opportunities to interact with people from many diverse backgrounds. Therefore, on many occasions, I had to adjust in order to form solid relationships with people who are different than me. The difference might be religion or ethnic background; it might be race, international culture, or sexual orientation. My personal reward is getting past these differences and learning to appreciate people for who they are and for what they can contribute.

Prior to assuming my current position, I was Vice-President for Corporate Communications at Saturn, "A Different Kind of Car Company." At Saturn, my primary responsibility was to protect and enhance the image of the company. That meant taking into consideration many factors that may impact our diverse customer base around the world.

I have taken my best practices from Saturn to my current position; a $100 billion enterprise, selling over 5 million cars and trucks to a very diverse customer base. It is my responsibility to ensure that our advertising, promotions, and public relations efforts send the right message to a worldwide audience.

General Motors is an organization with manufacturing, sales, and dealers all over the world. I cannot afford to damage my personal career or the image of the company by carrying around prejudices and biases. I greatly encourage you to open up your minds and hearts to all types of people. You will be richly rewarded in your career and personal life.

James E. Farmer, *Group Director, Public Relations & Communication,* General Motors Corporation

truck leaned out the window and called him a "n——" and spat in his direction. As the men drove off, Jerry saw a Rebel flag displayed at the back of the truck.

On reaching his residence hall, Jerry noticed the same truck, now empty, parked outside the hall. As he neared the front door, Jerry heard racial slurs being yelled at him from a third-story window directly above the entrance to the dorm. Clearly the students were very drunk. As Jerry unlocked the door, the slurs were mixed with threats to urinate on him. Jerry entered the residence hall just as drops of liquid fell around him.

How would you feel if you were Jerry?

_____

_____

_____

_____

What action, if any, do you think Jerry should take?

_____

_____

_____

_____

Do you think racial discrimination is a problem on college campuses?

_____

_____

_____

_____

Scenario #4

Tonya was a first-year student at a major research university. She had an excellent academic background. She had always loved science and math and was seriously considering a major that would allow her to incorporate her love of these subjects into a career. In her second semester at the university she enrolled in a calculus class taught by Dr. Ralph Bartlett. This class was especially important to Tonya for two reasons. First, Dr. Bartlett was the department chair for the program she was considering pursuing, and second, the course was her first college math course, so she wanted to start off strong.

On the first day of class Dr. Bartlett made some disparaging jokes about women in the field of science. Although these comments made Tonya uncomfortable, she thought perhaps she was being oversensitive. As the semester progressed, so did Dr. Bartlett's derogatory asides about women. Nonetheless, Tonya loved the course; she was earning A's and she felt that she had found her niche. She decided to major in this area. Tonya made an appointment to discuss possible career opportunities with Dr. Bartlett. Shortly into the appointment, Dr. Bartlett made it clear to Tonya that he didn't think she could cut it and suggested that she look for another program.

How would you feel if you were in Tonya's shoes?

_____

_____

_____

Thoughts ● ● ●

What action should Tonya take in regard to Dr. Bartlett?

_____

_____

_____

How would you feel if you were a male in Tonya's class?

_____

_____

_____

Do you think women face discrimination in higher education? In the workforce?

_____

_____

_____

Scenario #5

Gregg is in an orientation class for new students. He loves the class and most of the students in it. He is particularly close to Jessie. Gregg and Jessie were both raised in small towns, were active in their high school student councils, and love sports. They also have strong religious convictions, although they act on them differently. Gregg holds firmly to his own beliefs, but he also believes in free choice and people's right to choose their own religion. Jessie is extremely conservative as well as vocal in his approach to religion, and he readily condemns views that differ from his. Although Gregg believes that Jessie has a right to express his feelings and share his views with others, he also believes that Jessie should be more tolerant of others' beliefs.

Gregg has noticed that students avoid talking with Jessie in class and that they share less and less during class discussion. This concerns Gregg because he really likes Jessie, but he doesn't want the class to lose its openness. One day during a discussion on abortion, Jessie openly condemned a student when she shared that she had had an abortion. After class Gregg heard several students say how much they disliked Jessie's attitude.

Would you be willing to share your views in class if Jessie were one of your classmates?

_____

_____

_____

_____

If you were Gregg, how would you deal with Jessie?

_____

_____

_____

_____

How tolerant are you of people's differing religious views?

_____

_____

_____

_____

Can people be fanatically religious?

_____

_____

_____

_____

Do some religions carry a social stigma?

_____

_____

_____

_____

Thoughts ● ● ●

Scenario #6

Rebecca is a nontraditional student who is 38 years old. She is a single parent and has two young children. Although she is not a college graduate, she has been promoted through the ranks to a responsible position at a major bank. Because she has now reached the highest level she can achieve without a college degree, she has returned to school. Rebecca has developed excellent computer skills from her on-the-job experience. Working full time, parenting two young children alone, and going back to school constitute a heavy load for Rebecca.

You notice that Rebecca comes into class at the last possible moment since she must rush to school from work and find a parking place. As soon as class is over, she makes a dash for her car so she can get back to work. Her classmates have very little time to get to know her, and she tends to get left out of discussions.

Your professor has assigned groups for a project that must be completed outside of class. Rebecca has been assigned to your group. After class when you and your teammates are talking, it becomes apparent that they are concerned about Rebecca's ability to participate fully and to carry her share of the work.

How do you think Rebecca feels knowing that she must try to meet with traditional students who may have fewer demands on their time?

_____

_____

_____

_____

What can you say to the other members of the group to help them understand Rebecca's situation?

_____

_____

_____

_____

If Rebecca is unable to attend meetings held during her work hours, how can you help her catch up on what she needs to do to be an effective member of your team?

_____

_____

_____

_____

What suggestions can you make to the group that will help them be more inclusive of Rebecca and be more willing to plan meetings at a convenient time for her?

_____

_____

_____

What can Rebecca do to make up for the time she must miss during group meetings?

_____

_____

_____

_____

Thoughts

How can your team mix social activities with the professor's assignment to include Rebecca and make her feel more comfortable with traditional students?

_____

_____

_____

_____

What special skills and attributes can traditional students learn from a non-traditional student like Rebecca?

_____

_____

_____

_____

Thoughts ● ● ●

CORNERSTONES, INC. BUILDING A FOUNDATION FOR THE FUTURE

BLUEPRINTS
FOR CHANGE

NAME

DATE

C01P22

Now that you have read this chapter on diversity, choose the one of the six scenarios that elicited the most emotional response from you. Which scenario was it and why did it strike a chord with you?

_____
_____
_____
_____

As your class discussed the scenarios, what were some of the things that your classmates said that elicited strong emotional responses from you? List these feelings in Column A. In Column B, discuss why these statements caused a reaction from you.

Column A

_____
_____
_____
_____

Column B

_____
_____
_____
_____
_____

What are some steps you can take to ensure that you listen to all sides of an argument so that you completely understand other people's views and cultures?

Thinking

_____
_____
_____
_____

Think of someone from a culture, religion, or subculture other than your own whom you would like to know more about. Why would you like to get to know this person better?

_____
_____
_____
_____
_____

If you were having a conversation with this person from another culture, what three questions would you ask?

1. _____

2. _____
Change

3. _____

LIFE

THE One Minute *Journal*

In one minute or less, jot down the major ideas that you learned from this chapter.

_____

_____

_____

_____

_____

_____

_____

_____

_____

_____

THE COMPANION Website *Journal*

Log on to **www.prenhall.com/montgomery**, choose the version of this book you are using, and then choose Chapter 12 on the menu. Next, choose "Links" on the left side of the page. Explore one of the websites offered and summarize your findings.

_____

_____

_____

_____

_____

_____

_____

_____

_____

_____

Refer to page 306 of Chapter 12.
Review your **GOALS FOR CHANGE**.
Respond in writing as to the progress
you have made toward reaching one
of your three stated goals.

GOAL STATEMENT

PROGRESS

How is your life changing because of this goal?

CORNERSTONES

for celebrating diversity

Listen to people and try to *understand* them.

Develop relationships with people from a *variety* of backgrounds.

Your personal values and beliefs may need cultural *adjustments.*

Make an effort to *relate* to people.

Learn to appreciate *differences.*

Each person is a culture of *one.*

Read about various cultures.

Be willing to *change.*

The salvation of this human world lies nowhere else than in the

Live.

Amanda was a first-generation college student who had overcome tremendous odds to go to college. A single mother *and the sole supporter of her three children,* she moved back home to live with her mother so that she could afford to go to school. Amanda's mother cared for the children while Amanda was in class or working. Amanda worked the night shift so that she could spend time with her children. She attended classes while they were in school, went home and took a nap, and then got up to do homework with the children and help her mother with chores around the house.

Amanda came to my office two weeks after the fall semester began to tell me *that she would not be in class because her mother had passed away.* We worked out a plan for her to make up her assignments and to take her test at a later date. She was unable to return as quickly as we had hoped because *she had trouble finding someone to help her care for her children.* Finally, she arranged for her sister to care for the children, and she returned to school.

> **Amanda worked the night shift so that she could spend time with her children.**

Amanda made up her assignments and *scored one of the highest grades on the exam.* Several weeks later, she returned to my office in tears—*she had just learned that her son was diagnosed with leukemia.* She was devastated, but decided not to drop out of school because it was too late in the semester for her to be reimbursed for the tuition she had paid. She had to take her son to a medical center in another state. After her return, she worked diligently to keep her assignments current.

In spite of all this stress, Amanda completed the fall semester with very high grades. She preregistered for the spring semester and eventually completed her degree.

THE SERENITY PRAYER:
God, grant me the serenity to
accept the things I cannot change,
the courage to change the things I can,
and the wisdom to know the difference.
—*R. NIEBUHR*

STATEMENT	SCORE	Strongly Disagree	Disagree	Don't Know	Agree	Strongly Agree
1. My health is important to me right now.		1	2	3	4	5
2. I find it easy to take care of myself.		1	2	3	4	5
3. I know how to take care of my physical well-being.		1	2	3	4	5
4. I know what causes stress in my life right now.		1	2	3	4	5
5. I know how to control the stress in my life.		1	2	3	4	5
TOTAL		0–5	6–10	11–15	16–20	21–25

FEEDBACK

0 – 5 Extensive changes need to occur to ensure success.

6 – 10 Substantial changes need to occur to ensure success.

11 – 15 Considerable changes need to occur to ensure success.

16 – 20 Moderate changes need to occur to ensure success.

21 – 25 Minor changes need to occur to ensure success.

GOALS FOR CHANGE

Based on this feedback, my goals and objectives for change are . . .

Goal Statement _____

Action Steps 1. _____

2. _____

Goal Statement _____

Action Steps 1. _____

2. _____

Goal Statement _____

Action Steps 1. _____

2. _____

Results

Reading this chapter, completing the exercises, and reflecting on wellness and stress reduction will result in your:

- Determining your own health status.

- Understanding the key issues to developing a healthy diet.

- Developing a personal plan for wellness.

- Understanding the importance of activity in your life.

- Developing an activity plan for your college years.

- Determining your own mental state and recognizing the danger signs that require professional help.

- Distinguishing the different types of stressors.

- Determining your own stress level.

- Understanding how stress is related to your overall health.

- Developing a personal stress-management program.

What Does It Mean to Be Healthy?

Most people consider themselves healthy. They believe that if they are not sick, they are healthy. However, the absence of illness does not mean that you are healthy; it simply means that you are currently without illness.

The World Health Organization defines health as "not merely the absence of disease or infirmity, but a state of complete physical, mental, and social well-being." Realistically, health is a continuum: on one end you have death, and on the other you have excellent health. Most students are somewhere in the middle of the continuum, experiencing neither excellent health nor debilitating diseases. Often students slip slowly into a state of unhealthiness, which if ignored, could lead to serious health problems. Most of us take our health for granted. We place undue stress on ourselves and assume that our bodies will continue to take this abuse. This chapter will afford you the opportunity to review your own health status and to explore some issues that might help you to lead a healthier lifestyle.

A Holistic Approach to Wellness

You cannot divide your approach to wellness into specific categories because all aspects of your health are interrelated. You cannot address your mental health without taking into account your physical well-being; you cannot talk about fitness without including nutrition in your discussion. If your body, mind, and soul are to function in a healthy manner, then your approach to wellness should be balanced. You need a holistic approach to wellness.

The Mind

The mind is an incredibly complex organ. The health industry has not begun to tap the awesome power the mind has over a person's physical health. Very basic studies have shown that the mind is a vital link to physical health. For example, when patients were given placebos instead of

> Then deem it not an idle thing, a pleasant word to speak;
>
> The face you wear—the thoughts you bring—the heart may heal or break.
>
> —DANIEL CLEMENT COLESWORTH

medication, those who trusted their doctors and their prescribed treatments were more likely to report positive results from the placebos than were patients who did not trust their doctors or their prescribed treatment. There are thousands of anecdotal reports of people who have overcome tremendous physical illnesses through positive thinking and believing that they could overcome the illness. There is no question that the mind has power over the body, but just how and why are still a mystery.

Many of us tend to ignore mental health unless there is a serious problem. We are quick to visit a doctor if we have a broken bone, but we are much less willing to seek professional help if we are experiencing emotional distress. There is still a stigma attached to seeking professional counseling in regard to our mental well-being; yet mental health is often more important than physical health because of the important part it plays in maintaining physical well-being.

Ignoring your mental health can be dangerous. When was the last time you took a mental health break?

My freshman year started off with a bang. I was having the time of my life. Never before had I seen so many things that I could do in one place. It was great for the first semester, but the second semester changed things.

I began to get involved in intramural basketball officiating. It was fun, but added to my seventeen-hour class load and my other part-time job. It was too much. I never seemed to have time for anything. All I did was work and go to school. Most days, I didn't eat from breakfast until midnight, when nothing healthy is available. I studied at the worst times—like 1 a.m. or later. My sleep was less than adequate. I soon found myself starting to drag.

However, I told myself that I could do it, and do it I did. I told myself that I had played sports in high school and I was healthy enough to do anything. I was healthy in high school, but this was college. This time my mom wasn't putting home-cooked meals on the table for me, and I had to really study. Before I knew it, I was feeling tired all the time. Even after my week-end crashes, I was still exhausted. I didn't have the energy for anything. I tried to keep up my hectic pace, but this time something was seriously wrong.

When I got to the point that I didn't have the energy to get out of bed, I decided that I needed to go to the doctor. It was not a fun trip to see him. He told me that my health habits were poor. I wasn't eating right, sleeping enough, or taking time for myself. He said that, even though I was running while officiating basketball, I still needed to exercise more and better. The final diagnosis was that I had caught three or four viruses in a row and that my body's immune system was so weak that it could not fight off one infection before the other started. Rest and more rest was the cure.

I learned an important lesson that semester that I have kept with me. I always take time to eat well, exercise, and take time for myself. My daily schedule still remains frantic with activities, work, and school, but now I handle things with my wellness in mind.

J. D. White, *age 21*
University of Tennessee
Knoxville, Tennessee

Mental health, like physical health, is not simply the absence of mental illness. People who are psychologically healthy:

- Have a positive sense of self-worth
- Are determined to make an effort to be healthy
- Can love and have meaningful relationships
- Understand reality and the limitations placed on them
- Have compassion for others
- Understand that the world does not revolve around them

Mental health, too, should be viewed as a continuum, ranging from excellent mental health, to suffering from minor mental illness, to life-threatening illnesses. Psychiatrist Karl Menninger developed a continuum to represent the range of psychological states, from optimal mental health to severe mental illness.

In my job at Bank One, stress is an ever-present concern. However, somebody has to remain calm. I remember the first weeks of our bank conversion project, when we were managing 33 trainers at 7 sites; something that we had never done before. My insides were constantly torn up, but I had to remain calm on the outside. It is almost like the poised flight attendant when the plane is taking a nosedive. Someone has to be there, smiling and calm. I take a deep breath, think about the situation and ask myself, "Is this bad enough to make us shut down the project?" If the answer is no, then I can make it work. I have to put things into perspective and prioritize the tasks to be done. This is my way to control stress.

My job reminds me a lot of my college experience. In college, there are many requirements and some professor always needs something. You have only one semester to complete the tasks described in the syllabus and they must be done on time. One must learn how to manage time to accomplish those things. The way I saw it, I had two choices. I had an entire semester to do it all. I could set priorities and work on projects and papers on a daily or weekly basis, or I could try to play catch-up at the very end. I chose to set priorities. This was a great choice for me, because it helps me maintain perspective on my job today. At work, it is like I almost make a syllabus for each major project I have to accomplish. This is a way that I can set goals, work toward completion, and control my stress level.

Charles Steve Spearman, *Asst. Vice President & Project Manager for National Retail Education,* Bank One, Columbus, Ohio

DEPRESSION

Depression is used to describe feelings ranging from feeling blue to utter hopelessness. The use of "I'm depressed" to mean "I'm sad" or "I'm down" is a far cry from the illness of clinical depression. Depression is a sickness that can creep up on an individual and render that person helplessly lost if it is not detected and properly treated. Signs of depression include the following (Donatelle and Davis, 1994):

I must love this miserable state I'm in, because I've chosen to stay there since a quarter past ten. I know my mind can only think of one thing at a time so I keep focusing on making misery mine. But what if I choose to find a better space, could imagination find peace in a private place?

—*BARBARA GRAY*

- Lingering sadness
- Inability to find joy in pleasure-giving activities
- Loss of interest in work or school

Level of Dysfunction	
Optimal Mental Health	Normal coping devices and ego control
Level 1	Hyperreactions, anxiety, nervousness, minor physical symptoms
Level 2	Personality disorder, phobias
Level 3	Social offenses, open aggression, violent acts
Level 4	Severe depression and despondency, psychotic and bizarre behavior
Level 5	Severe psychological deterioration, loss of will to live

- Unexplainable fatigue
- Sleep disorders, including insomnia or early-morning awakenings
- Loss of sex drive
- Withdrawal from friends and family
- Feelings of hopelessness and worthlessness
- Desire to die

If you are feeling depressed, but your depression seems minor or situational, try some of these helpful hints for picking yourself up out of the blues:

1. Exercise. Exercise causes the release of endorphins, which help to stimulate you and give you a personal high.

2. Spend time talking with a good friend; share your thoughts and feelings.

3. Control your self-talk. If you're playing a negative tune, change to a positive song.

4. Do something special for yourself: Take a long walk in the park, watch a favorite movie, listen to a special CD, or eat a hot fudge sundae. It doesn't really matter what you do as long as it's something special.

5. Nurture yourself.

List special activities you could use to treat yourself when you are down or feeling blue.

_____

_____

_____

_____

The Soul

The human being is an insatiably inquisitive creature. Our quest for the greater meaning of life is equaled only by our quest for eternal life. For some, these two quests become one in the search for spiritual meaning. Some people find the true meaning of life in the teachings of Jesus Christ; others study the Koran or the teachings of Buddha or worship the wonder of Nature. Whether they follow a formal religion or not, people have their own beliefs about the universe, human nature, and the significance of life. How we approach our beliefs is related to our perception of our own spiritual nature, or the state of our soul.

Your time in higher education provides an outstanding opportunity for you to explore the true meaning of life. Many campus organizations can help you in your quest for spirituality. Take this opportunity to explore your spirituality and to provide food for your soul. To ignore this aspect of yourself is to shut off a potentially rich and wonderful source of joy.

Make a list of the campus organizations that are designed to help students in their spiritual quest.

_____

_____

_____

_____

_____

_____

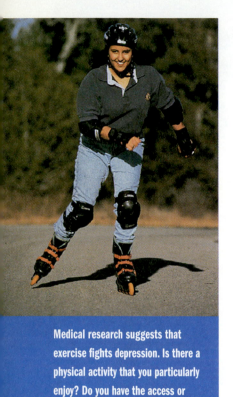

Medical research suggests that exercise fights depression. Is there a physical activity that you particularly enjoy? Do you have the access or opportunity to do it?

The Body

What does it mean to be physically fit? Basically, physical fitness means being physically capable of meeting life's daily demands without impairing your health. Physical fitness, using this definition, is different for everyone.

Why is physical fitness important? The list of reasons for maintaining an activity level that will keep you physically fit is lengthy.

Among other benefits, physical fitness:

- Helps you have more energy
- Gives you increased confidence
- Helps you deal with stress
- Improves the health of your skin
- Helps prevent insomnia
- Reduces your risk of heart disease

- Helps control blood-serum cholesterol levels
- Helps control high blood pressure and diabetes
- Increases longevity of bone structure
- Helps maintain your quality of life

There is no universal fitness plan or program that fits everyone, but there are universal components of fitness. Cardiovascular fitness, flexibility, muscular strength, and muscular endurance are the four components of fitness. **Cardiovascular fitness** is by far the most important component. Cardiovascular fitness means that your heart is able to pump oxygen-carrying blood to your cells and carry waste away from your cells. Excellent cardiovascular fitness is ensured by maintaining a level of aerobic exercise that conditions your body to be able to carry larger amounts of oxygen to working muscles. Some aerobic activities are walking, jogging, biking, swimming, jumping rope, dancing, and cross-country skiing. The benefits of aerobic exercise include reducing the risk of heart disease, keeping blood pressure down, increasing the level of HDL (good cholesterol), and helping control weight in addition to such psychological benefits as increased self-esteem, reduced stress, and decreased anxiety.

Flexibility is the ability of joints to move through the full range of their motion. Good flexibility is believed to prevent pulls, tears, and other damage to your muscles and is particularly important in preventing back pain. The key to flexibility is stretching correctly. You should stretch in a slow relaxed movement.

Muscular strength is the muscles' ability to exert force in one motion, such as a jump or lift. **Muscular endurance** is the muscles' ability to perform repeated muscular contractions. These two components are interrelated in that most muscular contractions use some degree of muscular strength. You can increase both strength and endurance by doing exercises that involve resistance, usually weights. You gain strength by conditioning your body to resist more and more weight; you improve endurance by increasing repetitions at the same weight.

All four fitness components are important to your own personal activity program. We use the term *activity* instead of exercise because we want you to understand that you do not have to be involved in a strenuous exercise program or play a competitive sport to be physically fit; rather, you need to develop an active lifestyle.

Although an active lifestyle should include all four fitness components to some degree, the extent to which each is included is determined by your goals and the level of activity you wish to achieve in your life. If you would like to have a

Finding an exercise buddy can increase your motivation to exercise regularly.

high level of activity so that you can work out or play a sport, here are some suggestions for getting started.

1. Start your program slowly.
2. If it hurts, stop!
3. Wear the proper gear.
4. Learn the proper form and technique.
5. Always warm up and cool down.

"I don't have time to join the gym," you might say. The following suggestions can help you be more active in your daily life.

1. Walk to class rather than drive or ride the bus.
2. Walk upstairs instead of taking the elevator.
3. Develop a hobby that involves physical activity, such as gardening or bowling.
4. Do volunteer work that involves physical activity.
5. Make a commitment to include some form of physical activity in your daily routine.

Almost everyone has at one time or another made a New Year's resolution or some other form of pledge to become more physically fit. Most people don't have trouble starting exercise programs; they only have trouble sticking with them.

The Body and Food

Eating has become Americans' favorite hobby. Rather than eating to live, many of us live to eat. We socialize around food—dinner and a movie, pizza and a beer with friends, and so on. Virtually every holiday or celebration we observe has a food focus. Marketing firms have made millions of dollars from our preoccupation with food and its effect on our bodies. They understand that we eat for reasons far different than mere fulfillment of a biological need for nutrients.

Your personal food choices are derived from a blending of culture, religion, and family habits. As you start your life in college, your eating habits may change dramatically. If you live in a residence hall, you may encounter familiar foods with different tastes; for example, your school's interpretation of turkey and dressing may differ greatly from what you knew at home. You may encounter other foods you've never tried. You may find yourself eating alone among strangers, when you were used to sitting down with parents or siblings. Or, you may be used to eating solitary meals because of your family's hectic schedule, and now find yourself eating with hundreds of others.

As you enter into this new stage of your life, you need to understand that your body will be undergoing tremendous biological stress. The hormonal changes that tend to coincide with the traditional college age, 18 to 22, will cause many of you to experience an alteration in your basal metabolic rate; you will no longer be able to eat like a horse and not gain a pound. At the same time, your lifestyle in college is likely to be more sedentary than was your lifestyle prior to college. As a result, you may well end up gaining the additional weight commonly referred to as the "freshman 15."

To assist you with developing a healthy eating plan, many guides are available to help you make the correct choices of foods. Probably the most widely used is the Food Guide Pyramid designed and released by the U.S. Department of Agriculture (USDA) and the Department of Health and Human Services (DHHS) in 1992. The pyramid is an excellent guide because it shows you how many servings of foods to eat.

When you're on the run it is easy to ignore your eating habits. How many times per day do you sit down to a balanced meal? Per week? Per month?

The Food Pyramid

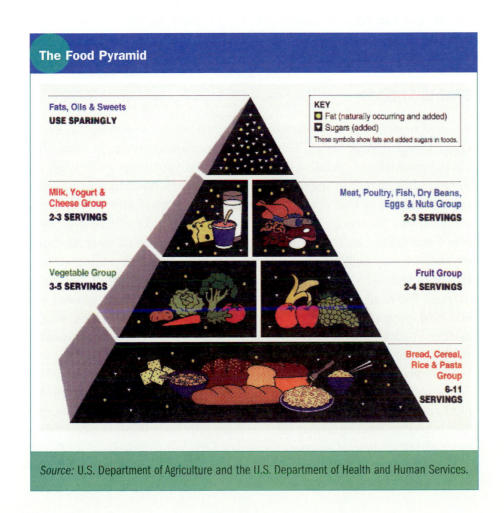

Fats, Oils & Sweets
USE SPARINGLY

KEY
- Fat (naturally occurring and added)
- Sugars (added)

These symbols show fats and added sugars in foods.

Milk, Yogurt & Cheese Group
2-3 SERVINGS

Meat, Poultry, Fish, Dry Beans, Eggs & Nuts Group
2-3 SERVINGS

Vegetable Group
3-5 SERVINGS

Fruit Group
2-4 SERVINGS

Bread, Cereal, Rice & Pasta Group
6-11 SERVINGS

Source: U.S. Department of Agriculture and the U.S. Department of Health and Human Services.

The pyramid was designed with the following eight goals in mind:

1. To promote overall health.
2. To provide recommendations based on the latest research.
3. To focus on the total diet rather than on specific parts of it.
4. To be of practical use to the target audience.
5. To meet nutritional goals in a realistic manner.
6. To allow maximal flexibility in food choices.
7. To be practical.
8. To be evolutionary.

Wellness and Stress

Many things can affect our wellness and cause stress in our lives. Our mental and physical wellness and stress levels may be affected by our weight. Our weight may be affected by our mental state of depression or fear. Most people know what stress is when they "feel" it, but few understand the adverse ramifications of stress on the human body, mind, and soul.

WHAT IS STRESS?

The word *stress* is derived from the Latin word *strictus,* meaning "to draw tight." Stress is your body's response to people and events in your life; it is the mental and physical wear and tear on your body as a result of everyday life. Stress is inevitable, and it is not in itself bad. It is your response to stress that determines whether it is good stress (eustress) or bad stress (distress). The same event can provoke eustress or distress, depending on the person experiencing the event; just as "one person's trash is another's treasure" (or so you know if you shop at secondhand stores), so one person's eustress may be another person's distress. For example, if you know that you are going to be graded on only oral presentations in class, you may experience eustress, while another student may perceive the situation as a fate worse than death and be deeply distressed.

The primary difference between eustress and distress is in your body's response. It is impossible to exist in a totally stress-free environment; in fact, some stress is important to your health and well-being. Only when the stress gets out of hand does your body become distressed. Some physical signs of distress are:

Headaches	Muscular tension and pain
Fatigue	Abdominal pain and diarrhea
Dry mouth	Hypertension and chest pain
Impotence	Heartburn and indigestion
Coughs	Menstrual disorders
Insomnia	Loss of appetite
Depression	Suicidal tendencies

Stress can also have an effect on your memory. Tim Friend of *USA Today* (August 20, 1998) suggests that stressful events that cause the release of a hormone called cortisol can make you forget things you know you should know. "The findings could explain why the mind sometimes goes blank before a key business presentation, a test, or an acting debut." Therefore, learning to control stress and stressful events may be a key to better memory.

STRESS TEST

To determine the level of distress you are currently experiencing in your life, check the items that reflect your behavior at home, work, or school, or in a social setting.

○ 1. Your stomach tightens when you think about your schoolwork and all that you have to do.

○ 2. You are not able to sleep at night.

○ 3. You race from place to place trying to get everything done that is required of you.

○ 4. Small things make you angry.

○ 5. At the end of the day, you are frustrated that you did not accomplish all that you needed to do.

○ 6. You get tired throughout the day.

○ 7. You need some type of drug, alcohol, or tobacco to get through the day.

○ 8. You often find it hard to be around people.

○ 9. You don't take care of yourself physically or mentally.

○ 10. You tend to keep everything inside.

○ 11. You overreact.

○ 12. You fail to find the humor in many situations others see as funny.

○ 13. You do not eat properly.

○ 14. Everything upsets you.

Research suggests that stress can trigger chemical releases in the body that might cause forgetfulness. Learning to relax, breathe properly, and maintain perspective can help reduce stress during tests.

○ 15. You are impatient and get angry when you have to wait for things.

○ 16. You don't trust others.

○ 17. You feel that most people move too slowly for you.

○ 18. You feel guilty when you take time for yourself or your friends.

○ 19. You interrupt people so that you can tell them your side of the story.

○ 20. You experience memory loss.

TOTAL NUMBER OF CHECK MARKS

0–5 = Low, manageable stress

6–10 = Moderate stress

11+ = High stress, could cause medical or emotional problems

Three Types of Stressors

TYPE	CAUSES	REDUCTION
Situational	Change in physical environment Change in social environment	Change your residence or environment. Find a quiet place to relax and study. Arrange your classes to suit your individual needs.
Psychological	Unrealistic expectations Homesickness Fear	Surround yourself with positive people. Surround yourself with people who support you. Talk to professors, counselors, family, and friends.
Biological	Hormonal changes Weight loss/gain Change in physical activities	Develop a healthy eating plan. Develop an exercise plan. Increase your daily activity.

Why is it important to approach your wellness from a holistic perspective?

_____

_____

_____

_____

Intelligence

LIFE

Using the space below, identify four strategies that can be used with the body, mind, and soul to design your own wellness plan.

Body

1. _____

2. _____

3. _____

4. _____

Mind

1. _____

2. _____

3. _____

4. _____

Soul

1. _____

2. _____

3. _____

4. _____

Self-Esteem

One Minute *Journal*

In one minute or less, jot down the major ideas that you learned from this chapter.

_____

_____

_____

_____

_____

_____

_____

_____

_____

_____

COMPANION Website *Journal*

Log on to **www.prenhall.com/montgomery**, choose the version of this book you are using, and then choose Chapter 13 on the menu. Next, choose "Links" on the left side of the page. Explore one of the websites offered and summarize your findings.

_____

_____

_____

_____

_____

_____

_____

_____

_____

_____

Refer to page 336 of Chapter 13.
Review your **GOALS FOR CHANGE**.
Respond in writing as to the progress
you have made toward reaching one
of your three stated goals.

GOAL STATEMENT

PROGRESS

How is your life changing because of this goal?

CORNERSTONES

for wellness & stress reduction

Develop a way to "*decompress*" after school or work.

Tackle your most difficult and important work *first.*

Reward yourself for achieving short-term goals.

Eat a diet high in complex *carbohydrates.*

Take *time out* to be with friends or family.

Surround yourself with *positive* people.

Keep yourself healthy with *exercise.*

Be *realistic* with your expectations.

Work at your relationships.

Limit your protein intake.

Do something you *enjoy.*

Organize your day.

Limit your fat intake.

Don't procrastinate.

Learn to say *no!*

Hold fast to dreams, for if dreams die, life is a broken-winged

Dream.

bird that cannot fly.   Langston Hughes

CHAPTER 14

Dream

I met Wilma when she was a first-year student in college. I was director of student activities and of the Student Government Association and she was a senator representing the first-year class. Her drive and enthusiasm distinguished her from other new students. She wanted to be a teacher. She had not gone to college immediately after high school; instead, *she had joined the armed forces and then entered the workforce.* During this time, Wilma had given her career a great deal of thought. She told me one day, *"I've had many jobs in my life, but I've never had a career."*

In the upcoming semesters, *Wilma made the president's list and the dean's list, was named to Who's Who among American College Students, won several academic scholarships, was elected to the Student Government Association,* and even placed second in a dance contest. She was the envy of her peers and colleagues. In addition to energy and drive, she had a desire to have a career, *to do something that she loved—*

She told me . . . "I've had many jobs in my life, but never a career."

to teach. She studied hard, tutored others, and graduated with honors. She received her associate's degree and transferred to a four-year college and became what she had planned for so many years to be—today, she teaches small children near her hometown.

Wilma's story does not seem extraordinary until you learn that Wilma began her career pursuit in her midsixties. *Today, in her seventies, she still teaches.*

She is an inspiration to all her students and colleagues who learn from her and love her dearly.

The key to success is to keep company only with people who uplift you, whose presence calls forth your best. *—EPICTETUS*

STATEMENT	SCORE	Strongly Disagree	Disagree	Don't Know	Agree	Strongly Agree
1. I know how to research a career.		1	2	3	4	5
2. I know my personality type.		1	2	3	4	5
3. I know how my personality type affects career decisions.		1	2	3	4	5
4. I understand the difference between a job and a career.		1	2	3	4	5
5. I have a career mentor.		1	2	3	4	5
TOTAL		0–5	6–10	11–15	16–20	21–25

FEEDBACK

0 – 5   Extensive changes need to occur to ensure success.

6 – 10   Substantial changes need to occur to ensure success.

11 – 15   Considerable changes need to occur to ensure success.

16 – 20   Moderate changes need to occur to ensure success.

21 – 25   Minor changes need to occur to ensure success.

GOALS FOR CHANGE

Based on this feedback, my goals and objectives for change are . . .

Goal Statement _____

Action Steps 1. _____

2. _____

Goal Statement _____

Action Steps 1. _____

2. _____

Goal Statement _____

Action Steps 1. _____

2. _____

Results

Reading this chapter, completing the exercises, and reflecting on your personal and professional dreams will result in your:

- Determining the difference between doing and being.

- Explaining the difference between a job and a career.

- Identifying personal traits that affect job selection and performance.

- Using the seven-step plan to decide on a major.

- Developing a personal success plan.

- Researching a career path.

- Identifying resources for future career study.

Do You Want to Do Something or Be Something?

If you were to ask most people on the street the simple question, "What do you do for a living?" they would respond, "I'm a welder" or "I'm an engineer" or "I'm a teacher." Most people answer the question without thinking about what is really being asked.

One of the first questions that you need to ask yourself when deciding on a career is, "Do I want to do something, or do I want to be something?" The title "welder," or "engineer," or "teacher" does not by itself make you a welder or engineer or teacher. The *art of being* is a mind-set that you have to develop on your own. There are many people who teach for a living, but there are very few teachers. There are people who do social work, but few are social workers. To be something, you have to make a philosophical decision regarding your future. The questions you have to ask are "How do I want to spend my time?" and "What is my purpose in life?" As an individual, you can do almost anything. You can do the work of medicine, you can do the work of upholding the law, you can do the work of instruction; but in order to be a doctor, lawyer, or teacher, you have to want to become the ideal for which those professions stand. Doing is the easy part, but doing the work is not enough to bring fulfillment to your life; it is being the person who heals, protects justice, or teaches that can bring you joy.

Whereas it takes only physical strength to do something, it takes vision to be something. So, what do you want to be? Take a moment to reflect on your dreams for a career.

I went into the woods because I wished to live deliberately, to front only the essential facts of life, and see if I could not learn what it had to teach, and not, when I came to die, discover that I had not lived.
—*HENRY DAVID THOREAU*

1. When you were a child, what was the first thing you ever wanted to be?

   _____

   _____

   _____

2. Are you considering this same career now? Why or why not?

   _____

   _____

   _____

3. Money aside, what would you do if you had the chance to do anything in this world?

   _____

   _____

   _____

4. Who is the person in your life who has the career that you want?

   _____

   _____

   _____

5. Why do you admire that person and his or her career?

   _____

   _____

   _____

6. How do you best like to spend your time?

   _____

   _____

   _____

7. Write a statement detailing what you perceive as your purpose in life.

   _____

   _____

   _____

● ● ● **Thoughts**

Deepak Chopra, in his book *The Seven Spiritual Laws of Success* (1994), refers to this situation as the Law of Dharma. "Dharma is a Sanskrit word that means 'purpose in life.' According to this law, you have a unique talent and a unique way of expressing it. There is something that you can do better than anyone else in the whole world. . . ." Have you found that something? Have you put your finger on your purpose? If not, don't worry right now. Read on. Maybe we can help.

You've Got a Job,
Now You Want a Career

Everyone at some time faces the age-old question, "Should I be what others think I should be or should I be what I want to be?" The life's work for many people turns out to be what other people think it should be. Well into the latter half of the twentieth century, women were expected to have traditional female careers, such as teaching, nursing, or homemaking. They had little opportunity to select a profession that suited them; society selected their professions for them. It was uncommon for women to enter the fields of engineering, construction, management, public safety, or politics; the avenues to such choices were not open.

College students, male and female, still face pressures to be what others want them to be. Parents actively guide their children toward professions that suit their ideas of what their children should do. Some students have little choice in deciding what they will do for the rest of their lives.

For nontraditional students, spouses, time, and finances may dictate a profession. Many choose courses of study that can be completed quickly because finances and family considerations pressure them in that direction. Money is often another consideration when choosing a profession. Regardless of the pressures you have in your life, be careful to research your choices, talk with people already in the profession you are considering, and consider the long-term effects of your decisions. You want your career decisions to be well thought out, well planned, and carefully executed.

You are the only person who will be able to answer the questions, "How do I want to spend my time?" and "What is my purpose in life?" No parent, teacher, partner, counselor, or therapist can fully answer these questions for you. Another

> I t is easy to live for others. Everybody does. I call on you to live for yourselves.
>
> —*RALPH WALDO EMERSON*

An informational interview is a useful way to research job options. These interviews can help you figure out how a career path can fit with your life goals.

person may be able to provide information that can help you make the decision, but ultimately, you will be the person in charge of your career path, your life's work.

What Do You Want to Be When You Grow Up?

More people than you would imagine have trouble deciding what they want to be when they grow up. Studies indicate that more than 20 percent of all first-year college students do not know what their majors will be. That's all right for the time being, but before long you will need to make a decision.

Find a job you like and you'll never have to work a day in your life.   *—UNKNOWN*

The questions that follow are designed to help you make that decision regarding what you want to do with the rest of your life—your career.

YOUR CAREER SELF-STUDY

What Is Your Personality Type?

You can best answer this question by taking a personality inventory, such as the Myers-Briggs Type Indicator. (An inventory based on the MBTI® is located in Chapter 3 of this book.) This question is important, because your personality may very well indicate the type of work in which you will be successful and happy. If you are a real people person, you probably will not be very happy, for example, in a job with minimal human contact and interaction.

Describe your personality type.

_____

_____

How will your personality type affect your career path?

_____

_____

What Are Your Interests?

Understanding your specific interests may help you decide on a career. If you love working on cars, you might consider becoming a mechanical engineer. If you love to draw or build things, you might be interested in architecture or sculpting.

● ● ● ● **Thoughts**

What are your major interests?

_____

_____

How can these interests be transferred to a career choice?

_____

_____

Do You Enjoy Physical or Mental Work?

Many people would go crazy if they had to spend so much as one hour per day in an office. Others would be unhappy if they had to work in the sun all day or use a great deal of physical strength. The answer to this question will greatly narrow your list of potential career choices. For example, if you are an outdoor person who loves being outside in all kinds of weather, then you should probably avoid careers that are limited to indoor work. You should also consider whether you have any physical limitations that might affect your career choice.

Do you enjoy physical or mental work or both? Why?

_____

_____

What does this mean to your career path?

_____

_____

Do You Want to Make a Lot of Money?

Most people, if asked, "Why do you work?" would respond, "For the money." There is nothing wrong with wanting to make money in your profession, but not all professions, regardless of their worth, pay well. Some of the hardest and most rewarding work pays the least. You have to decide whether to go for the money or do something that is personally challenging to you. Many times, you can find both!

Is your major goal in choosing a profession money or something else? What?

_____

_____

What does your goal mean to your career path?

_____

_____

Where Do You Want to Live?

Although this question may sound strange, many careers are limited by geography. If you are interested in oceanography, you would be hardpressed to live in Iowa; if you love farming, New York City would be an improbable place for you to live. Some people simply prefer certain parts of the United States (or the world) to others. You need to ask yourself, "Where do I eventually want to live?" "What climate do I really enjoy?" "In what size city or town do I want to work?" "Where would I be the happiest?" "Do I want to live near my family or away from them?"

Where do you eventually want to live? Why?

_____

_____

What does your preference mean to your career path?

_____

_____

Do You Want to Travel?

Some jobs require travel; some people love to travel, some hate it. Ask yourself whether you want to be away from your home and family four nights per week, or whether you want a job that does not require any travel.

Do you enjoy travel? Do you want to do a lot of traveling?

_____

_____

What does this mean to your career path?

_____

_____

How Do You Like to Dress?

Some people enjoy dressing up and welcome the opportunity to put on a new suit and go to work. Others prefer to throw on an old pair of blue jeans and head out the door. Jobs have different requirements in terms of dress, and you will be affected by them every workday, so you will want to consider your own preferences.

How do you like to dress?

_____

_____

● ● ● Thoughts

What does this mean to your career path?

_____

_____

_____

What Motivates You?

What are the one or two things in your life that motivate you? Money? Power? Helping other people? The answer to this question is an essential element to choosing a career. You have to find that certain something that gives you energy and then find a profession that allows you to pursue it with fervor and intensity.

What is your motivational force and why?

_____

_____

How could this help you in deciding on a career path?

_____

_____

There is often a typical style of dress or attitude associated with different professions. Will dress codes or other personal-behavior requirements affect your career decisions? Do you think they should?

What Do You Value?

Do you value relationships, possessions, money, love, security, challenges, or power? Once you have identified what you value in your life, you can identify careers that closely match your personal value system and eliminate careers that don't. If you have to constantly compromise your values just to get a paycheck, you may be unhappy.

What do you truly value in your life?

_____

_____

How might these values affect your career decisions?

_____

_____

What Are Your Skills?

Are you especially good at one or two things? Are you a good typist, a good manager of money, a good carpenter, a good communicator? Your skills will play a powerful part in selecting a career. If you are not good or skilled at manipulating numbers, then you will probably want to avoid careers that require their constant use. If you are not a good communicator, then you probably do not want a career that requires you to give daily presentations. Employers still stress the importance of three basic skills: writing, speaking, and listening. If you have these skills, you are ahead of the pack. If not, you need to enroll in a class that will help you to become better at all three.

What are your skills? What do you do well?

_____

_____

How could your strongest skills help you make a career decision?

_____

_____

Do You Like Routine?

The answer to this question will narrow down your choices tremendously. If you like routine, you will want a career that is conducive to routine and provides structure. If you do not like routine and enjoy doing different things each day, certain careers will be unrealistic for you.

Do you like routine or do you prefer variety? Why?

_____

_____

How does this affect your career path?

_____

_____

Are You a Leader?

One of the most important questions you must ask yourself is "Do I enjoy leading, teaching, or guiding people?" If you prefer to be part of the crowd and do not like to stand out as a leader or manager, some careers may not suit you. If you like to take charge and get things done when you are with other people, you will find certain careers better than others. How you relate to leadership will be a part of your personality inventory.

Do you consider yourself a leader? Are you comfortable in a leadership role? Why or why not?

_____

_____

● ● ● Thoughts

How will your feelings about leadership affect your career path?

_____

_____

Help Me: I'm Undeclared

No, it isn't a fatal disease. You're not dying. Being undeclared is not a disgrace, nor a weakness. It is a temporary state of mind, and the best way to deal with it is to stop and think. You should not declare a major because you are ashamed to be undeclared, and you shouldn't allow yourself to be pressured into declaring a major. Instead, you can take measures to work toward declaring a major and being satisfied with your decision. It is better to be undeclared than to spend several semesters in a field that is wrong for you, wasting hours that won't count toward a degree.

Not all who wander are lost.

—*J. R. R. TOLKIEN*

NINE STEPS TO CAREER DECISION MAKING

Step 1—Dream! If money were not a problem or concern, what would you do for the rest of your life? If you could do anything in the world, what would you do? Where would you do it? These are the types of questions you must ask yourself as you try to select a major and career. Go outside, lie on the grass, and look up at the sky; think silently for a little while. Let your mind wander, and let the sky be the limit. Write your dreams down. These dreams may be closer to reality than you think. In the words of Don Quixote, "Let us dream, my soul, let us dream" (Unamuno).

Step 2—Talk to your advisor. Academic advisors are there to help you. But don't be surprised if their doors are sometimes closed. They teach, conduct research, perform community service, and sometimes advise in excess of 100 students. Always call in advance; make an appointment to see an advisor. When you have that appointment, make your advisor work for you. Take your college catalog and ask questions, hard questions. Your advisor will not make a career decision for you, but if you ask the proper questions, he or she can be of monumental help to you and your career decisions.

Use students in your program as advisors, too. They will be invaluable to you as you work your way through the daily routine of college. Experienced students can assist you in making decisions about your classes, electives, and work-study programs. They can even help you join and become an active member of a preprofessional program.

Step 3—Use electives. The accreditation agency that works with your school requires that you be allowed at least one free elective in your degree program. Some programs allow many more. Use your electives wisely! Do not take courses just to get the hours. The wisest students use their electives to delve into new areas of interest or to take a block of courses in an area that might enhance their career opportunities.

Step 4—Go to the career center. Even the smallest colleges have some type of career center or a career counselor. Use them! Campus career centers usually provide free services. The same types of services in the community could cost from $200 to $2,000. The professionals in the career center can provide information on a variety of careers and fields, and they can administer interest and personality inventories that can help you make career and other major decisions.

Nothing is really work, unless you would rather be doing something else.
—SIR JAMES BARRIE

Step 5—Read, read, read! Nothing will help you more than reading about careers and majors. Ask your advisor or counselor to help you locate information on your areas of interest. Gather information from colleges, agencies, associations, and places of employment. Then read it!

Thoughts

Step 6—Shadowing. Shadowing describes the process of following someone around on the job. If you are wondering what engineers do on the job, try calling an engineering office to see whether you can sit with several of their engineers for a day over spring break. Shadowing is the very best way to get firsthand, honest information regarding a profession in which you might be interested.

Step 7—Join preprofessional organizations. One of the most important steps you can take as a college student is to become involved in campus organizations and clubs that offer educational opportunities, social interaction, and hands-on experience in your chosen field. Preprofessional organizations can open doors that will help you make a career decision, grow in your field, meet professionals already working in your field, and, eventually, get a job.

Step 8—Get a part-time job. Work in an area that you may be interested in pursuing as a career.

Step 9—Try to get a summer practicum or internship. Work in your field of interest to gain practical experience and see if it really suits you.

Networking: The Overlooked Source for Career Development

We are often so concerned with books, computerized databases, and interest inventories that we forget to look in our own backyards when thinking about careers. Networking is one of the most important aspects of career development. Look at the person sitting beside you in your orientation class. That person could be a future leader in your field of study. You might be thinking, "No way," but you'd be surprised at how many people lose out on networking opportunities because they do not think ahead. The person sitting beside you is important. You never know where or when you may see this person again—he may be interviewing you for a job in 10 years, or she may be the person with whom you will start a business in 15 years. "Too far down the road," you say? Don't close your eyes—15 years will pass faster than you think.

F*riends do business with friends.*

—J. W. MARRIOTT, JR.

You've all heard the expression, "It's not what you know, but who you know." Well, few statements could be more true, and college is the perfect place for making many personal and professional contacts. At this moment, you are building a network of people on whom you can call for the rest of your life. Your network may include people you know from:

High school and college	Student government
Clubs and professional organizations	Newspaper staff
Sporting teams and events	Family connections
Fraternities and sororities	College committees
Community organizations	Volunteer work

Mentors

A mentor is someone who can help open doors for you, who will take a personal and professional interest in your development and success. Often a mentor will help you do something that you might have trouble doing on your own. It may be too soon for you to determine now whether you have found a mentor, and you may not find that person until you begin to take courses in your field of study.

The student-mentor relationship is unique. You help each other. Your mentor may provide you with opportunities that you might otherwise not have. You may have to do some grunt work, but the experience will usually help you in the long run. While you are helping your mentor, your mentor is helping you by giving you experience and responsibility.

As a young, uncertain, first-year college student, Derrick applied for and was awarded a work-study position with Professor Griffon. His job was to help Professor Griffon ready a semester calendar of events from plays to lectures to dances to speakers. One of his responsibilities was to prepare mailings and other advertising materials for the humanities series. The work was monumental, the pay minimal, and Professor Griffon was not always in the best of spirits. On some days Derrick left the office swearing that he would never return. But he had little

Insider's View

My freshman year in college is one of the strangest, most stressful, and exciting times that I have ever encountered. I came to school not knowing anybody and not sure what to expect. As I stood and watched my family drive away, I came to the vague realization that I was on my own and it was now when I could really start my life.

I didn't know anyone and no one knew me. All of the people here knew nothing about my family, so they wouldn't say, "Aren't you Phyllis' daughter?" And they knew nothing of my past. I am here to start living my own life and start making my own decisions. The only problem is that I have to figure out what it is that I want.

I decided to major in history and political science because I liked both of those classes in high school. Also, everyone in college says that you don't really have to commit to a major your freshman or sophomore years. They say that I can change it later if I decide it's not really for me. Advisors urge freshmen to take a lot of different classes to expose you to a lot of different areas of study. This way if you find something that is very interesting, you will have the opportunity to learn more about it and maybe even change your major.

Many of my friends, however, find that although this sounds good in theory, it doesn't quite work this easily. Many of my friends have committed to a major because of scholarships that they have received. If they decide to change their major then they will lose the scholarships that they need to fund their education. Still others have already filled their schedule with classes to fulfill their major and are going to be taking their general requirement classes later. They fear that if they change majors they will have to stay in school for an extra year and may run short of money.

I made my choice to major in history and political science with the end result being, hopefully, that I will be able to get a job in government. I have also, besides my major, joined many clubs that will help me in my future career. These include several service organizations and the debate team. Also, I am looking into several internship possibilities for over the summer. This will help me to be sure that I am going into the correct career field.

I have discovered that my freshman year in college has given me a lot to think about. One of the biggest things that concerns me is how the decisions that I make now will affect my life in the future. Now, I have to just keep doing my best and always stay open to new ideas.

Amber Montgomery, *age 18*
Major: History and Political Science
Texas Lutheran, Seguin, Texas

College provides tremendous opportunities for students to prepare for the World of Work. As a student I was able to learn how to deal with competition in a non-monetary setting. This gave me the confidence to handle the competitive nature of my career as an attorney. College also provided me an opportunity to learn how to manage leisure vs. work/studying. Since time is my most important commodity, success in being able to prioritize my life issues is paramount to a successful career and home life. I have two wonderful daughters who have very active lives, which I don't intend to miss out on. I want to be able to spend time with them, attending their recitals, helping them with their homework, and introducing them to museums and the arts. I also have a husband who is not only my business partner but my soulmate, with whom I must spend time nurturing our relationship. I would not be able to manage all of my life goals if I had not learned how to prioritize my life and manage my time correctly.

If I could give one piece of advice to college students today, it would be to become active in extracurricular and co-curricular activities because it gives you a chance to become involved in the community. To be a successful career person you *must* give back. My work as an attorney cannot fulfill all of my needs. I've seen so many of my colleagues become so obsessed with work that they lose sight of the truly important aspects of life, family, friends, community. I'm very lucky that my career has provided me with skills that I can give back to the community through my work with volunteer organizations. Without this balance, my life would be incomplete.

Tanya Stuart Overdorf, *Attorney,* Indianapolis, Indiana

choice—the job paid more than unemployment. Derrick stayed with the job, and before too long, Professor Griffon began to give him more challenging work.

One day, an important member of the community came to the office. Derrick and the professor were both working at their desks. As the professor and the guest discussed a lucrative contract for an artist, Derrick overheard Professor Griffon tell the guest he could "bring the contract by tomorrow and leave it with Derrick, my assistant." "Assistant," Derrick thought, "that's interesting."

Before Derrick graduated with his two-year degree, he had a wealth of experience, knowledge, and, most important, contacts! He had learned how to run the lighting board in the theater, he had managed the box office, he had developed a marketing plan for one of the events, and he had been able to shadow many of the artists who came to the auditorium to perform. All this was possible because of his relationship with Professor Griffon. This student-mentor situation was rewarding for both of them. They helped each other, and both profited.

Benefits of Having a Mentor

- Mentors teach, advise, and coach.
- Mentors serve as a sounding board for ideas.
- Mentors serve as constructive critics.
- Mentors can promote you among their peers and contacts.
- Mentors provide information to help with career development.
- Mentors can increase your visibility on campus and in the work arena.
- Mentors introduce you to people who can advance your career.

HOW TO FIND A MENTOR

You can't go shopping for a mentor; you don't advertise; you can't use someone else's mentor. You find a mentor through preparation, work, and a feeling of being comfortable. The following suggestions may help you find a mentor:

How could a student assistant position with a professor help your career?

- Arrive at class early and work hard.
- Develop an outstanding work ethic.
- Seek advice from many professors and staff members.
- Ask intelligent, thoughtful questions.
- Offer to help with projects.
- Convey the impression that you are committed, competent, and hardworking.
- Look for opportunities to shadow.
- If a professor or staff member gives you an opportunity, take it.
- Look at grunt work as glory work.

Bringing It All Together

Throughout *Cornerstone,* we have tried to suggest that you can change your attitude, your behavior, your actions, and your life. If we did not believe this, we would not have spent seven years of our lives writing and revising this book, nor would we have spent a collective 55-plus years teaching and working with students.

Change is possible and, in many instances, practical and necessary. However, change does not come without sacrifice, hard work, and much determination. You already know that, don't you? You had to change to get this far in the text and in your college career. But change is not all that you face in the months, semesters, and years to come. You will also be faced with many hard, life-altering decisions that will affect you, your family, and your livelihood for many years.

One of the most important decisions that you will make, consciously or unconsciously, is deciding on what type of person you want to be, what you plan to do in your life, and what contributions you plan to leave this world when your time here is through.

Deciding on a career is only one part of the puzzle. Re-read Tonya Overdorf's "From the World of Work," found earlier in this chapter, and remember her words: "My work as an attorney cannot fulfill all of my needs. I've seen so many of my colleagues become so obsessed with work that they lost sight of the truly important aspects of life, family, friends, and community."

What Dr. Overdorf is suggesting is that the world is full of unhappy people who refused to consider that life is more than work and money and possessions. Consider the following from the book *Capstone: Succeeding Beyond College* (Sherfield, Montgomery, and Moody, 2001):

> The world in which we live is full of roadblocks that can potentially cause us to lose focus and fall out of balance. Consider the following facts: Americans reporting that they were *"very happy"* were no more numerous in the early 1990s than in 1957. In 1993, only 21% of 18- to 29-year-olds thought that they had a chance at the *"good life"* as compared to 41% in 1978. Today, Americans spend *40% less time* with their children than they did in 1965. Employed Americans spend *163 hours more* per year on the job than they did in 1969. Sixty-nine percent of Americans would like to *slow down* and live a more relaxed life.

Beyond these shocking facts, the book *Understanding* (Werner, 1999) reports that there has been a 545 percent increase in revolving credit debt since 1985, and that in 1997 alone, Americans held $455 billion in credit card debt. In 1998, almost 1.5 million people filed for bankruptcy in the United States. We give you these figures and statements so that you might think more diligently about your future and your decisions.

As a mature, rational, caring human being, you should realize that you are a part of a bigger picture. This world does not belong to us; we are only borrowing it for a while. Everything you do affects someone else in some way. You must realize that what you do—not just what you do for your career, but your daily actions—matters to someone. There is value in every job, and there is honor in all professions performed well and honestly. When making career and life decisions, you need to take into account the fact that other people, strangers and friends, will eventually be looking to you as a mentor, and a role model. This is a major responsibility that you cannot avoid; rather, you should relish the opportunity to inspire and teach. Embrace the moment. Finally, you must realize that unless you are out there, daily, creating a better future for yourself, you have no right to complain about the one that is handed to you.

Thoughts ● ● ●

BLUEPRINTS FOR CHANGE

NAME

DATE

C01P22

During your college career, you may explore numerous potential careers. As you know, it is very important that you settle on a major and determine a career track that will make you happy and fulfilled.

Before you select a major and career, you should find the answers to the following questions. The answers may help you narrow your choices and determine the best career for you.

1. The career I have chosen to research is

_____

2. Why are you interested in this career?

_____

3. What personality type is best suited for this career?

_____

4. Does this career require physical or mental work or both? Why?

_____

5. What is the average salary for this career?

_____

6. Where do most professionals in this occupation live? Is it region-specific?

_____

7. Does this career require travel?

_____

8. What type of dress is required of people who work in this profession?

_____

9. How much training and education are required to work in this career?

_____

10. What skills are required to do work in this job?

_____

11. Does this career involve routine?

_____

12. Does this career require you to work indoors or outdoors?

_____

13. Does this career require you to be a leader or participant?

_____

14. What is the call number for this profession in the *Dictionary of Occupational Titles*?

_____

15. What are the most positive aspects of this career?

_____

16. What is the worst thing about this career?

_____

17. Are you still interested in this career?

_____

18. Is there someone you might be able to shadow in this profession?

_____

19. What sources did you use to research this career?

_____

20. Whom did you interview to research this career?

_____

THE One Minute *Journal*

In one minute or less, jot down the major ideas that you learned from this chapter.

_____

_____

_____

_____

_____

_____

_____

_____

_____

_____

_____

THE COMPANION Website *Journal*

Log on to **www.prenhall.com/montgomery**, choose the version of this book you are using, and then choose Chapter 14 on the menu. Next, choose "Links" on the left side of the page. Explore one of the websites offered and summarize your findings.

_____

_____

_____

_____

_____

_____

_____

_____

_____

_____

Refer to page 358 of Chapter 14.
Review your **GOALS FOR CHANGE**.
Respond in writing as to the progress
you have made toward reaching one
of your three stated goals.

GOAL STATEMENT

PROGRESS

How is your life changing because of this goal?

CORNERSTONES

for career and life planning

Identify your physical and emotional *limitations.*

Make *educated* and researched *decisions.*

Identify your *best skills* and promote them.

Discover your personality type.

Shadow and do volunteer work.

Realize life is *more* than money.

Know your own *value* system.

Identify what *motivates* you.

Never be afraid to change.

Pinpoint your *interests.*

Make your *own* decisions.

Appendix

This appendix provides advice, suggestions, and hints for coping with some of the common problems and situations that you may face in college.

THE ACADEMIC ADVISOR

Your academic advisor is one of the most important people you will meet at college. You may never have your advisor for a class or even see your advisor except at registration time each semester, but he or she can be of enormous assistance to you throughout your college career.

Advisors are usually appointed by the college, although a few colleges allow students to select their own advisors. A good advisor will be of tremendous value to you; a poor advisor is one of the worst things that could happen to you. If you find that you and your advisor are completely incompatible, do not hesitate to ask for a reassignment.

Recognize that you are the person most responsible for the completion of your degree. You should know as much as your advisor about your degree.

Your roommates, friends, and peers can help you in the advising and registration process, but the last word should always come from your advisor. Your decisions about classes and scheduling should be made with the advice of faculty, staff, and the administration of the college.

If you do not know why you have to take certain courses or in what sequence courses should be taken, don't leave your advisor's office until you find out. Lack of understanding of your course sequence, your college catalog, or the requirements for graduation could mean the difference between a four-year degree, a five-year degree, or no college degree at all.

Academic advisors are not counselors or psychological counselors. They are assigned to assist students in completing their academic programs of study. They may offer advice on personal or career matters, but they are not trained to assist with psychological and emotional matters. However, if you are having problems not related to your academic studies, your academic advisor may be able to direct you to the professional on campus who can best help you address certain issues and problems. Your academic advisor may be the first person to contact in times of crisis.

Cornerstones

for making the most of the student-advisor relationship

- Locate your advisor as soon as you arrive on campus and introduce yourself. Begin your relationship on a positive note.

- Stop by to say hello if you see your advisor in his or her office. Don't stay for a long time without an appointment, but a brief hello can help you build your relationship.

- Prepare a list of questions before you go to your advisor. This will help ensure that you have all the answers you need when you leave.

- Call your advisor if you have a problem that can be dealt with over the phone.

- Don't go to your advisor unprepared. You should have an idea of which classes you would like to take or need to take for the upcoming semester.

THE COLLEGE CATALOG

Every college in the nation has a different catalog. Don't make the mistake of thinking that these catalogs are advertising tools and not that important. Your college catalog is one of the most important publications you will read during your college years. It describes the rules, regulations, policies, procedures, and requirements of the college and your academic degree. It is imperative for you to keep the college catalog that was issued during your first year, because college degree requirements can change from year to year and most colleges require that you graduate under the rules and requirements stated in the catalog under which you entered the college. This policy is sometimes referred to as the grandfather clause.

The college catalog includes information about adding and dropping classes, auditing, probation, plagiarism, attendance, honors, course descriptions, graduation requirements, faculty credentials, and college accreditation, and usually includes a campus map. It is an important tool.

PREREGISTRATION

Sounds simple: preregister, "to register beforehand." Preregistration is a process by which you reserve your seat in classes for the upcoming semester. Although it sounds simple, a large number of students fail to preregister or pay fees. If you are at a large institution, preregistration is a must. If 300 people want to take a class that has 45 seats, logic will tell you that you can't walk in on the first day of class and expect to get a seat. Your graduation may hinge on preregistration; if you are not able to enroll in certain classes, your course sequence could be thrown off and you may have to wait an entire year before a prerequisite class is offered again.

It is equally important to pay your fees on time to ensure that your seat is held until the semester begins. Many colleges have a purge date. If you do not pay your fees by the end of fall term exams, for instance, your schedule of classes for spring semester and your seats in those classes are purged from the computer and another student will get your seat. You may have to pay a late fee and go through the registration process again. More important, the classes you need may be full, and if so, you will have to wait another year to take them. Preregister and pay your fees! Consult your college schedule of classes to determine registration dates and fee payment dates.

Cornerstones

for developing a schedule and preregistering

- Never wait until the last day of preregistration to begin the process.
- Think ahead. If preregistration begins on October 15, you should review the college catalog before that date to begin planning your schedule.
- Make an appointment with your advisor early. Keep the appointment and be on time.
- When developing your schedule, work with several plans. If one class happens to be full, what are your alternatives? The students who graduate on time are those who know how to plan alternatives.
- Present your advisor with options. Don't suggest only one class or time. You may have to rearrange your life to get the class you need. Do it!
- There is no need to pay your fees on the first day of fee payment, but make sure that you do not miss the deadline.

INDEPENDENT STUDY AND DISTANCE-LEARNING COURSES

Independent study courses or courses taught by distance learning are great for students who work or have families and small children. These courses have flexible hours and few, if any, class meetings and allow you to work at your own pace. Do not let anyone try to tell you that these courses are easier than regular classroom offerings; they are not. Independent study and distance-learning courses are usually more difficult for the average student. Some colleges reserve independent study and distance-learning courses for students with GPAs of 3.0 or higher. You need to be a self-starter and highly motivated to complete and do well in these courses.

Cornerstones

for succeeding in independent study & distance learning courses

- If at all possible, review the material for the course before you register. This may help you in making the decision to enroll.

- Begin before the beginning! If at all possible, obtain the independent study packet or distance-learning tapes before the semester begins and start working. You may think you have the whole semester, but time will quickly slip by.

- Make an appointment to meet the professor as soon as possible. Some colleges will schedule a meeting for you. If it is not possible to meet, at least phone the professor and introduce yourself.

- Communicate with your advisor from time to time via email if your campus is equipped for you to do so.

- Develop a schedule for completing each assignment and stick to it! Don't let time steal away from you. This is the biggest problem with these courses.

- Keep a copy of all work mailed, emailed, or delivered to the professor or the college. When possible, send your materials by certified mail to ensure their delivery.

- Always mail, email, or deliver your assignment on time or even early if possible. Remember that you have deadlines and the mail system can be slow. Allow time in your schedule for revisions.

- Try to find someone who is registered for the same course so that you can work together or at least have a phone number to call if you run into a problem.

SUMMER SCHOOL

Some students can think of nothing worse than summer school. Others see it as a chance to get ahead or repeat a class in which they might have received a poor grade. Whether you attend summer school by choice or necessity, it can be a rough experience if you do not pace yourself and prepare from day one. Although you will have an instructor in summer classes, summer school is similar to independent study or distance-learning courses in that you must begin your studies, projects, and activities from day one! Most summer sessions last only a few weeks, and you will not have time to put things off until later. You will be exposed to the same amount of information and the same amount of work involved in courses offered during the regular semester.

Some academic programs require students to attend for at least one summer session during the four-year degree program. Some degrees cannot be completed in four years without taking a course during the summer or an overload during the fall or spring semesters. If this is your situation, a few classes in summer school may be an option for you.

You may want to save your more difficult courses for the summer session when you can take only one course at a time. Many students take courses with labs during the summer, because they can devote more time to them than is possible during the traditional semester.

If you are attending a college far from home, you might consider taking a class at a local college during the summer. Most colleges require you to get permission from your registrar or department head before enrolling in a summer program at another college if you want credit for your work. Check your college catalog for details and rules regarding status as a transient student.

DROPPING CLASSES, DROPPING OUT, AND STOPPING OUT

Sometimes students have to drop a class or their entire schedule because of family problems, medical reasons, work, or other reasons. We mention this because some students simply leave college, thinking that if they do not come back, their classes will automatically be dropped and everything will be fine. Then, when they return or transfer to another college, they are horrified to see five F's on their transcript. Never assume that your classes have been dropped from your records. At most colleges, classes are not automatically dropped. You must take care of this process. To make matters worse, some colleges never remove grades from your transcript, even if you repeat the course a thousand times and make an A every time. If you leave your classes without taking care of the paperwork, your grade of F can be with you and be calculated in your GPA for the rest of your college years.

If you have to drop all your classes, it is best to talk with each professor and explain why you are leaving. An open and honest relationship with your professors could help you when you return. Leaving your classes for an entire semester is called *dropping out;* if you decide not to return to college, the same term applies. Leaving college for one semester because of problems, work, or military service and planning to return is called by some colleges *stopping out.* Whether you drop a class, drop out for the semester, or stop out for a year, make sure your records are in order before you go. This will save you money, time, effort, and frustration on your return to college. Consult your college catalog for information dealing with dropping out, dropping courses, or stopping out.

THE PROFESSORATE

In high school, if a teacher is out because of illness or for some other reason, a substitute teaches the class. In college, substitutes are rarely used. When a college professor is absent because of illness, a conference, or another commitment, the class is usually canceled. Occasionally, guest lecturers substitute for an absent professor. Do not assume that you can cut class or give less than your full attention to a guest professor. Information provided by a guest professor often appears on tests and quizzes.

When the Professor Doesn't Show. At times during your college career a professor will not show up for class. This will be rare, but it will happen. Sometimes, a note on the board or door will explain the circumstances of the professor's absence. If there is no note, assume that the professor is running late. Do not leave class just because the professor is not there on time. You should normally wait at least 15 minutes for a professor. Use common sense and wait long enough to see whether the professor is just running late or is truly not going to show for the class.

You might consider starting a roster for students to sign before they leave so that you all have proof that you attended the class. You can present the list to the professor if there is a question about attendance.

Consult your college catalog or your class syllabus for details regarding a policy for waiting when a professor does not arrive.

When Professors Don't Speak English Well. Yes, you will have professors who do not speak English well. Universities often hire professors from around the world because of their expertise in their subjects. You may be shocked to find that it is difficult to understand a professor's dialect or pronunciation. If you have a professor with a foreign dialect, remember these hints:

- Sit near the front of the room.
- Watch the professor's mouth when you can.
- Follow the professor's nonverbal communication patterns.
- Use a tape recorder if allowed.
- Read the material beforehand so that you will have a general understanding of what is being discussed.
- Ask questions when you do not understand the material.

Understanding What Professors Want. College professors are unique. They all value and appreciate different things. What makes one professor the happiest person on earth will upset another. One professor may love students who ask questions and another professor will think these students are trying to be difficult. One professor may enjoy students who have opposing points of view, while the next professor may consider them troublemakers. One professor may be stimulated when students stop by the office to chat, while another may consider this an infringement on his or her time.

The best way to deal with your professors is as individuals, on a one-to-one, class-by-class basis. Take some time at the beginning of the semester to make notes about what you see in class, how students are treated who do certain things, and how the professor reacts in certain situations. This exercise will assist you in decoding your professors and in making the most out of your relationship with them.

There are, of course, certain characteristics that all professors cherish in students, so keep in mind that all professors like students who read the text, come to class and come on time, and hand in assignments on time.

FINANCIAL AID

You may feel that it is crazy to talk about financial aid at this point. After all, you had to have found the money to enroll in college or you would not be in this orientation class. Still, financial aid comes in many forms, and there may be some sources of aid you have not yet thought about that can help you through the rest of your college years.

The most well-known sources of financial assistance are the federal and state governments. Federal and state financial aid programs have been in place for many years and are a staple of assistance for many college students. Sources of aid include

- Direct Loans
- Federal Family Education Loans (FFEL)
- Federal Supplemental Education Opportunity Grants (FSEOG)
- Federal Work-Study (FWS)
- Pell Grants
- Perkins Loans

Not every school takes part in every federal assistance program. To determine which type of aid is available at your school, you need to contact the financial aid office.

Some students may be confused about the differences among loans, grants, and work–study programs. The following definitions are supplied by *The Student Guide,* published by the U.S. Department of Education:

- Grants—Monies that you don't have to repay
- Work-Study—Money earned for work that you do at the college that does not have to be repaid
- Loans—Borrowed money that you must repay with interest

An undergraduate may receive any of these types of assistance, whereas graduate students cannot receive Pell Grants or FSEOGs.

One of the biggest mistakes students make when thinking about financial aid is forgetting about scholarships from private industry and

Student Eligibility for Federal Financial Aid*

To receive aid from the major federal student aid programs, you must:

- Have financial need, except for some loan programs.

- Hold a high school diploma or GED, pass an independently administered test approved by the U.S. Department of Education, or meet the standards established by your state.

- Be enrolled as a regular student working toward a degree or certificate in an eligible program. You may not receive aid for correspondence or telecommunications courses unless they are a part of an associate, bachelor, or graduate degree program.

- Be a U.S. citizen.

- Have a valid social security number.

- Make satisfactory academic progress.

- Sign a statement of educational purpose.

- Sign a statement of updated information.

- Register with the selective service, if required.

*Some federal financial aid may be dependent on your not having a previous drug conviction.

Source: Adapted from *The Student Guide: Financial Aid from the U.S. Department of Education.* U.S. Dept. of Education, Washington D.C. 2000–2001.

social or civic organizations. Each year, millions of dollars are unclaimed because students do not know about these scholarships or where to find the necessary information. Below, you will find resources that can help you research and apply for all types of financial aid.

College Costs and Financial Aid Handbook (The College Board)

Don't Miss Out (Octameron Press)

Financial Aid for College (Peterson's)

Free Dollars from the Federal Government (Prentice Hall)

Free Money for Athletic Scholarships (Henry Holt)

Free Money for College (Facts on File)

How to Obtain Maximum Financial Aid (Login Publications Consortium)

Paying for College (Villard Books)

Paying Less for College (Peterson's)

Peterson's 4-Year Colleges (Peterson's)

Winning Money for College (Peterson's)

Winning Scholarships for College (Henry Holt)

You will also want to research:

Your college catalog (for scholarships at your college)

Your place of employment

Your parents' or spouse's place of employment

Social and civic groups within your community or hometown

Cornerstones

for applying for financial aid

- *Do not miss a deadline.* There are *no* exceptions for making up deadlines for federal financial aid!
- *Read all instructions* before beginning the process.
- Always fill out the application completely and have someone proof your work.
- If documentation is required, submit it according to the instructions. Do not fail to do all that the application asks you to do.
- Never lie about your financial status.
- Begin the application process as soon as possible. Do not wait until the last moment. Some aid is given on a first come, first served basis. Income tax preparation time is usually financial aid application time.
- Talk to the financial aid officer at the institution you will attend. Person-to-person contact is always best. Never assume anything until you get it in writing.
- Take copies of flyers and brochures that are available from the financial aid office. Private companies and civic groups will often notify the financial aid office if they have funds available.
- Always apply for admission as well as financial aid. Many awards are given by the college to students who are already accepted.
- If you are running late with an application, find out if there are electronic means of filing.
- Always keep a copy of your tax returns for each year!
- To receive almost any money, including some scholarships, you must fill out the Free Application for Federal Student Aid form.
- Apply for everything possible. You will get nothing if you do not apply.

COLLEGE WORK–STUDY PROGRAMS

A part of your financial aid package could include work–study. In this program you work a few hours each day and earn a paycheck at the end of each month to help defray the cost of your college education. A college work–study program confers several secondary benefits that can make this a vital aspect of financing your tuition.

A college work–study position provides additional experiences that may allow you to explore jobs and activities that you may not previously have considered. Work–study jobs are often connected to the department or discipline of your college major, and the knowledge and experience you can gain are immeasurable.

College work–study can also provide the opportunity for you to meet people who may eventually help you get a job, help you get into graduate school, or assist you through difficult times in your degree program. College work–study is more than earning money; it is a chance to explore new options, meet exciting people, and gain experience in your discipline. Work–study money is taxed, but does not count against your earned income when you apply for financial aid for the next year.

PAYING TUITION

Paying tuition is another process that sounds simple, and it is if you do it. Yet each semester, countless students for one reason or another do not pay their tuition on time, or at all, and lose their spots in classes for which they were preregistered. Painful as it may be, you must observe the deadlines for payment dates. Paying tuition on time can save you $25 to $50 in late fees, not to mention the hassle and frustration of having to re-register. Take this seriously. If you can pay your tuition by mail, you can avoid wasting valuable time standing in long lines. However, never send cash in the mail. Keep your paid receipts from tuition payments.

BUYING A MEAL PLAN

Some colleges offer a meal plan, some do not. Some colleges require on-campus students to purchase some variation of a meal plan, others do not. You will need to consult your student handbook for details. Be careful about purchasing something that you may not use. If you purchase a three-meal-a-day plan, but never get up early enough to eat breakfast, you have wasted a great deal of money. If you have pizza delivered to your room a lot and don't eat dinner at the dining hall or cafeteria, again, you have wasted money. Purchase a meal plan that matches your habits!

CASH CARDS

Some colleges offer cash cards so that students do not have to carry a lot of money with them. A cash card works similarly to a debit card from a bank. Cash cards may be accepted at the campus bookstore, cafeteria, library, and copy center, for example. You purchase a cash card in a certain amount, say, $500, and each expenditure electronically reduces the available amount on the card until it is all spent. If your cash card works on a Personal Identification Number (PIN) system, be sure that you never let anyone know your PIN. Do not tell even your closest friend. Students have lost every cent to "friends" they trusted. Be cautious.

BUYING TEXTBOOKS

The biggest gripe that students today have about college life is the cost of textbooks. We have mentioned that it is not wise to sell your texts after each semester. Of course, you may have to do so because of financial concerns, and most colleges purchase used texts from students at a reduced rate. This policy may be helpful to you, but it may also create a problem. Someone may see your books lying on the floor of the student center and decide to take them and sell them to the bookstore. This could cost you upwards of $300 to $400. Guard your textbooks. Never leave them in your car overnight, in an unlocked residence hall room, or in a library study room.

Do not purchase a used textbook from a student until you have checked to see that the same book will be used in the course again. A professor may opt to use a new edition of the text or a different book altogether.

Also, do not buy a lab manual or workbook that has been used. If the assignments have been completed, then you do not have a chance to complete the assignment yourself, which may cause problems later on. Always buy new lab books and workbooks.

PARKING ON CAMPUS

The second biggest gripe on college campuses is parking. Sometimes it seems as though there are 16,000 students, 750 employees, and 100 guests, but only 37 parking slots on campus! Although the situation is not really that bad, on almost every college campus the parking situation is frustrating. We cannot create more parking spaces or valet park your car for you, but we can give you some advice learned by hard knocks about parking on campus.

- Purchase a parking decal if it is required. One ticket for not having a decal could probably have covered the cost of the sticker.
- If your sticker reads "Z Lot Only," park in the Z lot only! Parking in the wrong lot can cost you up to $50 per instance.
- Never, under any circumstances, park in a handicapped spot unless you have a decal that allows you to do so. Fines can range from $200 to $1000 for each violation. Also, by parking in a handicapped zone, you may be creating a hardship for someone who needs the space for more than mere convenience.
- Arrive early so that you have a slight chance of finding a parking space within an hour's hike of your classroom. The Z lot is usually in another county. Plan for this in your schedule.
- Pay your fines when you get them. Do not let them add up or you could quickly owe $100 to $500 in a semester. When you go to pay your tuition, your parking fines will be added to it, and you will not be allowed to register for classes until the fines are paid in full. (This is also true of library fines.)

- Do not park in a faculty member's parking place. The last thing you need is to be seen getting into your car in the faculty lot when the professor had to park in Canada because you took that slot. Big mistake!

- Keep change in your car in case you have to park in a metered space owned by the college or the city. Meter fines can range from $5 to $50.

- If parking is restricted to residents of the hall or community, drive on. Without a decal identifying you as a resident, the campus or city police will ticket or tow your car.

- Carpool when possible. You'll save money and your frustration level will decrease.

- Be polite to the traffic officer or the secretary in the transportation office. Do not use profanity; it will get you nowhere except perhaps jail!

Glossary

Academic freedom Academic freedom allows professors in institutions of higher education to conduct research and teach their findings, even if the subject matter is controversial. Academic freedom gives college professors the right to teach certain materials that might not be allowed in high school.

Accreditation Most high schools and colleges in the United States receive accreditation from a regional agency, which ensures that all its members meet or exceed a minimum set of standards. The Southern Association of Colleges and Schools is an accreditation agency.

Adding Adding a class means enrolling in an additional class. The term is usually used during registration period or during the first week of a semester.

Administration The administration of a college is headed by the president and vice presidents and comprises the non-teaching personnel who handle all administrative aspects of running the college. The structure of the administration varies at each college.

Advising An academic advisor is assigned to each student on arrival on campus. It is the advisor's responsibility to guide students through their academic work at the college, to be sure that they know what classes to take and in what order. An advisor is most often a faculty member in the student's discipline or major who will work with the student through the student's entire college career.

African American studies Courses in African American studies consider the major contributions of African Americans in art, literature, history, medicine, sciences, and architecture. Many colleges offer majors and minors in African American studies.

AIDS This acronym stands for **a**cquired **i**mmuno**d**eficiency **s**yndrome, a disease that is transmitted sexually, intravenously, or from mother to fetus. There is currently no known cure for AIDS, but several medications, such as AZT, DDC, 3TC, DT4, Sequinavir, DDI, and Indinavir, help to slow the deterioration of the immune system. AIDS is the number one killer among people aged 25 to 44 years.

Alumna, alumnus, alumni These terms describe people who attended a college. *Alumna* refers to a woman, *alumnus* refers to a man, and *alumni* refers to more than one of either or both. The term *alumni* is the most often used.

America Online America Online (AOL) is the nation's largest commercial on-line computer service. It offers a gateway to the Internet, magazines, software, live interactive services, and financial services, and can be one of the most informative and exciting learning tools for college students today.

Articulation An articulation agreement is a document signed by representatives of two or more institutions that guarantees that courses taken at one of the participating institutions will be accepted by the others. For example, if Oak College has an articulation agreement with Maple College, course work completed at Oak College will be accepted toward a degree at Maple College.

Associate degree An associate degree is a two-year degree that usually prepares the student to enter the workforce with a specific skill or trade. It is also offered to students as the first two years of a bachelor's or four-year degree program. Not all colleges offer the associate degree.

Attendance Every college has an attendance policy, such as "any student who misses more than 10 percent of the total class hours will receive an F for the course." This policy is followed strictly by some professors and more leniently by others. Students should know the attendance policy of each professor with whom they are studying.

Auditing Most colleges offer the option of auditing a course. Whereas a student enrolled in a course pays a fee, must attend classes, takes exams, and receives credit, a student auditing a course usually pays a smaller fee, does not have to take exams, and does not receive credit. People who are having trouble in a subject or who simply want to gain more knowledge about a subject but don't need or want credit are the most likely candidates for auditing. Some colleges charge full price for auditing a course.

Baccalaureate The baccalaureate degree, more commonly called the bachelor's degree, is a four-year degree granted in a specific field, although it can be completed in as few as three or as many as six or more years. This degree prepares students for careers in such fields as education, social work, engineering, fine arts, and journalism.

Board of trustees The board of trustees is the governing body of a college. For state schools, the board is appointed by government officials (usually the governor) of the state. The board hires the president, must approve any curriculum changes to degree programs, and sets policy for the college.

Campus The term *campus* refers to the physical plant of a university or college, including all buildings, fields, arenas, auditoriums, and other properties owned by the college.

Campus police All colleges and universities have a campus police or security office. Campus security helps students with problems ranging from physical danger to car trouble. Every student should know where this office is in case of emergency.

Carrel A carrel is a booth or small room, often large enough to accommodate one person only, located in the library. Students and faculty can reserve a carrel for professional use by the semester or the week. Personal belongings and important academic materials should never be left in a carrel, because they could be stolen.

Catalog The college catalog is a legal, binding document that states the degree requirements of the college. It is issued to all students at the beginning of their college career and it is essential to developing a schedule and completing a degree program. Students must keep the catalog of the year in which they entered college.

Certificate A certificate program is a series of courses, usually lasting one year, designed to educate and train an individual in a specific area, such as welding, automotive repair, medical transcription, tool and die, early childhood, physical therapy, and fashion merchandising. Although certified and detailed, these programs are not degree programs. Associate and bachelor's degrees are also offered in many of the areas that have certificate programs.

CLEP The College Level Examination Program (CLEP) allows students to test out of a course. The exams are nationally averaged and are often more extensive than a course in the same area. If a student CLEPs a course, it means the student does not have to take the course in which he or she passed the CLEP exam.

Cognate A cognate is a course or set of courses taken outside of the student's major but usually in a field related to the major. Some colleges call this a minor. A student majoring in English may take a cognate in history or drama.

Communications College curricula often mandate nine hours of communications, which commonly refers to English and speech (oral communication) courses. The mixture of courses is typically English 101 and 102 and Speech 101; the numbers vary from college to college.

Comprehensive exams Exams that encompass materials from the entire course are comprehensive exams. That is, a comprehensive exam covers information from the first lecture through the last.

Continuing education Continuing education or community education courses are designed to meet specific business and industry needs or to teach subjects of interest to the community. These courses are not offered for college credit, but continuing education units may be awarded. Continuing education courses range from small engine repair to flower arranging, from stained glass making to small-business management.

Co-op This term refers to a relationship between a business or industry and the educational institution that allows a student to spend a semester in college and the next semester on the job. Co-ops may be structured variously, but the general idea of a co-op is always to gain on-the-job experience while in college.

Corequisite A corequisite is a course that must be taken at the same time as another course. Science courses often carry a corequisite; for example, Biology 101 may have as a corequisite the lab course, Biology 101L.

Counseling Most college campuses have a counseling center staffed by counselors trained to assist students with problems that might arise in their personal lives, with their study skills, and with their career aspirations. Counseling is different from advising—academic advisors are responsible for helping students with their academic progress. Some colleges combine the two, but in most cases the counselor and the advisor are two different people with two different job descriptions.

Course title Every course has a course title. A schedule of classes may read: ENG 101, SPC 205, HIS 210, and so on. The college catalog defines what these terms mean. For example, ENG 101 usually stands for English 101, SPC could be the heading for speech, HIS could mean history. Headings and course titles vary from college to college.

Credit hour A credit hour is the unit of academic credit. Most classes are worth three credit hours; science, foreign language, and math courses that require labs are often worth four credit hours. A class that carries three credit hours typically meets for three hours per week. This formula varies in summer sessions and midsessions.

Critical thinking Critical thinking is thinking that is purposeful, reasoned, and goal directed. It is the type of thinking used to solve problems, make associations, connect relationships, formulate inferences, make decisions, and detect faulty arguments and persuasion.

Curriculum The curriculum is a set of classes that the student must take to earn a degree in an area of study.

Dean *Dean* is the title given to the head of a division or area of study. The dean is the policy maker and usually the business manager and final decision maker for that area. A college might have a dean of arts and sciences, a dean of business, and a dean of mathematics. Deans usually report to a vice-president or provost.

Dean's list The dean's list is a listing of students who have achieved at least a 3.5 (B+) on a 4.0 scale (these numbers are defined under "GPA"). Although it varies from college to college, the dean's list generally comprises students in the top 5 percent of the college.

Degree A student is awarded a degree for completing an approved course of study. The type of degree depends on the college, the number of credit hours in the program, and the field of study. A two-year degree is called an associate degree, and a four-year degree is called a bachelor's degree. A student who attends graduate school may receive a master's degree (after two to three years) and a doctorate (after three to ten years). Some colleges offer postdoctorate degrees.

Diploma A diploma is awarded when an approved course of study is completed. Diploma requirements are not as detailed or comprehensive as the requirements for an associate degree and usually consist of only 8 to 12 courses specific to a certain field.

Dropping Students may elect to drop a class if they are not enjoying it or think that they will not be able to pass it because of grades or absenteeism. A class that has been dropped will no longer appear on the student's schedule or be calculated in the GPA. Rules and regulations governing dropping courses vary from college to college and are explained in the college catalog.

Elective An elective is a course that a student chooses to take outside his or her major field of study. An elective can be in an area of interest to the student or in an area that complements the student's major. For example, an English major might choose an elective in the field of theater or history because these fields complement one another. An English major might also elect to take a course in medical terminology because of an interest in that area.

Emeriti This Latin term applies to retired college personnel who have performed exemplary duties during their professional careers. A college president who procured funding for new buildings, enhanced curriculum programs, and increased the endowment might be named president emeritus (singular of emeriti) on retirement.

Evening college An evening college program is designed to allow students who have full-time jobs to enroll in classes that meet in the evening. Some colleges offer an entire degree program in the evening; others offer only some courses in the evening.

Faculty The faculty is the body of professionals at a college who teach, conduct research, and perform community service. Faculty members prepare for many years to hold the responsibilities carried by the title. Some may have studied for 25 years or more to obtain the knowledge and skill necessary to train students in their specific fields.

Fallacy A fallacy is a false notion. It is a statement based on false materials, invalid inferences, or incorrect reasoning.

Fees Fees refer to the money charged by colleges for specific items and services. Fees may be charged for tuition, meal plans, books, health care, and activities. Fees vary from college to college and are usually printed in the college catalog.

Financial aid Financial aid is money awarded to a student from the college, the state or federal government, private sources, or places of employment on the basis of need or of merit. Any grant, loan, or scholarship is formally called financial aid.

Fine arts The fine arts encompass a variety of artistic forms, such as theater, dance, architecture, drawing, painting, sculpture, and music. Some colleges also include literature in this category.

First-year student The term "first-year student" as used by colleges and refers to a student who has not yet completed 30 semester hours of college-level work.

Foreign language Almost every college offers at least one course in foreign languages, and many colleges offer degrees in this area. Some of the many foreign languages offered in U. S. colleges are Spanish, French, Russian, Latin, German, Portuguese, Swahili, Arabic, Japanese, Chinese, and Korean.

Fraternity A fraternity is an organization in the Greek system. Fraternities are open to male students only. Induction for each is different. Many fraternities have their own housing complexes on campus. Honorary fraternities, such as Phi Kappa Phi, are academic in nature and are open to men and women.

GPA The grade point average, GPA, is the numerical grading system used by most colleges in the United States. A student's GPA determines his or her eligibility for continued enrollment, financial aid, and honors. Most colleges operate under a 4.0 system: an A is worth 4 quality points, a B 3 points, a C 2 points, a D 1 point, and an F 0 points. To calculate a GPA, for each course the number of quality points earned is multiplied by the number of credit hours carried by the course; the numbers thus obtained for all courses are added together; finally, this total is divided by the total number of hours carried.

Example: A student is taking English 101, Speech 101, History 201, and Psychology 101, all of which carry three credit hours. If the students earns all A's, the GPA is 4.0; if the student earns all B's, the GPA is 3.0. However, if he or she had a variety of grades, you would calculate as such:

COURSE	GRADE	CREDIT HRS.		QUALITY POINTS		TOTAL POINTS
ENG 101	A	3	x	4	=	12 points
SPC 101	C	3	x	2	=	6 points
HIS 201	B	3	x	3	=	9 points
PSY 101	D	3	x	1	=	3 points

GPA = 30 points divided by 12 hours = 2.5 (C+)

Graduate teaching assistant In some larger colleges and universities, students working toward master's and doctorate degrees teach lower-level undergraduate classes under the direction of a senior professor in the department.

Grant Usually a grant is money that goes toward tuition and books that does not have to be repaid. Grants are most often awarded by the state and federal governments.

Higher education This term applies to any level of education beyond high school; all colleges are considered institutions of higher education.

Honor code Many colleges operate under an honor code, which demands that students perform all work without cheating, plagiarizing, or engaging in any other dishonest actions. A student who breaks the honor code may be expelled from the institution. In some cases, a student may be expelled if he or she does not turn in a fellow student whom he or she knows has broken the code.

Honors Academic honors are based on a student's GPA. Academic honors may include the dean's list, the president's list, and departmental honors. The three highest honors, summa cum laude, magna cum laude, and cum laude, are awarded at graduation to students who have maintained a GPA of 3.5 or better. Although the breakdown varies from college to college, these honors are usually awarded as follows: cum laude, 3.5 to 3.7; magna cum laude, 3.7 to 3.9; and summa cum laude, 4.0.

Honors college The honors college is a degree or a set of classes offered for students who performed exceptionally in high school.

Humanities The humanities are sometimes as misunderstood as the fine arts. Disciplines in the humanities include history, philosophy, religion, cultural studies, and sometimes literature, government, and foreign languages. The college catalog defines what a college designates as humanities.

Identification cards An identification (ID) card is an essential possession for any college student. An ID card allows students to use the library, participate in activities, use physical fitness facilities, and often to attend events free of charge. ID cards can also be useful beyond the campus borders. Admission to movie theaters, museums, zoos, and cultural events usually costs less and is sometimes free for students with IDs. ID cards also allow access to most area library facilities with special privileges. Some colleges issue ID cards at no charge, and some charge a small fee. ID cards are usually validated each semester.

Independent study Many colleges offer some independent study options. Independent study courses have no formal classes and no classroom teacher; students work independently to complete the course under the general guidelines of the department and with the assistance of an instructor. Colleges often require that students maintain a minimum GPA in order to enroll in independent study classes.

Inference An inference is a thought that is arrived at by logical evidence. An inference does not include opinion, hearsay, illogical thought, or unjust reasoning.

Journal In many classes, such as English, orientation, literature, history, and psychology, students are required to keep a journal of thoughts, opinions, research, and class discussions. The journal often serves as a communication link between the student and the professor.

Junior A student who is in his or her third year of college or who has completed at least 60 credit hours of study is a junior.

Learning style A learning style is one's preferred method of processing information and learning new material. There is no right or wrong learning style. The three styles are visual, auditory, and tactile. A visual learner learns best by seeing new information. An auditory learner learns best by hearing new information, and a tactile learner learns best by doing, touching, and feeling.

Lecture The lecture is the lesson given by an instructor in a class. Some instructors use group discussions, peer tutoring, or multimedia presentations. The term *lecture* is usually used when the material is presented in a lecture format, that is, when the professor presents most of the information.

Liberal arts A liberal arts curriculum ensures that the students are exposed to a variety of disciplines and cultural experiences, that they take courses beyond those needed for a specific vocation or occupation. A student at a liberal arts college who is majoring in biology would also have to take courses in fine arts, history, social sciences, math, hard sciences, and other areas, for example.

Load The number of credit hours or classes that a student is taking is the student's load. The normal load is between 15 and 18 hours or five to six classes. In most colleges, 12 hours is considered a full-time load, but a student can take up to 18 or 21 hours for the same tuition.

Logical A logical thought is a thought that is based on evidence, reasoned and critical thought, and proven past events and situations. Logical thoughts avoid fallacies, manipulation, opinions, and invalid inferences.

Major A major is a student's intended field of study. The term *major* indicates that the majority of the student's work will be completed in that field. Students are usually required to declare a major by the end of their sophomore (second) year.

Meal plan A student purchases a meal plan at the beginning of a semester that allows the student to eat certain meals in the cafeteria or dining hall. These plans are regulated by a computer card or punch system. Meal plans can be purchased for three meals a day, breakfast only, lunch only, or a variety of other meal combinations.

Mentor A mentor is someone who can help a student through troubled times, assist in decision making, and provide advice. A mentor can be a teacher, staff member, fellow classmate, or upper-level student. Mentors seldom volunteer. They usually fall into the role of mentor because they are easy to talk with, knowledgeable about the college and the community, and willing to lend a helping hand. Sometimes students are assigned mentors when they arrive on campus.

Minor A student's minor usually comprises six to eight courses in a specific field that complements the student's major area of study. A student majoring in engineering might minor in math or electronics, subjects that might help later in the workforce.

Natural sciences The natural and physical sciences refer to a select group of courses from biology, chemistry, physical science, physics, anatomy, zoology, botany, geology, genetics, microbiology, physiology, and astronomy.

Orientation All students are invited and many are required to attend an orientation session when they enter college. These sessions are extremely useful. They present important information about college life as well as details of the rules of the specific college.

Plagiarism Plagiarism refers to the act of using another person's words or works as one's own without citing the original author. Penalties for plagiarism vary and can include asking the student to withdraw from the institution. Most institutions have strict guidelines for dealing with plagiarism. Penalties for plagiarism are usually listed in the student handbook.

Prefix The code used by the Office of the Registrar to designate a certain area of study is called a prefix. Common prefixes are ENG for English, REL for Religion, THE for Theater, and HIS for History. Prefix lettering varies from college to college.

Preprofessional programs Preprofessional programs usually refer to majors that *require* further study at the master's or doctoral level in order to be able to practice in that field. Such programs include law, medicine, dentistry, psychiatry, nursing, veterinary studies, and theology.

Prerequisite A prerequisite is a course that must be taken *before* another course. For example, in most colleges students are required to take English 101 and 102 (Composition I and II) before taking any literature courses. Therefore, English 101 and 102 are prerequisites to literature. Prerequisites are listed in the college catalog.

President A college president is the visionary leader of the institution. He or she is usually hired by the board of trustees. The president's primary responsibilities include financial planning, fund-raising, developing community relations, and maintaining the academic integrity of the curriculum. Every employee at the college is responsible to the president.

Probation A student who has not performed well in his or her academic studies, usually manifested by a GPA below 2.0 in any given semester or quarter, may be placed on academic probation for one semester. If the student continues to perform below 2.0, he or she may be suspended. The rules for probation and suspension must be displayed in the college catalog.

Professor Not all teachers at the college level are professors. The system of promotion among college teachers is adjunct instructor, instructor, lecturer, assistant professor, associate professor, and full professor, or professor. A full professor is likely to have been in the profession for a long time and usually holds a doctorate degree.

Provost The provost of a college is the primary policy maker with regard to academic standards. The provost usually reports directly to the president. Many colleges do not have provosts, but have instead a vice-president for academic affairs or a dean of instruction.

Readmit A student who has stopped out for a semester or two usually has to be readmitted to the college but does not lose previously earned academic credit unless the credit carried a time limit. Some courses in psychology, for example, carry a five- or ten-year limit, which means that the course must be retaken if a degree is not awarded within that time period. Students who elect not to attend summer sessions do not need to be readmitted. There is typically no application fee for a readmit student.

Registrar The registrar has one of the most difficult jobs on any college campus, because the registrar is responsible for all student academic records as well as for entering all grades, recording all drops and adds, printing the schedule, and verifying all candidates for graduation. The Office of the Registrar is sometimes referred to as the records office.

Residence hall A residence hall is a facility on campus where students live. Residence halls can be single sex or coeducational. Many new students choose to live in residence halls because they are conveniently located and they provide a good way to meet new friends and to become involved in extracurricular activities. Each residence hall usually has a full-time supervisor and elects a student representative to the student council. In addition, a director of student housing oversees the residence halls.

Residency requirement Many colleges have a residency requirement, that is, they require that a minimum number of credits must be earned at the home institution. Many two-year colleges require that at least 50 percent of credits applied toward graduation must be earned at the home college. Many four-year colleges require that the last 30 hours of credits must be earned at the home college. All residency requirements are spelled out in the college catalog.

Room and board Room and board refers to a place to stay and food to eat. Colleges often charge students who live on campus a fee for room and board. Students may opt to buy a meal plan along with their dorm room. Issues involving room and board are usually discussed during orientation.

Scholar *Scholar* typically refers to a student who has performed in a superior manner in a certain field of study.

Section code When many sections of the same course are offered, a section code identifies the hour and instructor of the student's particular class. A schedule that includes section codes may look something like this:

English 101	01	MWF	8:00–8:50	Smith
English 101	02	MWF	8:00–8:50	Jones
English 101	03	T TH	8:00–9:15	McGee

The numbers 01, 02, 03, and so on refer to a specific section of 101.

Senior Senior refers to a student who is in the last year of study for the undergraduate degree. To be a senior a student must have completed at least 90 credit hours.

Social sciences The social sciences study society and people. Social science courses may include psychology, sociology, anthropology, political science, geography, economics, and international studies.

Sophomore *Sophomore* refers to a student who is in the second year of study and who has completed at least 30 credit hours.

Sorority A sorority is an organization in the Greek system open to women only. Many sororities have on-campus housing complexes. Initiation into a sorority differs from organization to organization and from campus to campus.

Staff College personnel are usually divided into three categories: administration, staff, and faculty. The staff is responsible for the day-to-day workings of the college. People who work in admissions, financial aid, the bookstore, housing, student activities, and personnel, for example, usually hold staff titles, whereas the people who head these departments are usually in administration.

Student Government Association One of the most powerful and visible organizations on the college campus, the Student Government Association (SGA) usually comprises students from all four undergraduate classes. Officers are elected annually. The SGA is the student voice on campus and represents the entire student body before the administration of the college.

Student loan A student loan is money that must be repaid. Student loans generally have a much lower rate of interest than do bank loans, and the payment schedule for most student loans does not begin until six months after graduation. This delayed start is intended to allow the graduate to find a secure job and a steady income before having to make payments. If a student decides to return to school, the loan can be deferred, with additional interest, until the graduate degree is completed.

Suspension Students may be suspended for a variety of reasons, but most suspensions are for academic reasons. GPA requirements vary, but students are usually suspended if their GPA falls below 1.5 for two consecutive semesters. The college catalog lists the rules regarding suspension.

Syllabus In college, a syllabus replaces the class outline of high school. A syllabus is a legally binding contract between the student and the professor; it contains the attendance policy, the grading scale, the required text, the professor's office hours and phone number(s), and important, relevant information about the course. Most professors include the class operational calendar as a part of the syllabus. The syllabus is one of the most important documents that is issued in a class. Students should take the syllabus to class daily and keep it at least until the semester is over.

Tenure Tenure basically guarantees a professor lifelong employment at an institution. Tenure is usually awarded to professors who have been with the college for many years in recognition of their successful efforts in research, their record of having books and articles published, and their community service.

TOEFL The Test of English as a Foreign Language, TOEFL, is used to certify that international students have the English skills necessary to succeed at the institution or to become a teaching assistant. Some colleges allow international students to use English to satisfy their foreign language requirement if they score high enough on the TOEFL.

Transcript A transcript is a formal record of all work attempted and/or completed at a college. A student has a transcript for every college attended. Many colleges have a policy of listing all classes, completed or not, on the transcript. Some colleges allow Ds and Fs to be removed if the student repeats the course and earns a better grade, but many others retain the original grade and continue to calculate it in the GPA. Rules regarding transcripts vary from college to college. Many employers now require that a prospective employee furnish a college transcript.

Transfer The term *transfer* can refer to course work as well as a student. A student who enrolls in one college and then moves to another is classified as a transfer student. The course work completed at the original college is called transfer work. Many colleges have rules regarding the number of credit hours that a student can transfer. Most colleges will not accept credit from another college if the grade on the course is lower than a C.

Transient A transient student is a student who is taking one or two courses at a college other than his or her home institution. For example, a student who enrolls in a college near home for the summer while maintaining student status at his or her chosen college is a transient student.

Transitional studies Many colleges have an open admission policy, meaning that the door is open to any student, and colleges frequently offer a transitional studies program to help students reach their educational goals. For example, a student who has not performed well in English, math, or reading may be required to attend a transitional studies class to upgrade basic skills in that area.

Veterans' Affairs Many colleges have an Office of Veterans' Affairs to assist those students who have served in the military. Colleges often accept credit earned by a veteran while in the service. Veterans' financial packages are also often different because of the GI Bill.

Vice president Many colleges have several vice-presidents who serve under the president. These are senior-level administrators who assist with the daily operations of the college and may include vice presidents of academic affairs, financial affairs, and student affairs, among others.

Volumes A volume refers to a book or a piece of nonprint material that assists students in their studies. If a college library has 70,000 volumes, it means that the library has 70,000 books *and* other pieces of media. Many colleges have millions of volumes.

Who's Who This is the shortened title of *Who's Who in American Colleges and Universities*. Students are nominated by the college for this national recognition because of their academic standing and their achievements in cocurricular activities and community service.

Women's studies Some colleges offer majors and minors in women's studies. The curriculum is centered on the major contributions of women in art, literature, medicine, history, law, architecture, and sciences.

References

Adler, R., Rosenfeld, L., and Towne, N. *Interplay. The Process of Interpersonal Communication*. New York: Holt, Rinehart and Winston, 1989.

American College Testing Program. *National Drop Out Rates*. ACT Institutional Data File, Iowa City, 1995.

Armstrong, T. *Multiple Intelligences in the Classroom*. Alexandria, VA: Association for Supervision and Curriculum Development, 1994.

Astin, A. *Achieving Educational Excellence*. San Francisco: Jossey-Bass, 1985.

Beebe, S., and Beebe, S. *Public Speaking: An Audience Centered Approach*. 2d ed. Englewood Cliffs, NJ: Prentice Hall, 1997.

Benson, H. *The Relaxation Response*. New York: Caral Publishing Group, 1992.

Benson, H., and Stuart, E. *The Wellness Book: The Comprehensive Guide to Maintaining Health and Treating Stress-Related Illness*. New York: Birch Lane Press, 1992.

Benson, H., and Stuart, Eileen. *Wellness Encyclopedia*. Boston: Houghton Mifflin, 1991.

Berenblatt, M., and Berenblatt, A. *Make an Appointment with Yourself: Simple Steps to Positive Self-Esteem*. Deerfield Beach, FL: Health Communication, 1994.

Beyer, B. *Developing a Thinking Skills Program*. Boston: Allyn and Bacon, 1998.

Bosak, J. *Fallacies*. Dubuque, IA: Educulture Publishers, 1976.

Boyle, M., and Zyla, G. *Personal Nutrition*. St. Paul, MN: West Publishing, 1992.

Bozzi, V. "A Healthy Dose of Religion," *Psychology Today,* November, 1988.

Buscaglia, L. *Living, Loving, and Learning*. New York: Ballantine, 1982.

Cameron, J. *The Artist's Way: A Spiritual Path to Higher Creativity*. New York: Penguin Putnam, 1992.

Checkley, K. "The first seven . . . and the eighth." *Educational Leadership, 55,* no. 1, September, 1997.

Chickering, A., and Schlossberg, N. *Getting the Most out of College*. Boston: Allyn and Bacon, 1995.

Christian, J., and Greger, J. *Nutrition for Living*. Redwood City, CA: Benjamin/Cummings Publishing, 1994.

Chopra, D. *The Seven Spiritual Laws of Success*. San Rafael, CA: New World Library, 1994.

Cohen, L. *Conducting Research on the Internet*. University of Albany Libraries; 1996.
http://www.albany.edu

Cohen, L. *Evaluating Internet Resources*. University of Albany Libraries; 1996.
http://www.albany.edu

"Commonly Abused Drugs." National Institute on Drug Abuse
http://www.nida.nih.gov/DrugsofAbuse.html

Cooper, A. *Time Management for Unmanageable People*. New York: Bantam Books, 1993.

Donatelle, R., and Davis, L. *Health: The Basics*. Englewood Cliffs, NJ: Prentice Hall, 1994.

Ellis, D., Lankowitz, S., Stupka, D., and Toft, D. *Career Planning*. Rapid City, SD: College Survival, Inc., 1990.

Elrich, M. "The Stereotype Within." *Educational Leadership,* April 1994, p. 12.

Freshman Survey Data Report. Cooperative Institutional Research Program Sponsored by the Higher Education Research Institute (HERI). University of California, Los Angeles, 1999.

Fulghum, R. *All I Really Need to Know, I Learned in Kindergarten*. New York: Ivy Books, 1988.

Gardner, H. *Frames of Mind: The Theory of Multiple Intelligences*. New York: Basic Books, 1983.

Gardner, H. "Reflections on multiple intelligences: myths and messages." *Phi Delta Kappan, 77,* no. 3, November, 1995, p. 200.

Gardner, J., and Jewler, J. *Your College Experience*. Belmont, CA: Wadsworth, 2000.

Gardenswartz, L., and Rowe, A. *Managing Diversity: A Complete Desk Reference and Planning Guide.* New York: Irwin/Pfeiffer, 1993.

Grilly, D. *Drugs and Human Behavior.* Boston: Allyn and Bacon, 1994.

Gunthrie, H., and Picciano, M. *Human Nutrition.* Salem, MA: Mosby, 1995.

Hall, D. *Jump Start Your Brain.* New York: Warner Books, 1995.

Hales, D. *Your Health.* Redwood City, CA: Benjamin/Cummings Publishing, 1991.

Helpern, D. *Thought and Knowledge: An Introduction to Critical Thinking.* Mahwah, NJ: Lawrence Erlbaum, 1996.

Kirby, D. "The worst is yet to come." *The Advocate,* January 19, 1999, p. 57.

Kleiman, C. *The 100 Best Jobs for the 90's and Beyond.* New York: Berkley Books, 1992.

Kübler-Ross, E. *On Death and Dying.* New York: Macmillan, 1969.

Lecky, P. *Self-Consistency: A Theory of Personality.* Garden City, NY: Anchor, 1951.

Nevid, J., Fichner-Rathus, L., and Rathus, S. *Human Sexuality in a World of Diversity.* Boston: Allyn and Bacon, 1995.

Olesen, E. *Mastering the Winds of Change.* New York: Harper Business, 1993.

Ormondroyd, J., Engle, M., and Cosgrave, T. *Distinguishing Scholarly Journals from Other Periodicals.* Cornell University Libraries; 1996a.
http://www.library.cornell.edu

Ormondroyd, J., Engle, M., and Cosgrave, T. *How to Critically Analyze Information Sources.* Cornell University Libraries; 1996b.
http://www. library.cornell.edu

Pauk, W. *How to Study in College.* 6th ed. New York: Houghton Mifflin, 2001.

Paul, R. *What Every Person Needs to Survive in a Rapidly Changing World.* Santa Rosa, CA: The Foundation for Critical Thinking, 1992.

Popenoe, D. *Sociology.* 9th ed. Englewood Cliffs, NJ: Prentice Hall, 1993.

Powell, E. *Sex on Your Terms.* Boston: Allyn and Bacon, 1996.

Rathus, S., and Fichner-Rathus, L. *Making the Most out of College.* Englewood Cliffs, NJ: Prentice Hall, 1994.

Rathus, S., Nevid, J., and Fichner-Rathus, L. *Essentials of Human Sexuality.* Boston: Allyn and Bacon, 1998.

"Retention Rates by Institutional Type," Higher Education Research Institute, UCLA, Los Angeles, 1989.

Rogers, C. *On Becoming Partners: Marriage and Its Alternatives.* New York: Delacorte Press, 1972.

Romas, J., and Sharma, M. *Practical Stress Management.* Boston: Allyn and Bacon, 1995.

Sciolino, E. "World Drug Crop Up Sharply in 1989 Despite U.S. Effort." *New York Times,* March 2, 1990.

Shaffer, C., and Amundsen, K. *Creating Community Anywhere.* Los Angeles: Jeremy P. Tarcher Publishing, 1994.

Shenitz, B. "The worst is over." *The Advocate,* January 19, 1999, p. 56.

Sherfield, R., Montgomery, R., and Moody, P. *Capstone: Succeeding Beyond College.* Upper Saddle River, NJ: Prentice Hall, 2001.

Silver, H., Strong, R., and Perini, M. "Integrating learning styles and multiple intelligences." *Educational Leadership,* 55, no. 1, September, 1997, p. 22.

Tieger, P., and Barron Tieger, B. *Do What You Are: Discover the Perfect Career for You Through the Secrets of Personality Type.* Boston: Little, Brown, and Company, 1992.

Warnick, B., and Inch, E. *Critical Thinking and Communication—The Use of Reason in Argument.* New York: Macmillan, 1994.

Werner, R. *Understanding.* Newport, RI: TED Conferences, 1999.

Whitfield, C. *Healing the Child Within.* Deerfield Beach, FL: Health Communication, 1987.

Woolfolk, A. *Educational Psychology.* 6th ed. Boston: Allyn and Bacon, 1995.

Yale Study of Graduating Seniors. Yale University, New Haven, CT, 1953.

Index